THE SECRET LIFE OF THOMAS HARDY

The Secret Life of Thomas Hardy
'Retaliatory Fiction'

EDWARD NEILL

ASHGATE

Published by
Ashgate Publishing Limited
Gower House
Croft Road
Aldershot
Hampshire GU11 3HR
England

Ashgate Publishing Company
Suite 420
101 Cherry Street
Burlington, VT 05401-4405
USA

Ashgate website: http://www.ashgate.com

British Library Cataloguing in Publication Data
Neill, Edward
    The secret life of Thomas Hardy : 'retaliatory fiction'. -
    (The nineteenth century series)
    1. Hardy, Thomas, 1840-1928 2. Hardy, Thomas, 1840-1928 -
    Criticism and interpretation
    I. Title
    823.8

Library of Congress Cataloging-in-Publication Data
Neill, Edward
    The secret life of Thomas Hardy ; "retaliatory fiction" / Edward Neill.
        p. cm. - (The nineteenth century series)
    Includes bibliographical references and index.
    ISBN 0-7546-3841-3 (alk. paper)
        1. Hardy, Thomas, 1840-1928–Fictional works 2. Experimental fiction,
    English–History and criticism 3. Wessex (England)–In literature. I. Title. II. Nineteenth
    century (Aldershot, England)

PR4757.F5N45 2003
823'.914–dc22

2003065060

ISBN 0 7546 3841 3

Printed and bound in Great Britain by MPG Books Ltd, Bodmin, Cornwall

Contents

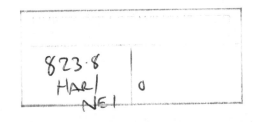

The Nineteenth Century Series
General Editors' Preface

The aim of the series is to reflect, develop and extend the great burgeoning of interest in the nineteenth century that has been an inevitable feature of recent years, as that former epoch has come more sharply into focus as a locus for our understanding not only of the past but of the contours of our modernity. It centres primarily upon major authors and subjects within Romantic and Victorian literature. It also includes studies of other British writers and issues, where these are matters of current debate: for example, biography and autobiography, journalism, periodical literature, travel writing, book production, gender and non-canonical writing. We are dedicated principally to publishing original monographs and symposia; our policy is to embrace a broad scope in chronology, approach and range of concern, and both to recognize and cut innovatively across such parameters as those suggested by the designations 'Romantic' and 'Victorian'. We welcome new ideas and theories, while valuing traditional scholarship. It is hoped that the world which predates yet so forcibly predicts and engages our own will emerge in parts, in the wider sweep, and in the lively streams of disputation and change that are so manifest an aspect of its intellectual, artistic and social landscape.

Vincent Newey
Joanne Shattock
University of Leicester

Preface

This book is an attempt to recall us to a sense of what we mean when we utter the words 'Thomas Hardy'—who is, after all, a man made out of words. He was also particularly good at making women out of them. Indeed, Hardy may himself be figured as a Pygmalion of sorts who breathes fleshly life into female 'phantoms of his own figuring'.

Hardy himself seems to have been well aware of this. His last novel, *The Well-Beloved* (1897), until recently a sidelined little opus, depicts the artist as a kind of Pygmalion reversed—in the form of the sculptor Jocelyn Pierston. Pierston turns (female) flesh to stone in achieving the Pyrrhic victory of art. This 'victory' seems finally to pre-figure the death of desire itself. In life, this was a consummation to be devoutly 'unwished'. As art, it made the perfect finish.

Why, then, is *The Well-Beloved*, which has attracted some recent critical acclaim, still left virtually unread? This is because Hardy made another attempt, and a much more speciously authoritative one, to 'finish himself off' twenty-five years on. As a kind of 'posthumous' novelist who had abandoned the genre in the 1890s, he made a rather bad decision to 'write his life' in the form of an autobiography disguised as a biography by his second wife.

But Hardy had already performed a 'typeover' operation on his flesh-and-blood self as one happy to determine his essential identity in the prison-house of genre. One of *The Life*'s little ironies was that, as an attempt to spike the guns of biographers, it merely encouraged them in their wild goose chase after a 'real Thomas Hardy' who had already not merely stood up to be counted, but, by his own account, 'stood up to be shot at'—when he wrote *Tess of the d'Urbervilles* (1891).

As Leo Bersani puts it, 'the aesthetic effect depends on an absence, the absence of a subject as the authoritative source or origin of fantasies or ideas'. The Death of Thomas Hardy may be said to have taken place as a result of his 'life of – and in – writing'. But this paradoxically happy fate was unhappily reversed by various attempts (including, of course, his own) to 'write his life'. And thus was born the 'other' Thomas Hardy who has wasted so much of our time. For example: 'the author of *The Well-Beloved*' is a sardonically alienated analyst of High Society, whereas 'the author of *The Life*', if likeable enough, must be accounted something of a snob. It is *The Well-Beloved*, itself a creative work, rather than *The Life*, which offers a condensed *resumé* of the preoccupations of his life in fiction(s) as a piquant 'metacommentary' on his artistic concerns.

Extrapolating from *The Life*, biographers, however accomplished in their own areas of expertise, reproduce a figure in many respects the opposite of the one who made what was intended to be his creative debut with a work intent on '*miching mallecho*'—mischief-making—as his timid publisher noted. This led, apparently, to his being quashed on the spot. To be published at all, it seems, required the practice of sleights and stratagems. Fortunately, though, Hardy was quick to learn his lesson.

Some of his ancestors may have been involved in *smuggling*, and in a sense he continued this tradition in textual form, with an illicit cargo of cultural disruption and dissent, in what would prove an impressively sustained 'dance of the intellect among narratives'. It might, then, be taken as a sort of allegory that, thanks to the efforts of officious and self-appointed custodians who crowded in to appropriate him, Hardy was ghoulishly dismembered in death. His heart was, appropriately, buried in 'Wessex', but the rest of his corpse, in the official ceremonies of interment, in Westminster Abbey. 'He's the man we were in search of, that's true', claims Hardy's constable in his story, *The Three Strangers*, 'And yet he's not the man we were in search of. For the man we were in search of is not the man we wanted'. Perhaps biography is similarly inclined to figure (and finger) the wrong suspect, replacing the artist, or the artist as work or text, with an implied, or pretended 'explanation' which 'entombs' the work of which biographers would formally claim to be the humble custodians. Lacan's seminar on Poe's 'Purloined Letter' examined a tale in which the 'letter' remained unexamined precisely from its being something of an open secret. As Poe's detective remarked, 'the best clues' are 'perhaps a little *too* self-evident'. In 'reviving' Hardy, one may find that 'the *letter* giveth life', while the *spirit,* in the sense of the ectoplasm pursued by biographers, is a treacherous phantom.

The present study, then, implies a 'subject' opposed to that retrieved by biographers—mischievous and subversive, not cowed and compliant, fertile in expedient, not a humble literary 'jerry-builder', brilliantly 'conceited', not a plodding 'serialist' who 'went about the business mechanically'. Hardy, in what we might describe as 'propria persona', is reticent if not inaccessible in his decorous Victorian privacy. In his creative writings, though, as if by way of compensation, he openly conducts something of an inquisition into desire, language and society. Hardy, in other words, is never done with tweaking Mrs Grundy's tail. Yet 'Mrs Grundy' is herself something of a comic misnomer, if not a 'gender studies item', in being largely made out of the responses of hysterical *male* editors.

The traditional view of Hardy as a writer of rustic sincerity suggests someone of fairly unambitious intellectual gait. Yet on closer inspection, Hardy seems set on following unusual rubrics of representation, which might almost be described as '*conceited*' in a specific sense reserved for discussions of some kinds of poetry. To read Hardy, we must realize that the word 'realism' is an inadequate characterization of his mode, and those who attempt film adaptations may not have merely their work cut out, but also his. His feline, metamorphic approach to representation suggests the sophistications of modernism, while there is much in Hardy which 'modernism cannot reach'. And Hardy's intellectual brilliance proves to be a source of critical inquiry, spelling potential trouble for the author, not just innocuous, if pyrotechnic, entertainment for his audience. (It also cuts across the pleasantly geriatric image of the Older Hardy and recalls us to a sense of the younger man making his—in context— highly experimental way.) We are given to understand that 'Wessex' is, among other things, rather *chalky*, and a certain 'porosity' in acts of (re-) presentation will turn out to help Hardy in what we might almost call his running battle with the authorities. His silences are often rather eloquent, and the present study was particularly keen to hear from them.

'Wessex', incidentally, is an attractive fancy which becomes a menace only when used for the purpose of pre-emptive canon-creation, instantly producing a list of officially major works—which, as it happens, serve to produce *it*. The insidiousness of this resides in the fact that the helpful offer of 'rational' criteria actually favours a limiting set of conventions, attitudes and styles of representation. 'Wessex', in other words, is suspiciously twinned with nostalgia and conservatism, a strand in Hardy's work, but perhaps a little too *reassuring* as a shorthand indication of what Hardy is 'about'. It seems important to recognize that Hardy's creative intentions are not quite so easily assessed or characterized. For example, he also gets a good deal of creative mileage out of a sort-of Shelleyan inquisition into metaphysics, mores and social structures. Hence the sub-title here is a phrase annexed from words Grace Melbury uses to maximize discomfort in her erring husband in *The Woodlanders* (1887) – 'retaliatory fiction[s]'. Hardy's unusual techniques of presentation ensure that his own implicit commitment to 'retaliatory fiction' is also sustained. His novels present a persistent investigation into the results of social arrangements as well as natural causes and metaphysical conundrums.

The argument began here with reference to Hardy's last work of fiction, but might equally be said to stem from his first—Hardy's 'début which was not one'. What was intended to be his 'inaugural' novel—*The Poor Man and the Lady* (1868)—was indeed quashed. But, as we shall see, Hardy declined to become the 'good little Thomas Hardy' (in the sadly patronising phraseology of Henry James). In a new look at the startlingly original ways in which Hardy's novels may be said to work, this book itself naturally aspires to be rather startling—although not, of course, wholly original. Some advanced and adventurous recent writing about Hardy has superseded a mass of previous criticism which failed to note that Hardy announces metaphysical contradictions but explores ideological ones. Accordingly, such work has got rather impressive mileage out of defining Hardy as a sociologist of sorts. On a different front, other studies have indicated the strange psychological undercurrents of Hardy's writing rendering it 'darkly, deliciously disturbing' (in a vogue phrase whose alliteration Hardy would certainly have admired) without bothering too much about the implications of the perturbation he induces. In other words, both the 'canny' and the 'uncanny' Hardy are impressive (and the Hardy who involves the canny with the uncanny particularly so). With a sophisticated sense of the practice of writing, the present study unites both critical strains in providing a new understanding of Hardy's creative procedures and a heightened appreciation of their results.

The chapter on Hardy's poetry is a much altered and re-written version of an article originally published in *Victorian Poetry*. I also owe something here to the articles of mine published in *Victorian Literature and Culture* and the *Oxford Literary Review* listed in the bibliography. And sentences from this book were used in an essay-chapter on Hardy in *A Companion to the Victorian Novel* (2002), edited by Professors William Baker and Kenneth Womack. Of those who have helped me, I am particularly indebted to Professor John Chalker, who read several chapters with impressive care and attention and made a number of useful suggestions and comments. I should also like to thank Professors Alan Durant, Donald Hawes, Stephen Wall and Christopher Ricks for their support, and also take the occasion to express my gratitude to Ann Donahue in particular at Ashgate for her assistance.

Chapter 1

Introducing Hardy's Pharmacy:
Desperate Remedies

'Did she put on his knowledge with his power?'[1]

It is still quite widely assumed that Hardy, a sadder and a wiser man after his first work failed to win acceptance by a publisher, humbly recanted and reverted to type— or rather, what we take his type to be. This typecasting is after the manner of Henry James' painfully patronising 'good little Thomas Hardy'.[2] And many critical discussions of Hardy seem to have liked it that way. With misunderstanding still being added to, it is particularly interesting to reconsider what Hardy himself might call 'his first ventures in this kind',[3] in which a certain Lutheran *ich kann nicht anders* ('I cannot do otherwise') attitude is very much in evidence.

In later life Hardy himself rather startlingly described his 'original' first novel, *The Poor Man and the Lady*, as 'socialistic, not to say revolutionary'.[4] This sense of 'danger' is fully reflected in Macmillan's obvious disquiet over the discarded text. Initiating a perceptive comparison with Thackeray, Macmillan concluded that 'he meant fair, you mean mischief'.[5]

As a result, it seems to be taken as read in subsequent critical and especially biographical accounts rendered, that Hardy was instantly called to heel. Thereafter, it is assumed, he became suitably compliant, coming up with the 'goods' in the form of genial rustics depicted with at best a 'distinctly patronising affection'.[6] The result would of course entail abandoning his commitment to what Alexander Macmillan called 'mischief'. So we might expect his literary début to be undertaken as a kind of already desperate remedy for a career apparently still-born (as, incidentally, the author of *Desperate Remedies* had himself been taken to be).

Desperate Remedies was, then, an even more apposite title than its readers could possibly have guessed, and so perhaps even more apposite than its author would have liked. The novel, advertising itself as a *pharmakon*, a remedy, or possibly a remedy for life itself (as it was for Socrates, who drank it [the celebrated hemlock]), was obviously perceived as more poisonous than remedial by its first perusers, and quickly remaindered. In fact, as *Desperate Remedies* demonstrates with clarity, Hardy definitely bore in mind some slightly unconvincing rhetorical questions of Macmillan's he had ringing in his ears about his first book: questions like, 'Is it possible that a gentleman would pursue his wife at midnight and *strike* her?'[7] which seem to depend on circular definition to keep themselves out of trouble.

It is perhaps particularly interesting that what looks like the 'violation' of a lady survives, not less mischievously, in this, his first *published* novel—as it is precisely the original 'violation' (or at the least, seduction and betrayal) of Miss Aldcliffe which motivates *Desperate Remedies* itself (see p.321).[8] This was precisely what was supposed to have been firmly 'under erasure'. But it was *not* erased, even if represented in a suitably encrypted fashion.

Perhaps, then, we are in the presence of an already 'retaliatory' fiction, in the suggestive phrase used in connection with Grace Melbury in *The Woodlanders*. This particular novel would be 'retaliatory' in a special sense, however: hidden from the reader here was the painful rejection of Hardy's 'real' first novel, *The Poor Man and the Lady*, as a potential 'stirrer-up of strife', the chastening advice he received in consequence—and the birth of *Desperate Remedies* as a reaction to the quashing and admonishing he had received as a result. And arranging for such paradoxical secondary scenes of cowed, compliant retaliation would prove to be at once his *métier* and his forte.

Confident readers like George Meredith and John Morley advised perusal of the Wilkie Collins sensation-novel, which Hardy was indeed able to press into service as a kind of stalking-horse.[9] In fact this excess of well-meant exhortation by these impressive, if slightly hectoring readers, would certainly have killed off a lesser novelist. Accused of producing a disturbing text, Hardy ironically capitulates, 'complies' with advice and exhortations to 'cool it'—and produces a rather more disturbing one. To appreciate the persistence of this impulse makes subverting the process which leads to the premature canonisation of those perennial Hardy novels held to project a reassuring Myth of Wessex, almost a critical duty—if hardly a solemn one. In particular, one should appreciate the brilliance and mischief of Hardy's 'conceited' procedures (using 'conceited' in a favourable sense usually reserved for discussions of some forms of poetry) in *Desperate Remedies*, and subsequently in other novels.

Adding to the provocation, but more for modern readers this time, it seems that the quite possibly violated Miss Aldcliffe of this book, though 'notoriously abused', does indeed 'bear responsibility' as well as the child which results from her (possibly 'enforced') seduction. This child will turn out to be (and turn up as) the amusingly *im*pious *Aeneas* Manston. His not-so-Christian first name supplies him with a distinguished literary pedigree (as if to compensate for his dubious personal pedigree). Indeed, Hardy himself becomes a kind of T.S. Eliot *avant la lettre* here, 'manipulating a continuous parallel between contemporaneity and antiquity',[10] as Cytherea (Venus) was the mother of Virgil's Aeneas. And in the novel itself, Cytherea II was herself given the unusual name of the Goddess of Love by her still lovelorn father. She will thus become a *nominal* daughter of Cytherea I in a text in which, as we shall see, the act of naming will constitute a fateful performative, not just a 'token performance'.

Indeed, as nothing if not a 'bitch goddess' here, machinating Cytherea I (Miss Aldcliffe) will wrongfully appoint *Aeneas*, the offspring of an 'original sin' (which was perhaps 'not hers') to stewardship of the Knapwater estate she subsequently inherited. Manston's application is looked on with favour and preferred to that of Edward Springrove, against the legal advice Aldcliffe herself had solicited only in order to present an appearance of equity over the appointment. She also (loathsomely) conspires to transfer to Manston the 'other occupation' (that of Cytherea II herself) through false representations of the state of 'Cythie' II's heart in relation to

Springrove—a man formally acknowledged as better qualified both as suitor *and* steward.

Auden has reminded us that 'Those to whom evil is done/ Do evil in return'.[11] Perhaps Hardy is ironically implying here that as a result of the Victorian pressure on femininity the character of 'fallen woman' will show itself unbidden after Cytherea I has put on 'guilty knowledge', however innocently. Hardy conveys as much in subtle intellectual manoeuvres combined with pyrotechnic effects in plotting, so that the novel's original *commercial* failure is irrelevant to a current assessment of its achievement(s).

The novel might be described as a study in—or even entitled—'(*De-) cadences*'. Indeed, in what might be described as an 'ultimate' act of empathy with the 'fallen' Miss Aldcliffe, her still effectively lovelorn suitor, Cytherea's father, still in emotional terms 'affianced' to Cytherea (as Aldcliffe), *falls* to his death from a church spire, an unsupervized superisor watched by the helpless Cytherea (a daughter named 'for' Aldcliffe) (p.8).

So the Father who may be 'named' as 'doubly *Cytherea's*' fell, finally, because Cytherea (I) had *nominally* done so, watched by the Cytherea (II) *named* for her who thereby imbibes, perhaps, a certain 'knowledge of the fall'. We are to infer, then, that, as if in refutation of the Yeats who claimed in a late poem ('All Souls' Night') that 'names are nothing', names are as meaningful in themselves as the person they are associated with. For Bertrand Russell, names, a problem for analytical philosophers, were a kind of 'description', but Hardy seems to be applying the idea 'with a vengeance' here.

Cytherea II of course also bears the *surname* Aldcliffe would have borne had she not been 'violated' [fallen]). Hardy implies that her father's last thoughts (and this is why they became those) were perhaps, and perhaps confusedly, of *Cytherea*. Whether those were of the 'wife that wasn't one' or 'the daughter that wasn't Cytherea's but was Cytherea (II)', it might be said to have been thoughts of 'fallen' woman which caused him to fall. But the fall also pre-emptively allegorized what it will initiate, as the Graye family will fall further as a result of this misfortune which has befallen them. (Cythie's brother will fall ill, and she will fall into the hands of Aldcliffe, and subsequently Manston.)

Hardy may not have had all this wordplay in mind, but foregrounding it shows something of the way his imagination is working here, providing something of a 'reveal codes' key to his 'political unconscious'. And it is also notable that the later notorious 'sex scene'—between Cytherea and Cytherea—at Knapwater, is an attempt to mingle what is already *nominally* identical (apparently under the rubric 'what *naming* has joined let no *man* put asunder', or possibly something like '*nominally* we are as one'). (Previous critics have conducted an understandably heated 'lesbian' vs. 'not lesbian' debate[12] in assessing the effect of the scene.)

Cytherea I, then, entering Cythie's bedroom in a slightly deranged condition (p.64), attempts to 'repeat' the sexual initiation of 'Cytherea' (II) from, as it were, the 'other [gender] side', putting on her ravisher's knowledge with his power, compounding the offence by repeating the role he played against 'her self as Cythie'. She will don this, as a kind of 'occupying power', one which has just provided Cythie II with a somewhat servile 'occupation'. (Her son Aeneas, fruit of the violation, will subsequently be substituted for her in this attempt to subdue Cytherea II sexually, and interestingly embark on the pursuit [and conquest] of the woman named 'as' his mother.) As a 'fallen woman who was not one', Miss Aldcliffe (Cytherea I) entertained the daughter of 'the man who fell', if *only literally*, as a long-range result.

'Name-calling', then, seems particularly fateful in *Desperate Remedies*, even when ludically so, in the case of brother Owen (one suspects that 'more than he could pay' is the simple motif here; no need to ascribe some arcane interest in the Celtic). This signals that Owen, ill and feckless, is largely a device used to put his sister Cytherea under pressure to 'tie the knot' with Aeneas Manston. Manston was himself the offspring of the 'illegitimate use' of Cytherea (I)'s body. At the same time, we might see Cytherea II as her spiritual child, and this is retrospectively confirmed by Cytherea's final inheriting of the Knapwater estate. (See the suggestively named short story by Hardy, 'An Imaginative Woman' [1893] for a child of the imagination, of an 'elective affinity' in a Goethean sense he himself had entertained with respect to Mrs Florence Henniker and perhaps with less for her husband, Major Henniker, damned with the not-so-faint praise in a letter as a type of the 'practical soldier' [sc. 'unimaginative man'].)

Thus, if Cytherea II were united with Manston they would become a kind of parody of those Shelleyan 'twins' who haunt Hardy's imagination—'twinned with "Laon and Cythna"', as it were (and cf. the romantic sentiment of the Shelley of 'Epipsychidion': 'Would we two had been twins of the same mother').[13] Manston owed his being to Cytherea (I)'s 'fall'. And Cytherea II's 'marriage' to Manston (she 'becomes a Manston') was also retrospectively considered as a great fall from grace on her part, if perhaps mainly by herself, though the idea was imputed by her to the whole community.

After this 'marriage' of Manston and 'Cytherea', a frantic pursuit of 'Cythie' and Manston was initiated by Owen, the Rector Mr. Raunham, and Edward Springrove, on hearing from the porter Chinney that Manston's wife still lived (p.212) (which proved to be no longer true). Like Edward, but covertly, Mr Raunham was himself clearly in love with Cytherea (II) and thus with an amusingly unclerical 'libidinal investment' in a delirious anxiety for 'Cythie' to remain 'intact'. Unfortunately, it seems to have been the pursuit which itself helped destroy the reputation of Cytherea they were trying to preserve, despite its being a kind of 'hue and cry from mistaken premises'. What justified it was not what initiated it.

Edward, Cytherea's gentle first suitor, is the eventual winner here. But his official triumph is, finally, rather mawkish, as he refers to Cytherea as his 'stolen pet lamb', which seems itself to be a literary filch from Keats[14] (p.208). This would seem to be specifically ironized by Cytherea's earlier spotting of the Springrove sheep branded in the buttocks with Edward's initials (p.68) (in fact they are those of his 'humble and rustic' father, Ted). (As 'pet lamb' [p.257] she might almost considered to be aspiring to their condition.)

With the pursuit of Cytherea after her legitimate-looking marriage to Manston, the Yeatsian question relating to Cythie's putting on (carnal) knowledge ('with *his* power') *returns* in a new and menacing form. Manston and Cytherea II are 'not married' in a double sense. It had been a universal assumption that Manston's first wife Eunice had been destroyed in the fire at Carriford which also destroyed the old

Springrove buildings, including the Inn to which Eunice had repaired in distress (Manston had failed to meet her off the train due to his careless perusal of Bradshaw, revealing his lack of real affection for her.) The fire, resulting from smouldering couch grass, was a particularly pernicious one, destroying the cottages of the Springroves, and their financial prospects—particularly as neither Manston nor Cytherea I is inclined to be merciful to tillers of the soil, treating them rather as Mrs Charmond will later treat Giles in *The Woodlanders* (1887).

In fact, Manston had subsequently killed Eunice by accident partly through disappointment that her continuing existence meant that his legitimate pursuit of Cytherea was over, and he appeared to be left with a 'nag, a drag and a drunk' (who was already taunting him over his love for Cythie). He had discovered that Eunice had left the burning buildings, including the Inn, at Carriford, unscathed. A pursuit of the well-beloved was later re-legitimized for Manston as Eunice did indeed die, yet Manston was not exactly the murderer he was later (again) universally taken to be.

Crowned only with precarious success, suspected of bigamy but guilty of something darker, Manston *also* remains unmarried to Cythie in the sense that the marriage is unconsummated. Paradoxically, then, he 'remains unmarried' in a very real sense, as Hardy's contemporary John Ruskin found to his cost in 1854 when his marriage was declared a nullity as a result of his failure to consummate it. Yet speculation on these marital conditions seems analogously out of control with the fire which brought the Springroves low and provided Manston with his great opportunity. It is as if the reader as well as the locals require to be 'introduced to Cytherea's story'[15] in an inadmissibly intimate way, as in the indecent innuendo or insinuation of Mallarmé's '*M'introduire dans ton histoire*'. (And the apparently enamoured Hardy did at least induce Mrs Henniker to collaborate with him in narratives, intimate enough at least to be introduced to her stories.)

'How *hymeneal* was it, this marriage of yours?' whisper the intimately malicious voices which Cytherea seems to hear (p.237), with narrative interest heavily invested in such ultimate intimacies. Rude questions, it seems, are being asked concerning Cythie's marital (or hymeneal) condition, considered as a painful matter of common knowledge ('utterly fictitious details of the finding of Cytherea and Manston had been invented and circulated' [p.294]).

So, cunning beyond editorial requirement, in a highly 'conceited' way, the narrative invests heavily in this little aporia of *a non-consummated marriage which might (otherwise) be a legitimate one.* Or, in other words, Manston did *not* have a wife still living, the supposition which initiated the chase. (So what presented itself to the appalled [male] imaginings of their pursuers is that of *a consummated 'marriage' which was not one.*)

Without whipping up a too-conspicuous prurience, Hardy is already at the threshhold of the 'contrapuntal' treatment of hymeneal conditions much more famously explored twenty years later in *Tess* and made something like a structural principle in *Jude*. Adumbrating the problem(s) of Tess herself, insistently considered and pursued as a mere sex object, Cytherea makes a plea to her brother Owen to be considered as a person with one chance in or of life. This argument, re-used, impressed Gilles Deleuze in relation to Tess, a figure who inspires cognate feelings in Hardy's narrator in his most famous later novel to those inspired by Cytherea in his rarely perused début here—she seems to be as much a 'sex-object' as (say) Etty's *Nude* (c.1835), a woman highly prized as a physical phenomenon.

Hardy seems to be implying here, not pleasantly, that 'Woman can always be defined', specifically as that in which one finds one has a kind of 'libidinal investment', as without this she ceases to 'be one'. Manston's almost slavering appreciation of Cythie reminds the reader of Alec's feeling for Tess, whose problems stem from her being highly prized on account of either an imputed beauty, or an imputed state of virginity.

Angel also thought that Tess' (physical) 'integrity' was guaranteed in much the same way, as that of a bona fide 'Virginity' Tess, yet Tess' 'integrity' was actually guaranteed by her *failing* that particular examination. In 'a repetition which is not one' of the fate of the earlier Cytherea, Cytherea II also takes the rap for the 'sins of the fathers', takes on the character of the 'fallen woman' in the latter half of the novel (pp.237ff.), with psychological implications—although she is physically intact, rumours seem to have 'touched' her reputation. These voices of critique which Cytherea is said to hear after she is rescued from Manston in the nick of time remain remote and conjectural: but compare the humorous echo of this in Hardy's rollicking early poem 'The Bride-Night Fire' (published 1875) in which the first, unsuitable match for the girl was conjecturally consummated (although the drunken old bridegroom was burned to death). At the wedding, the ruder guests cried '"after Sweatley". She said: "I declare/ I stand as a maiden today"',[16] and this is the result which Cytherea plainly fears for herself. Cytherea II, then, seems to take on the knowledge "of" Miss Aldcliffe in suffering undeserved ill-fame in sexual matters, just as she later takes on her power in inheriting the estate. Paradoxically, at the point of dénouement, 'the knot there's no untying' unties the knot intrinsicate of Cytherea's 'love-hate relationship' with the House of Aldcliffe.

But finally, clinching the idea that Hardy's 'conceits' here are not merely a figment of our imaginings, Manston's later 'substitute for Eunice' *also* substituting for the second wife who was thought not to 'be one' (Cytherea II), is herself more emphatically a 'fallen woman' than either Cytherea—'Anne Seaway' (p.281). Interestingly, the narrator persistently refers to Anne by her Christian name, ironically confirming that 'surnames are despised in Paphos' [p.283] ('Paphos' itself suggests the 'area' of 'substitutes for wives' in general, but, in disturbing analogy, 'paid' for their 'services': as an ancient city of Cyprus with a temple to Aphrodite this is another version of 'Cytherea country'). But the familiarity of reference also insinuates the idea that the narrator has a partiality for her or that he would like the reader to share this, despite the plain fact that, *stricto sensu*, 'Paphos' names the (sub-) urban realm of prostitution from which Anne has been plucked, Manston having been an *habitué* there, it seems.

So, revelling in his own revelation that Anne also ironically derives from a Cytherean place or place of Cytherea, the mother of Aeneas, the narrator himself relishes the use of Anne's Christian name, takes her part, as she herself will in turn go about the business of saving herself from the desperate Manston (pp.288ff.). So this familiarity in 'name-calling' of his also seems to signal, what will appear to be proved, that Anne is just as human and likeable as anyone else, *despite* the fact that Anne's *surname* quite pruriently signals that, in Miss Aldcliffe's idiom about Cytherea II, her 'heart' has been 'had' (p.67) a very great many times indeed.

Desperately clever (worth noting once more, given the long tradition of vague assent to the idea of a 'good little Thomas Hardy' and emotional investments in the reassuring image of 'the older Hardy'), *Desperate Remedies* also confirms Joe Fisher's idea, in his *The Hidden Hardy* (1992) that there is something quite sardonic lodged in humble Hardy's editor-compliant texts, as he introduces a woman who really has fallen with a vengeance at this point and shows that her sexually 'fallen' condition is not correlated with the qualities of hardened villainy—malevolence or cruelty. We see this, for example, in her solicitude over the detective who falls victim to Manston's shovel as he vainly attempts to 'dig for victory', secreting the body of first wife Eunice (see pp.299-300).

Brilliantly 'conceited', then, *Desperate Remedies* is perhaps only a failure in the light of "Wessexian" criteria which demand that all Hardy should be roughly like *Far from the Madding Crowd* (1874). It does however seem to be working to establish one basically proto-Wessexian attitude. Favouring ingenuousness over ingenuity, it seems to oppose the baleful effects of those who attempt to take advantage of the unsophisticated ways of simple folk. Yet, even in this, the novel seems to reverse its manifest signs as to how it is to be taken. As we approach its latter end, the novel suddenly shifts sharply from a sense of the *powerlessness* of 'local hearts and heads'[17] against metropolitan or high-life characters. Initially, the implications of *Desperate Remedies* seem very much opposed to the spirit of Yeats' paean to a cultural rootedness in 'The Municipal Gallery Revisited', which enables whatever is local or parochial to 'grow strong'—'Antaeus-like', as he puts it.

By contrast, what is Antaeus-like, it seems, grows weak in *Desperate Remedies*: Hardy seems to underscore the point when he shows an apparently defeated son of a local peasant farmer, Edward Springrove, turning up at Cythie's wedding (to Manston) looking 'spectre-thin' (p.201), reminding us of Keats' Nightingale Ode, in which 'youth grows pale, and spectre-thin, and dies'. And 'indigenous', 'native', seems to correlate with 'indigence' (penury): 'they have no money: what can they prove?' whispers Manston to Aldcliffe as they conspire against their social inferiors (p.294).

Throughout the novel's opening three-quarters, to be a 'native', it seems, is to be doomed to weakness, if not impotence. In stark contrast, 'aliens' like Aldcliffe and Manston are highly successful agents of oppression. In the end, though, the novel does indeed stage something like a 'Return of the Native' in a sense of a return [to power] of the formerly repressed and outmanoeuvred 'local hearts and heads'. Another way of putting this would be to say that *Desperate Remedies*' complete succumbing to a 'detective fiction' ending 'overdetermines' what is unleashed against its 'villains'. This in turn gives the fates of Miss Aldcliffe and Manston the pathos of an 'expunged and razed' otherness. Their very destruction rescues them for empathy.

Indeed, the novel's apparent black and white 'morality play' quality may even seem a duplicitous one (and the Knapwater estate does indeed literally end up as a 'Graye' area). There is a detectable sleight-of-hand with 'words as "conceits"' here: Cytherea Graye transparently owed her (sur-) name to the poet Thomas Gray, whose phrase about the 'purple light of love', applied to the goddess Cytherea herself, was often pressed into service by Hardy, and also reminded him of Virgil as the origin of this particular phraseology).[18] (There are significant uses of these connections in both the 'Poems 1912-13' and *A Pair of Blue Eyes*.)

A sense of its moral ambiguity and rapidly alternating currents of empathy and estrangement helps to throw new light on the culminating scenes of the novel: when Anne Seaway watches Miss Aldcliffe watching the detective watching Manston (re-) interring his first wife in a scene in which, as Hardy puts it, 'night herself seemed to have become a watcher' (p.302), the novel does indeed seem to develop into a rustic panopticon in which everyone seems privy to the fate of Manston. The 'desperate remedy' against his acts of desperation itself seems 'undecidable' after all: good triumphed over evil, but the devils (as Blake said of Milton's) had a good deal of the novelist's (imaginative) life: Manston, 'a voluptuary with activity' (p.91), is a handsomely Byronic figure who arouses Cytherea against her will as she watches 'with parted lips' (p.113) as he plays the organ during a thunderstorm, and its harmonies are said to 'enter into her with a gnawing thrill' (p.113).

And finally, the insipidity of the officially approved lovers is metaphorically as well as literally terminal, as Edward cloyingly re-stages his first kiss with Cytherea at Creston to create a *rondo* effect of some mawkishness. Indeed this *terminus ad quem* makes the reader wonder a little about the fate of desire itself (p.330). It seems that the novel might be implying that Desire is always involved with devilishness, with Manston's insinuating little touch to the effect that Cytherea 'would soon acquire the touch for an organ' (p.111), or with the hissed jealousies of Miss Aldclyffe in 'Cythie's' bed-chamber (p.67). The idea is also implied by the sado-masochistic dream which precedes Cytherea's marriage to Manston in which she dreams of being 'whipped with bones suspended on strings' (p.195) as a result of the action of frozen snow on the boughs outside—perhaps also as a warning characteristic of the 'natural supernaturalism' of Romanticism.

Indeed, the weather-god seems to be trying to prevent the wedding to Aeneas Manston by freezing up the countryside around, but finally doesn't, so that consoling idea is definitely 'under erasure', and the idea that Cytherea is indeed being warned is at once cancelled and preserved. Yet Manston's (evil) desire for Cythie seems horribly *vivid*, instinct with life, so that the 'immanent will' of the novel seems finally to be, as Philip Sidney puts it, 'desiring naught but how to kill desire' rather than fulfil it. If, as Leo Bersani says, 'the message in *La Peau de Chagrin* is simple: desire disintegrates society, self and the novel',[19] this Hardy novel itself is not too far away from the idea.

So the final irony is that the fulfilment of desire in the form of the mawkish re-uniting of Edward and Cythie seems disturbingly implicated in its erasure. This 'novel of ingenuity' according to Hardy's 'basically factitious'[20] categories includes (while appearing to subsume) the psychological and the ideological. More precisely, its message would appear to be that 'the conventions of the novel and society which officially enable or fulfil desire are precisely those which annul it'.

'I am now about to enter into my normal condition. For people are almost always in their graves' (p.319), writes Manston in his Prison Notebook on the verge of self-slaughter. This might be described as the 'ultimate' Hardy point, and the passage itself is soundly if a little surprisingly based on Dr Johnson's manner in *Rasselas* (1759), a frequent point of reference for Hardy. With the restitutions of rusticity, Aldcliffe and

Manston are revealed in their anti-social alienation, and, suggestively, society's very figureheads seem to be the 'antisocial element of the *present time*' here.[21] Yet their very defeat tilts Hardy's emotional see-saw in favour of the 'expunged and razed' 'villains' themselves, as a whole community seems suddenly to spring into life to debate, and abet, the pursuit of Manston (pp.307ff.). 'We must not make him desperate', says kindly Jane Bennet of Wickham in *Pride and Prejudice*. But this is *Desperate Remedies*, and Hardy does need to make Manston rather desperate after all (his 'remedy' or *pharmakon*, Socratic in its own fashion, was the 'pyrrhic victory' of death).

In doing so, however, he seems to take his part. The 'desperate' Manston was, after all, homing in on someone he had 'married' (pp.309-311) in church, as, disguised in a smock-frock, he breaks and enters Cytherea's secluded cottage, in a final attempt to compensate for his 'hymeneal' frustrations. In the light of his later fascination with marital nuances, Hardy would also presumably enjoy this as a curious form of heinousness, as dereliction of such marital duty could render a marriage null and void.

This sexual assault by Manston, if successful, would stage a repetition of the fate of Manston's mother on someone named 'after' her, a nominal daughter who was also a virtually 'adopted' one. In a sense she 'replaced' Manston, as Cytherea I, if in a suitably unorthodox fashion, 'had Manston adopted'. We understand that baby Aeneas was secreted by some absurd stratagem in Clapham [Miss Aldcliffe watched and ran after ringing the bell (p.321)]). This orphan-drama goes easily into a mode of parody, which now seems almost reserved for comic melodrama, as in Gilbert and Sullivan or Oscar Wilde.

This device suggestively recalls Emma's rather poisonous musings on the revelation of Harriet Smith's origins in *Emma* (1816), in which 'the stain of illegitimacy, unbleached by nobility or wealth, would have been a stain indeed'.[22] In fact Aldcliffe/Cytherea and Manston/Aeneas possess whatever is to be had here of 'nobility' or 'wealth', but the novel declines to entertain ideas of their having been 'bleached' as a result.

Aeneas' upbringing is elided, so presumably we are to suppose that his genes themselves contain trace elements of the ethical derelictions to which he owes his very being. His literal pedigree is interestingly 'crossed' with his literary one. It appears that he is mysteriously tainted and doomed to cynical adventurism, composing an interesting gloss on his Virgilian origin, and the 'pious' Aeneas he succeeds or embodies rather as, according to the Marx of *Dix-Huite Brumaire*, legendary figures are merely parodied by the 'nominal' embodiments who follow.

Indeed, '*Aeneas delenda est*' seems to be the highly ironic tag with which Hardy 'informs' the novel's last movement. The fact that Aeneas arrived in Virgil's land from Carthage itself makes the idea particularly suggestive. And perhaps Hardy's destructive characters here, Manston and Aldcliffe, are too full of life, their terminal places too full of pathos, for the reader wholly to savour the restitution of 'order' here. On the other hand, *Aeneas* Manston's unkindness to inferiors no less than his inability or unwillingness to treat people as other than instrumental to his ends provides a specific ironizing of the Virgilian emphasis on imperial need (or greed) transposed into an ethical destiny by the grandiosity of Virgilian rhetoric. Perhaps, then, Hardy is even traducing the Latin lore he sweated for with autodidactic intensity. And perhaps this lively début of his is something of a Trojan horse to the classicism he entertains and subverts. Aeneas and Virgil bring ideas of (imperial) order, but Hardy's Aeneas seems to dissolve them.

Ideas of Order do seem to dominate the novel's last ('dying') moments: 'There's no such thing as a random snappen off of what was laid down to last longer', muses Springrove the Elder (p.313), as Manston's body, 'snapped off' by himself, not randomly, but with philosophic deliberation, trundles past in its inglorious coffin. Springrove's philosophic observation may find an ironic justification here, but he is obviously a philosophic naïf, and the text in which he appears will not provide him with further support. If this text does comprise one of 'Darwin's plots',[23] it seems to imply that Darwin was plotting against the idea that there any longer was one. The earlier speculation by Rector Raunham to the effect that Manston's 'recovery' of his wife through newspaper advertisement 'cleared everything up' with the 'suspicious patness of an old play' (p.276), was well founded, and the 'recovery' so far from clearing things up, constituted merely another piece of deliberate obfuscation (as a desperate remedy for the suspicious circumstance that first wife Eunice would now be permanently missing).

Indeed, the idea of a 'suspicious patness' itself returns to haunt the novel's own 'sense of an ending', as Edward kisses Cytherea in mawkish reminiscence of their original moment of attraction at Creston, surrounded by the estate made over to them. 'Beautiful to see it', remarks a passing rustic, but the reader, his/her sympathies stirred in other directions, might almost feel like heckling it all in terms of the satirical ending of 'The Bride-Night Fire', with the words 'After Manston!'. They would, after all, be startlingly true in a sense, as would an adaptation of D.H. Lawrence's provocative words about Tess and Alec D'Urberville to the effect that 'in a way, Manston was her mate'. As we saw, it is *he* who demonstrates just what passionate love is like, even if the sight of it 'in action' is profoundly unsettling. All in all, then, the reader may feel that Hardy has perpetrated more mischief in this, the first novel he was 'allowed' to publish than in the one he was not. And he began as he meant to continue for the rest of his novel-writing career.

Chapter 2

'Honey or Money?' *Under the Greenwood Tree*

The particular outrageousness of *Desperate Remedies* (1871) derives from Hardy's relative unawareness at that particular point of a need to turn himself into 'Thomas Hardy'—the one we imagine we know and love (but are also rather inclined to patronize). It is of course for this very reason that, for us now, his brilliantly *outré* (and quickly remaindered) first novel is so very well worth a visit.

With *Under the Greenwood Tree*, given the favourable response to the country matters so well handled in *Desperate Remedies* itself, Hardy had sensed that reviewers and editors might wish him to invent himself as a dedicated chronicler of rustic modes and mores. *Under the Greenwood Tree* definitely offers a more 'editor-compliant' Hardy than '*Desperate Remedies* Hardy', so that surely not the littlest of life's ironies at this point was his ongoing failure to publish with 'major league' Macmillan. For the time being, Hardy the Obscure was currently doomed to remain with 'minor league' Tinsley, a fact which was itself to lead to yet more frustration and annoyance in the form of Tinsley's astute but curmudgeonly refusal to sell back the copyright to the novel with which the young Hardy (as yet a stranger to *Copinger* [on copyright]) had naively parted.

Hardy seems initially to be broaching two ideas here, one of a traditional community rooted in one dear perpetual place, arranging a festive closure suggesting all of it still going reassuringly on. His other idea, irreconcilable with this, is that this long-running rural idyll must close, just when we are starting to get really interested. But a further idea, also in tension with the others, is that the rural idyll is not now and never had been particularly idyllic. The tension between these propositions makes *Under the Greenwood Tree* a memorable, if minor, music of dissonance, itself a discordant surprise for those expecting to be entertained by a kind of rustic 'harmonium' (an instrument which makes a brief appearance here). This is a version of pastoral in which you would (consequently) expect nature and culture to unite, in a 'hymeneal' reflection of the theme of the novel itself as it moves towards its nuptial conclusion. But just as 'Hymen' in *As You Like it*, a precursor-text here, 'bars' the 'confusion' she stands for in a paradoxical yet appropriate way, *Under the Greenwood Tree* defers this particular kind of mingling.

The short novel initially looks well set to be both idyllic and 'all, all of a piece throughout'. Yet instead of showing nature, culture and society in happy continuum, the book is full of 'faultlines'. Indeed, the text's 'warring significations' seem to show it contesting its own 'version of pastoral'. The 'communal' ideal associated with being 'under the greenwood tree' is continually fractured by a quietly frantic emphasis on social gradations, particularly by women.

Men and women are related, it seems, by what Coleridge called the 'war embrace' of power relations which see 'the girls' drowning out the tired and hence underperforming male 'quire' in a prelude to ousting them.[2] as being insufficiently genteel. Gender is, as they say, 'always imbricated with other categories', and seems to come with innate assumptions reflected in Dick's mother Mrs Dewy's endless rebukes to kindly Reuben Dewy, leader of the Mellstock quire, to be more refined and less sweaty ('dewy'), although the 'ghastly dew' (p.40) (a phrase neatly picked up from Tennyson's 'Locksley Hall' [1842])[3] rained by country dancers (male) is innocently *au naturel* and only to be expected.

Interestingly, too, in the last chapter, with young and old gathered under 'the ancient beech tree' (p.155), low dialect, too much indulged by 'natural men', is barred from its festive conclusion. So also is such low (if natural) behaviour as wiping mouths with hands. The two expressions of male rusticity are intrinsically connected (p.155), and the injunction to 'wipe dialect, not cider' threatens to banish 'natural man' from the closing ceremonies of a novel set fair to celebrate him. Hardy spoke of dialect in Darwinian terms as 'worsted in the struggle for existence',[4] and dialect is the linguistic expression of the social forms which precede bourgeoisification (as described by Weber: 'A man does not by nature wish to earn more and more money, but simply to live as he is accustomed to live and to earn as much as is necessary for that purpose. Wherever modern capitalism has begun its work of increasing the productivity of human labour by increasing its intensity, it has encountered the immensely stubborn resistance of this leading trait of pre-capitalist labour').[5] Ironically, it is the *mouth-wiping* which Hardy deliciously describes as '*dying out* among the upper classes of society', ascribing the knowledge to the young bride Fancy. Traditional village life is being at once 'cancelled and preserved' in this final tableau. But the 'preservation' is finally guaranteed only by the act of writing itself.

This 'note of sadness' in the minor key of narrative ironies also celebrates a union finally less than inevitable or perhaps even plausible. What joins young Dick Dewy and Fancy Day together might quite easily be put asunder, one feels, and particularly so given the unremitting pressures towards 'gentrification' which the novel unobtrusively suggests. In particular, Dick, as, basically, a horse-and-cart man, would be very much out of the final 'reckoning' if the novel actually 'pressed its case' here. (In fact, as if himself feeling the pressure, Hardy, in an attempt to 'balance' the book, occasionally gives Dick [humble son of Reuben and Mellstock Quire member] an improbably bourgeois register, almost as if Harold Steptoe had stepped into an Austen novel: his closing, unconsciously ironic remarks to Fancy as new-married bridegroom ('why we are so happy is because there is such entire confidence between us' [p.159]) does sound a little like an unlikely recapitulation of Mr Knightley addressing Emma.

A tell-tale point for Hardy's narrative future is that his own transparent love for Fancy is inseparable from what in other contexts might easily be seen as misogyny. Fancy seems to be auditioning quite hard for the role defined by Mr De Courcy in 'Letter Four' of Austen's *Lady Susan* as 'the most *accomplished* coquette in England', and 'coquette' is a word that occurs to and troubles Dick himself in connection with her (p.84) after her summary dismissal of him from the schoolhouse at the approach of

Maybold (p.116) when their fingers had just been prettily mingled under water in anticipation of Tess and Angel on the occasion of their doomed honeymoon at Wellbridge Manor (p.82). By contrast the narrator, not exactly unreliable but perhaps a little infatuated, explains that Fancy was possessed of 'a certain coquettishness . . . which in its turn was never so decided as to banish honesty' (p.39). The narrator in Hardy is always interesting, often protesting too much and implicitly contradicted by the characters he champions: Fancy, as Dick grimly notes, is keen to be admired by the 'handsome man' in the 'brand-new gig' which overtakes them on the Budmouth road (p.98), and all too set on turning the heads of the young men of Yalbury with the 'blue dress' she snips and sews while Dick's half-holiday is lost (p.112), metonymically defining herself through 'dress[es]', rather like light-minded Lucetta in *The Mayor of Casterbridge* (1886).

Indeed, a certain 'character note' of pettiness persists to the end as she experiences 'innumerable little tremors of pleasure' on hearing of the 'sorrowful envy' of the maidens as her [wedding] banns are called (p.146). This is disturbing, as, remembering the Miltonic description in 'L'Allegro' of 'Sweetest Shakespeare, Fancy's child, / Warbling his native woodnotes wild',[6] Milton seems to see Shakespeare as a (cultural) child of Nature, and it looks as if Hardy's own 'Fancy', reversing Milton's genealogy, is being imagined by Hardy as an offspring of Shakespeare here. To Hardy, Fancy is a 'perfect woman' (p.107) in the sense of one who is susceptible to admiration, with no reluctance to gratify the male gaze, whose 'art itself is nature' in an unreassuring sense. He seems to approve of this in the way in which he will approve of Elfride's 'little artful ways which partly make up ingenuousness', in *A Pair of Blue Eyes* (1873).

Fancy is the bearer of educated refinements which threaten the communitarian ethos of village life: given the sexual infatuation she induces in Vicar Maybold and churchwarden Shiner, reported as '*crazy* to see [her] *playing*' (p.98), the old quire is decisively doomed, while her shilly-shallying in courtship induces insecurity based on the pride and prejudice of class consciousness. No doubt Molly Bloom's idea of 'as well him as another', said of her acceptance of hapless (and subsequently cuckolded) Leopold in Joyce's *Ulysses*, is a harsh point of comparison, but not so much so considering Fancy's (slightly 'against the grain') relinquishing of timid young vicar Maybold. Indeed the 'rejection' itself was in fact a reluctant recantation of an initial acceptance (p.138). And it was Maybold himself who enjoined this when Dick insouciantly revealed the fact of his own engagement on their walk towards Casterbridge, (p.141) just after poor Maybold, flushed with temporary success, seems already to have set about arranging a transfer to Yorkshire (pp.138-139) with Fancy in tow.

Reported earlier as 'looking across at Miss Day in a warmer way than Christianity asked for' (p.56), Maybold and his late-surging suit bid fair to succeed thanks to his impressive umbrella (p.136). Hardy is nothing if not a dab hand at metonymy here: Derrida devotes pages to Nietzsche's 'I have forgotten my umbrella'[7] as a kind of hermeneutic imponderable, but here we can definitely interpret Maybold's phallus of gentrification as coming dangerously close to success, particularly as Dick has just been caught looking a sorry sight without one (p.136). Indeed, Dick's final success in courtship paradoxically flows from Fancy's being thwarted in her desire for Dick because her very achievements deny him access to Fancy as an appropriate suitor. Her talents and acquisitions, combining cultural capital and crass cash, are marshalled against Dick himself by father Geoffrey—quite suggestively a 'head *keeper*' by profession. Ironically, Geoffrey, unlike Dick himself, apparently often expresses himself in thick dialect ('Ay, let en come . . . Leaf, th'rt welcome, 'st know' [p.153]), but Fancy's refinement is clearly some kind of overcompensation for this.

So Geoffrey's initial quashing of Dick's 'suit' (pp.123-124) is even more plausible than his final acceptance of it, and Fancy's own inclination for Dick required the desperate remedy of feigned illness, apparently: the results of these 'power relations', with Dick temporarily routed, eventually forced Fancy to consult a 'wise woman' (p.125), and the result brings gruff but basically fawning father round with a burst of simulated anorexia suggested by (sc. 'Agony') Aunt Endorfield, her very name somewhat bewitching (see 1 *Samuel* 28). Similarly, sex appeal, also a part of power's window-dressing, helps show the old quire the church door as churchwarden Shiner and vicar Maybold succumb to Fancy's charms.

So Maybold's late-flowering offer of marriage would also have been a victory of class and culture over Dick and Fancy's natural attraction. It would also constitute an attack on the idea of remaining 'rooted in one dear perpetual place', in Yeats' phrasing, as Maybold invites Fancy to join him in a 'quiet parsonage-house' as 'the place in which I shall pass my days, wherever it may be situated' (p.137). The paradox of Fancy's triumph is that it is a triumph over the stronger side of the book's implication, even a kind of 'own goal', as it hints that, sentimental journey into the past notwithstanding, the discreet charms of bourgeoisification will conquer, despite Hardy's obvious sympathy with Jane Austen's concern that rank or class should not determine the course of natural affection: Maybold's only slip gives him a momentary resemblance to the egregious Mr Collins as he clumsily reminds Fancy that she would be 'foolish' (p.138) to turn him down.

It is a somewhat darkened idyll which leads up to a (short) series of painful rejections: the *ancien régime* as (paradoxically?) expressed in the form of 'humble and rustic life' is much more obviously something of a 'pushover'. The 'quire', particularly in its approach to a Vicarage containing only the timid young Maybold, seems a disconcerting source of fun as Rusticity Exhibited (pp.62-69), and, later in the short novel these older men tamely retire to the nave from the gallery, dispersed and 'disseminated' without anything more than token opposition. The original terms of retention which they endearingly, if almost half-wittedly, propose, are much too 'soft', proceeding from their fundamental deference ('instead of turning us out neck and crop, let us stay on till Christmas' [p.59]), and they are easily routed by unredoubtable Maybold, who beats them back to Michaelmas (at the end of September).

Fancy is implicated in this also, and Hardy may indeed relish her fashioning rather more than we can, as a 'bunch of sweets' in Part Three, Ch. I, (p.93). She is the eternal-feminine parodically 'self-fashioning' by means of fashion, whose 'whimsical and politically neutral vicissitudes', as Susan Bordo claims, 'supply endless amusement for woman's eternally superficial values'.[8] Yet it is precisely here that fashion, its 'sartorial semiotics' inspiring confidence, may entail the cast(e)ing off of class constrictions. Fancy may even seem finally set, less as a spouse for Dick, than as something of a 'device' with which to defy the daughters of the local gentry, as she enters church (pp.133-134) in provocative ringlets and hat (as opposed to the more demure bonnet). She will thus draw gratifying gasps from the temporarily upstaged daughters of the manor.

Her ambiguous schoolmistress status[9] is eked out not only by Geoffrey Day's hoarding (he is said to have accumulated nine hundred pounds), and a (vague) 'gentlewoman' in the family background; but also her cultural capital as a 'Queen's Scholar' (p. 154), and her exhibitionistic performances on the organ, dooming the ancient quire to extinction in the Darwinian world of church music, apparently. The biographer Robert Gittings is highly instructive on the perilously liminal status of Victorian school teachers and their need to be preternaturally alert to nuances of social context as a matter of professional survival, and the theme is broached as Fancy and Dick drive back from Budmouth to Mellstock and take tea at the inn [p.130]). Milton's parochial beauty was 'the cynosure of neighbouring eyes', but the neighbouring eyes in this case may also have something of Jane Austen's 'neighbourhood of voluntary spies' who induce a justified paranoia. As a response to social provocation Fancy's culture, combined with the significant impact of her *couture*, makes her, not merely defiantly 'miss-ish', almost indeed a (social) missile.

So if Fancy is the 'master-mistress' of the novel's proceedings, not only does Dick's 'passion lend [her] power', in *Romeo and Juliet*'s phrasing, power also flows freely from other sources, including, as he himself frankly avows, Geoffrey's laying up treasure for the daughter he sees as herself an investment of sorts, his calibrations of social status based on pelf, acquirements, and 'the convergence of the twain'. His care and dear concern in these matters will be 'cashed out' later in the form of George Melbury's anxious investments in his daughter Grace in *The Woodlanders* (1887). In that novel, which grows so naturally out of this earlier one, its Fancy-like heroine Grace will ironically protest her status as 'chattel' or commodity, but everyone around her seems to accept that that is indeed exactly what she is.

As himself little more than an 'upper' servant—to 'The Earl of Wessex', naturally—Geoffrey is also 'invested' with a sense of the absoluteness of class fractions, fracturing ideas of pastoralism as a communitarian idyll. Indeed, Hardy himself seems intent on showing that even (or especially) the 'lower orders' have a 'pecking' order: it is by no means clear that Day's second wife's almost deranged preoccupation with the need to produce best linen and china, and a household regimen so exacting it prevents her attendance at the wedding itself [p.157]), should not finally be laid at Geoffrey's own door, despite his own critical tut-tuttings to others over her disturbingly obsessive behaviour (p.157).

So much for those who are at least well enough off to keep up appearances of being so. There are other nuances, nuances of the other(s): for example, Thomas Leaf, the only character named for his maker (who was himself pronounced dead at birth, and whose only children were *leaves*),[10] is introduced as '*a human skeleton and a smock frock*' (p.12). He is also brother to '*ten still-born children*'—and 'Jim', who died aged four hours and a bit. We are not introduced to Mrs Leaf. For some, it seems, this *Under the Greenwood Tree* 'idyll' issues from something like a rather beleaguered 'ghetto'. For a work which seems to have the word *charm* running through it like a reliable watermark, its local effects can be excruciating. By way of comparison we might note Joshua Sobol's play *Ghetto*, in which the inhabitants of a Nazi-policed and eventually 'liquidated' ghetto keep their spirits up with song and dance routines when the fit is on them.[11] In performance this can be embarrassing, and the conditions of living in *Under the Greenwood Tree* can also be wince-making, and the high level of 'cultural expression' achieved seems almost equally against the cultural odds. In the light of Thomas Leaf et al., Mrs Penny's pre-marital injunction to the young bride of "'tis to be, and here goes', thrice repeated, supposedly a reassuring mantra of sorts (p.147), begins to sound rather grim—Jane Austen's heartfelt exclamation over a bride-to-be's prospect of incessant child-bearing even at the level of relatively privileged society might be considered here. Hardy himself underscores the point in Reuben's hints of straitened means which attend the 'torrent of babies' (in Tennyson's hysterical phrase), with hints of a particular pressure-point when 'the oldest daughter's boots be only a size less than her mother's, and the rest o' the flock close behind her' (p.157).

It seems characteristic of Hardy not to be able to resist a hint of half-starved peasants living in desperately unsanitary conditions while simultaneously serving up an entertainment of 'humorous rustics' (Leslie Stephen) consisting of 'distinctly patronising' (Raymond Williams)[12] affection. His statement that he was describing the two village 'castes' (*sic*),[13] seems to co-exist with 'communal' gestures of continuity. And a humbler version of Yeats' grandiose 'custom and ceremony' under Geoffrey Day's spreading beech tree in the final tableau may itself be something of 'a fake model of festive inclusivity'.[14] Leaf himself, for example, does seem to get a bit of reluctant 'care in the community', although he is patronized (e.g., pp.60-61), always just on the point of being excluded. It seems almost as if our attendance, or at least attention is required, just at the moment at which these social ties would seem to be dissolving, as church organs, manned by women, announce the death of the 'organic' community.

What might be described as, in a double sense, 'the feminisation of "culture"' also sees to it that a strong sense of social gradation is well to the fore, correlating rustic expression(s) less with charm than uncouthness—'no 'thee's' and 'thou's' and no wiping mouths with the backs of hands at *my* wedding, thanks' (p.155). Hardy himself uses a Darwinian image for the ousting of dialect, but *his own* attitude towards its use is defensive, reminding us of Roland Barthes' military image for the struggle of linguistic registers.

Aware of being not so very far from the Mudie's crowd[15] — those urban perusers who associate country living with congenial escapism and so bring editorial pressure to 'keep sociology out of it' in the interests of 'prose idyll', 'pastoral', etc., Hardy seems to be furtively letting it in anyway, rather like a ferret, quietly hinting at the unpleasant effects of cultural pretension, frantic penny-pinching, class discrimination, and the results of rural slum-living. Geoffrey's relationships with his slightly deranged second wife and rather flighty daughter are disconcerting, but so also is his social role. As a result of his 'game keeping', Geoffrey has an odd nose due to his receiving a blow during a poaching fray (pp.74-75). Nothing is actually said to this effect, but Geoffrey's job is the slightly embarrassing one of protecting his Lord's enclosed excess from the 'local natives', inconveniently returning as 'skeletons in smock-frocks' [Hardy's phrase] trying to get something to eat.

As if in the interests of balance, Fancy will give the daughters of the local gentry their comeuppance, wearing a hat and (literally) letting her hair down, and that blue dress (pp.132-133), in order to show that, although she is only a schoolteacher, Geoffrey has so much stashed away she can afford to 'flout 'em and scout 'em'. Far from being 'free' as that line from *The Tempest* goes on to indicate, 'thought' is, it seems, terribly expensive (not that the signs of it here are particularly pronounced). Education too seems a 'token' here, something to be cashed in, not quite itself. (The 'exchange-value' of Fancy's formal certification greatly outweighs the 'use-value' of what Hardy calls 'subtle thought on things'.) Certainly Dick and Fancy, unlike the later Sue and Jude, are hardly exemplars of 'intellectual intercourse' (the phrase seems just right for the later couple). Indeed Hardy makes it very clear indeed that, although basically nice young people, they are indeed 'joined at the hip'. As the Mellstock fiddlers 'kick back their chairs and saw madly at the strings with legs firmly spread and eyes closed', Dick and Fancy ('You think their names are not puns?' as one commentator alarmingly puts it)[16] dance so close together that 'they were practically one person' (p.42).

Dick and Fancy are clearly 'part of nature', but Dick also has a socially 'liminal' position, humbly 'entranced' by a Fancy who will provide a kind of 'entrée' to the 'just-about-"bourgeois"', given Fancy's more comfortably ensconced occupation of her 'class fraction'. But social imaginaries provide shifting vectors of class here: we initially see Dick as a member of the choir ('quire') and a horse-and-cart man, yet we are told at one point that he has been so well educated his siblings can hardly look him in the eye (p.85). Described as 'penniless', twice, but with an expanding business another minute, more horses needed, and a business card (p.141), it is not entirely clear what Fancy is getting either, except as expressed by a sense of social 'differences without positive terms' rather confusingly applied to the 'same person'.

Pastoral, it seems, needs the soft-focus treatment,[17] but that paradoxically brilliant 'blurring' he does so well and so disconcertingly also entails Hardy's showing *the process of 'blurring' itself*, with a strong sense of social imaginaries and self-deceptions. Perhaps even the absent Earl of Wessex has something to answer for here, infecting underlings like Geoffrey and Mrs Day with defensive notions of property and propriety which re-enact social exclusion.

However class calibrations actually apply to these country matters, someone is certainly getting stung here: indeed, Geoffrey seems almost grateful when the bees do it to him (pp.117-118) (as a small price to pay to those who, unlike humans, otherwise give something for nothing?). It is bees who seem, after all, to 'yield a better return' (as the homologous George Melbury of *The Woodlanders* [1887] would put it), than Day's hen-pecking second wife and slightly worrying daughter. As Virgil, fellow-countryman, puts it, '*Sic vos non vobis mellificatis, apes*' ('Thus ye make honey not for yourselves, o bees!'). 'Honey-taking' suggests processes of courtship and bee-keeping, and when Fancy too is stung, the 'swelling' of her 'lip', (p.121), her dismay, and the involvement of her suitors in the affair also seems symbolic and anticipatory of that 'honey of generation' about which Hardy has made us feel rather ambivalent, or queasy. As if presenting mutually exclusive activities, the 'murmur of innumerable bees'[18] near the conclusion almost causes Dick to miss his own wedding. We are reminded that a wedding may be held at any time, but a swarming, part of the course of nature, takes primacy over what a contemporary Hardy might have called 'the *Schwarmerei* of ecclesiastical superstructuralism'.

Itself caught in a brief snapshot as 'part of nature', the wedding seems to be virtually 'achieved' as the local folk pass through a 'natural temple' (in Baudelaire's phrasing)[19] on the way to what sounds like the ironic 'redundancy' of a church wedding itself elided here ('Now among dark perpendicular firs, like the shafted columns of a cathedral [pp.153-154] . . .'): those *vivants piliers*' ('living pillars'), phallicly ecclesiastical, suggest, with Ezra Pound's phrasing, the 'adequacy of the *natural* symbol' to the matter in hand.[20] These 'shafted columns' also give echo to Wallace Stevens' idea that 'all our ideas come from the natural world'.[21] Oddly, Stevens' own example was 'umbrellas = trees'. Formally, we might say, 'Dick-ian' trees win out over 'Mayboldian' umbrellas here, but the implication is that the case may be reversible, and Hardy insinuates the implausibility of the happy outcome: formally, *Maybold* (getting his correspondence in first) renounced *Fancy*, not, as one would expect, vice versa [p.141].

This version of pastoral may sound like a paradoxically exclusive genre in the sense of *attempting to exclude all that which might be thought of as incipiently exclusive*—and hence with a 'no admittance' sign for 'bourgeois' habits and assumptions. Yet suggestively even some of the 'natural' descriptions sound suggestively suburban ('fuchsias and dahlias were laden till eleven o'clock with small drops and dashes of water' [p.102]). We are similarly flummoxed if we turn to forms of exchange and recompense, as things turn here on a honey/money 'antithesis which is not one'. 'Outside' pastoral, it seems, is the dumb god, riches, while 'inside', honey provides the significant reminder that 'you can't eat money'. Teresa Brennan articulates Marx's insight that 'in a market system a commodity is always produced for exchange, and has exchange-value. But it also and always has use-value, and there can be no use-value without nature, or natural substance'.[22]

Yet even for Geoffrey Day's grouchy under-helper Enoch, it is 'without *money*' that 'man is a shadder' (shadow) (p.148): this sounds almost like a parapraxis for 'honey', a linguistic stumbling on a truth which makes Enoch disturbingly irrecuperable, a shadowy figure alienated from the wedding celebrations (p.187). Perhaps, then, Hardy's 'village castes'[23] finally correspond to a difference between those who understand or accept only use-value, and those more sophisticatedly alert to exchange value: 'Marx describes the money form as a symbol of the commodity *as such*, or of the commodity exchange-value . . . over against use-value, which he aligns with production and consumption. The money form is not, then, any particular commodity . . . but the "material representative of general wealth"'.[24]

Under the Greenwood Tree celebrates 'use value' with relish, and almost seems to be identifying against itself in being forced to acknowledge the power of money. Yet money, it seems, is finally more potent than honey, the 'other' representation of that without which 'man is a shadder', whose difference may decline into mere *différance*: the Hardys' piano teacher was occasionally 'paid' in honey[25] (the recipient's good manners would presumably entail shrugging one's shoulders and asking 'what's the difference?'). And indeed the Hardy of *Far from the Madding Crowd* (1874), putting words into the collective family mouth here, might indeed have enthusiastically described it as 'the divinest form money can wear'. As if in tandem with this, *ancien régime* masculinity, awed by 'united 'ooman', succumbs to the 'progressive feminisation' of 'culture': fatherly Reuben,[26] for example, head of the ousted quire, stands for all investments in cultural nostalgia—combining use-value, maleness, and the user-friendly version of oedipality implied by his tendency to address all as '*my sonnies*' (even, amusingly enough, when females are present).

Hardy, then, while in some ways coming up with 'the goods' as a metropolitan editor might require them, hardly paints rusticity in exclusively rosy colours here: pastoral, it would seem, *is* overdeterminedly 'hymeneal' in dramatising a 'permitting and prohibiting of "access"' in a class as well as marital sense. The narrative is punctuated by an intrusive relay in which honey is threatened by money, the organic community by organs, Dick by Maybold, men by women, and use value by exchange value. Use value puts an emphasis on things made almost venerable by human association(s), threatened by a more abstract discourse of the value(s) of exchange.

Chapter 3

Fogeys and Fossils: *A Pair of Blue Eyes*

Although in formal terms it may be said to attract a reasonable share of critical attention, for any imaginable reading public *A Pair of Blue Eyes* seems more or less to have dropped out of the canonic frame—categorized as par-ergonal rather than perennial. Yet if one wished to proceed in the mode of recommendation, it would be perfectly possible to advance the claim for this to be considered as nothing less than the ultimate in Victorian novels. It is interesting in this connection to find that Tennyson and Coventry Patmore adored the book and saw in it the work of a 'natural born poet', a point which a still young but already much-abused Hardy must have found deeply gratifying.[1] Lord Northcliffe, another representative figure, if a slightly more disconcerting one, claimed to 'know it backwards' and greatly to prefer it to *Tess* and *Jude*, for example.[2]

Indeed, at the level of a kind of journalistic incitement to the reader which would still function as showing what a cultural archive it is, the novel might be described as being full of fogeys, railway elopements, slender hypergamous Youths with Prospects, encrusted snobberies, misremembered Latin quotations, gout, Rectories, broken-hearted peregrinations with a Baedeker, Family Vaults, geology, chess, church restoration, forelock-touching rusticity, strenuous autodidacticism, heavy fathers pursuing flighty runaway daughters and bitter widows muttering in the shades of the shrubbery, with the spirit of Samuel Smiles over all, more particularly in the form of the 'Every Man His Own Maker' Club of St. Launce deftly caricaturing the Victorian worship of push and pelf. It also projects a wonderful post-Romantic sense of 'the world's body' in the form of dramatic descriptions of a wild Cornwall conscripted to underscore and orchestrate the human emotions, particularly feminine ones, which animate it.

Yet the fact remains that these emotions turn out to be, for the most part, extremely painful and unpleasant ones. The novel finally offers a spirited critique of the Victorian world it projects and phallogocentric imperatives and patriarchal propensities it propounds. Seascapes convey a symbolic sense of a 'destructive element' in which an imperious 'linguistic mastery of the drives',[3] a male (and bourgeois) prerogative, must founder. As bossy Henry Knight, verbally abusive barrister and 'killer reviewer', doubts and suspects, yet still quite strongly loves his enchanting, if flighty fiancée Elfride, Hardy writes that the sea . . . could as usual be heard from this point along the whole distance between promontories . . . floundering and entangling itself among the insulated stacks of rock which dotted the water's edge – the miserable skeletons of tortured old cliffs that would not even yet succumb to the wear and tear of the tide'[4](p.260).

The startlingly emotive charge suggests a kind of 'objective correlative' for the human emotions which fill the novel itself. Students of William Blake would recognize this as a depiction of a familiarly patriarchal agon of the kind he liked to depict, with stony 'Urizenic' figures, insecure yet imperious, exhibiting a frantic mistrust of what is uncontained, immeasurable or unpredictable – and particularly of 'the drives', the semiotic sounds and rhythms of pleasureable 'fantasies of the feminine'. The contemporary reader would instantly compose a suggestive anticipation of the work of Julia Kristeva here: as a master of 'hard, square sentences' (p.123), Knight is set on linguistic victory as a kind of 'anti-Pygmalion' bent on 'petrifying' the once dashing and apparently uncontrollable Elfride.

The narrative will show the process by which Elfride is reduced to what Hélène Cixous would describe as a *'personne'*,[5] that is to say, declined from a 'person' who was 'so *living*' (p.19; Hardy's italics) to 'nobody'. Her enchanting spontaneity is annulled by Knight's terrifying notions of what is 'proper' to femininity. Informally put, in a context particularly alert to such terms, Elfride is finally reduced from a tomboy of sorts to a kind of 'tomb-girl'. And perhaps Hardy's most powerfully operative irony here is that it was the *unreconstructed* Elfride who, thanks to her dash and pluck, was able to save the life of Knight himself, trapped on 'The Cliff without a Name'—with unorthodox methods he was hardly in a position to frown upon.

But the (finally) ignoble Knight was subsequently to erase these very qualities through his Victorian patriarchal insistences, firstly in cowing and quashing Elfride in various spheres, but also by an emphasis on sexual purity and absolute right to an (attenuated) 'sexual initiation'. Knight had commended this, in itself a prurient rather than innocuous practice, to the young Stephen Smith in his ('no-lady's') chambers in Bede Court. Ironically, it was Stephen himself who had in fact kissed Elfride before he did, thus making her something of a 'love-adept' (Shelley), if only by comparison with Knight, already, as eminently the 'young fogey' type, something of a 'confirmed bachelor'.

Inflexible and domineering Knight will prove to be the archetypal 'control freak', and Elfride, unfortunately, is particularly provocative and challenging for him here— 'ultra-feminine in being something of an emanation of wild Cornwall itself: as Jane Thomas helpfully points out, she has had 'restricted access to the regimes and jurisdiction of society'.[6] Her femininity is, as it were, 'overdetermined' by her upbringing. And her lineal descent from 'nobby' (p.230) female 'bolters' makes her something of a proto-Bathsheba (the better-known heroine said alarmingly to be capable of conceiving and carrying out 'sexual' exploits in the immediately-following *Far from the Madding Crowd* [1874]).

But Hardy also rehearses as a master-elegist here, imbricating desire and death with what seem to be mandatory visits to the (Luxellian) Family Vaults, quietly intimating that in narrative no less than biological terms this is indeed where it will all come to an apposite, if untimely, end. From toiling workmen therein—who provide a kindly choric sense of parochial doings—we learn that Elfride's aristocratic grandmother ran off with a singer (and died 'at her first groaning' [p.202]). This also predicts Elfride's own death from a miscarriage. As a kind of intermediate term in this tradition of 'family "fugue"-ing', the daughter which resulted from the match, Elfride's mother, eloped with Elfride's father, the handsome but stupid Rector, Christopher Swancourt.

Christopher seems to have developed an intellectual carapace, and his ideological inflexibilities as a 'Fossilized Tory' (p.35) [his description] seem to be offering a kind of atonement for his amusingly unpatriarchal flightiness of yore. But Christopher's class prejudice is *also* reinforced by his lack of talent. This is revealed in a quiet aside hinting at blundering share dealings, which have unduly impoverished his formerly 'comfortable' family, bringing him perilously close (in crass cash terms at any rate) to the level of amiable rural builder John Smith. Unfortunately Smith turns out to be the father of Stephen, the young architect's assistant sent from London to restore Swancourt's almost allegorically crumbling ecclesiastical 'heritage'. Stephen's boyish charm and attractiveness lead to his being treated initially as 'one of the family' and, more compromisingly, as a worthy suitor for Elfride. The crisis provoked by the revelation of his social unworthiness leads to a painful re-emergence of some familar Victorian postures. Indeed, it is 'pain' which provides the link to the novel's processes of social rupturing and female abjection.

Stephen, staying at Endelstow on equal terms and already far gone in love for the flighty, slightly captious Elfride, blurted the fateful disclosure of his paternity on hearing exaggerated reports of John's hand having been 'squashed to a pummy' by a descending 'beetle' (p.61). Unfortunately, with his emphasis on 'good dinners, genealogy, and patrician reminiscences' (p.62), Swancourt's kindliness was promptly overtaken by his prejudices. Stephen, though callow and ingenuous, had already intuited that his decline in status would render him a 'different person' and, quite suddenly, a highly *ineligible* one, challenging Elfride's (it would seem, incontrovertibly redundant) assumption that 'an architect in London is an architect in London' (p.58). In a scene of fogeyism and 'distinction(s)', Swancourt ejected Stephen, with much stereotypical grumbling: he had, *inter alia*, served Stephen, now proved a son of one of his 'peasants', one of his last dozen bottles of '40 Martinez (port wine) (p.66), which particularly rankled, believing him to be a bona fide metropolitan with the correct class coefficients—and consequently one of 'orthodox' educational and social 'formation'. Of course by his actions Swancourt virtually foments the lovers to undertake one of those desperate remedies Hardy is ever ready to dispense. Elfride, with all the volatility predicted by the immemorial rustics speaking from the family vaults with hollow authority, is more than genealogically proven as scion of a line of 'nobby' (p.230) female bolters as she rushes off with Stephen on the up train to London—with the best of marital intentions.

However, despite this being an affair of 'hot youth', things are unhappily unconsummated, as the dismayingly dull journey and the unpleasantness of London as glimpsed from Paddington leads to a (temporary) death of desire (p.88). They take the next down train, not unobserved by the bleak and malignant widow Jethway (p.90). She will subsequently use her knowledge of the incident to rupture Elfride's involvement with Harry Knight, Stephen's unwitting supplanter, with poison-pen correspondence, which will arrive only *d'outre-tombe* to quash tomb-haunting Elfride's engagement (p.267). This was after Swancourt's apparently strong church tower—made emblematical of Knight's love by a passing Elfride already alarmed at Knight's jealous estrangement—had fallen suddenly in their very sight (p.253). This tower-toppling is realistically explained as a result of what would appear to be a disastrously obliterating church 'restoration', but in the text it has a largely symbolic function.

Apparently another 'objective correlative' of sorts, this abrupt phallic descent will prove to have killed Jethway, sight unseen for the moment (but whose lifeless body Knight will later discover, in gruesome circumstances, and see to, with unpleasant narrative effects). The disturbingly embittered and malignant widow seems to have 'got mad' in both the American and British senses, and she will, if unwittingly, finally 'get even' by toppling Knight's already tottering love for an Elfie he already suspects to have been 'sexually active' in the ridiculously attenuated degree defined by Knight here (a peck on the cheek is deeply compromising, apparently). Peeping Jethway, deranged through her bereavement, is fully cognisant of these pitifully innocuous acts of 'carnal knowledge'. But at least (thanks to the toppling of the ironically 'phallic' tower), she will not have lived to witness the efficacy of her malevolence in toppling Knight's—in the form of his domineering suitorship.

The reader may well feel that, neglected as this text is, we might simply emphasize how Hardy succeeds brilliantly here. But where he does perhaps 'put his thumb in the scales' just a little is that his avowed theme (as enunciated by his narrator) is that Knight's palpable jealousy and emotional perturbation over Elfride's imagined behaviour was a sign that his love was *weakening*, whereas (in Blake's idiom), it is clear that his 'selfish love' has 'increased', as his own power dissolves at the thought of a sexually initiated Elfride. He is obviously disturbed by the very idea of 'female power', even if only in bestowing (sexual) favour(s). And this is particularly unfair when all other forms of access to 'power' for Elfride have been sealed off here, *and by Knight himself*. His final desertion of Elfride is thus a kind of pyrrhic victory.

Knight partly 'inherited' Elfride due to his initially attractive personal and intellectual characteristics, but, ironically, the 'position' became 'overdetermined' here against her first real suitor, young Stephen Smith, as Elfride's father Christopher Swancourt also 'improved his position' in the chess game of social advancement by a method quite likely to occur to the talentless: ironically, as Elfride's mad 'elopement which was not one' foundered, Swancourt himself went off to marry, without hitch, the richest heir(ess) – after Lord Luxellian himself – in the county (the middle-aged and physically unalluring Mrs Troyton, a merry widow). This successful matrimonial adventure, in sardonic counterpoint with the young lovers' failure, also pulled the Swancourt family well out of Stephen's social reach, despite his own obvious 'family vaulting' (see *Macbeth* [1.7.27]) ambition (e.g., p.32).

Hardy makes the reader herself complicit with some narrative bolting here, and his narrative bustle seems to require some 'looking before and after' to appreciate: in fact, Elfride had quite early been 'in trouble' over her 'lovers', and was later accused by Henry Knight of confessing to having sat on one 'lover's' tomb with another (p.257) while attempting to exonerate herself to a third (i.e., himself). Knight finally had his suspicions about possible amorous predecessors aroused, unfortunately just after revealing, what was most terrible of all for Elfride, that in *his* case there was *nothing to reveal* (p.235). Elfride herself was forced to reveal her history, as 'a woman with a past' through her vetoing of Knight's choice as a souvenir of their relationship. Unfortunately he selected Stephen's original gift to her of a myrtle plant – itself, of course, a traditional emblem of love (p.240). This required an explanation after its refusal only because Elfride was so admirably 'scrupulous' about 'an iota', to use Knight's own phrasing.

The bustle of Hardy's narrative here is as technically delightful as it is emotionally upsetting: climaxing Elfride's unfortunate fall from grace, Knight, helped by a Lord Luxellian who is himself to become the actual husband of Elfride, will deposit the body of the tower-crushed Jethway in her 'deserted' cottage (pp.264-5). He will discover some rather bafflingly wispy drafts of the perfectly intelligible poison-pen letter he will receive next day with the full details of the Stephen-and-Elfride elopement (not quite a full-blown one after all, however), together with an enclosed (and touchingly anguished) epistolary request from Elfride herself to the malignant Jethway not to expose her. This will lead to jealous Knight's pitiless rupturing of the engagement (and to the breaking of 'Elfie's' heart). Subsequently, he will be importuned in his London chambers by the distraught damsel who is herself amusingly pursued by an understandably gruff and bewildered Christopher Swancourt (p.275). Like Knight himself, Swancourt is similarly scandalized by thoughts of possible scandal thanks to this latest outbreak of mini-bolting on Elfride's part, which proves, at least to Christopher's own satisfaction, that she who runs may ruin. Ironically, his own subsequent alienation from the girl will play its part in her self-alienation, which will lead to her listless surrender to a Lord Luxellian she may still have learned to love before her final sequestration from Stephen and Knight alike. Stephen, meanwhile, pathetically convinced of Elfride's staunchness and of the hopelessness of his suit in the circumstances, betakes himself to India to seek an architectural fortune in building projects. These will come fruitlessly to fruition as Elfride's inconstancy, revealed in those pointedly 'terminal' Family Vaults yet again, sees Stephen sickened unto death by the confirmed defection of the woman he idolized to the man he had idolized (pp.209-10).

Hardy, aware of his own humble genealogy (while his personal circumstances were of course close to those of Stephen, as himself an architect's assistant and scion of a humble rural builder), cites canonic texts with 'self-legitimising' frequency. For example, Chapter 23 deals with Stephen's first tremulous homecoming from India (ostensibly to order quantities of Birmingham cast iron, actually to see if his entrepreneurial architectural 'yuppie-ism' renders him any more acceptable as a suitor to Swancourts). Its epigraph pertinently inquires if 'auld acquaintance' should 'be forgot?' (p.178). Burns' hint of dialect has its point as Stephen descends, without personal arrogance, on the humble family home. Of course Burns' line forms a rhetorical question, but here, unfortunately, the answer seems, overwhelmingly, to be—'Yes – they must be'. Stephen has been condemned by the stereotypically Victorian Mr Swancourt with an equivalent of the 'base born churl' insult which Hardy's wife Emma's father, a derelict solicitor, it seems, as well as a drunkard, thought fit to throw at Hardy himself as a young suitor.[7] And Swancourt, as we saw, has been particularly outraged to have offered house and home to the son of humble John Smith, who potters about his estate doing not-so-little-little jobs with skill.

Stephen had been on his mettle as at least a mimic bourgeois, who has learnt chess and Latin by correspondence courses with seemingly noble Knight, the genuine varsity man. Stephen at this stage is a serious case of social liminality, in terms of his social 'class-ification' made out of differences without positive terms combined with differences made out of too many of them—'not good enough' for Swancourt, apparently, but now rather too good for his own dad: 'Sir says I to my own son. But ye've gone up so Stephen', says the gentle stonemason (p.180), fairly innocent in such matters, but highly impressed by Stephen's gentlemanly mien. His homely surname underscores the unromantic genealogy which has its place in Stephen's displacement by Knight—whose very name, by contrast, bespeaks his superiority—seeming by itself to require the address of 'Sir'. Despite 'sirring' his own son, though, John, unlike his wife, has not quite got the point about the importance of jealously guarding any signifiers of social status or social ascent, however incipient. (Here Hardy's women tend to be 'united' in a less mysteriously Lacanian way than Marjorie Garson intimated in her impressive book on Hardy.) And it seems particularly ominous that for Stephen's homecoming, Smith, to the deprecations of his spouse Jane, has freely invited from the lowest social tier—what we must call 'comic turns' like William Worm, an ex-servant of snobbish Mr Swancourt himself (and thus awkward for Stephen as wooer of Swancourt's daughter Elfride to have about the place). Worm's large wife Barbara is in attendance, as is Robert Lickpan, a pig-killer whose talk is of porkers (pp.180-7). William's tales, in apparent contrast, are of his incessant (but apparently undiagnosed) tinnitus—although he does sustain the porcine theme in hearing something like 'frying bacon' as they all tuck into new-slaughtered pig. What Raymond Williams called Hardy's 'distinctly patronizing affection' for those of rustic rank is fully in evidence here once more, but Hardy cleverly bisects the audience response by making the homely rustic fun congenial. At the same time, he provides sympathetic handling of Stephen's fear (as a suitor) of being all too well suited to humble and rustic life through his links with the local links-man (Robert) and possibly even as 'kin[dred] to [the] Worm', as Wordsworth might put it (*Prelude* 8.488). But as he will shortly discover, Stephen has already been supplanted, thanks to Elfride's love of 'sheer force in a man' (p.203), and Knight's refined bullying obviously has some kind of erotic charge for her. She has also just participated in an incident on a nameless precipice which has precipitated a special intensity and sense of 'intimacy' with Knight, arising from its very proximity to death.

Despite his accusations of feminine folly— or rather behaviour he induces in order to label it *as* folly, and despite the admonitory lectures on 'wind science' (at which he would obviously be highly adept), Knight cannot prevent his own suspension on the slope over 'the Cliff without a Name' as he foolishly attempts to retrieve his hat (suggestively, '*head*gear') (p.166). The 'Cliff without a Name' provides symbolic perils, of 'falling' either (in-) to 'death' or 'sex', those always potentially frightening and ineluctably *carnal* appointments lying just beyond the pale of linguistic mastery. Indeed, the Cliff will now provide a (fore-) taste of both. We have had one demonstration after another of Knight's 'linguistic mastery of the drives', asserted unwittingly in the first instance in his quashing of Elfride's claims to any linguistic mastery *herself* in her novel-writing experiment (p.124). In those patronizing, superior metropolitan tones and terms with which Hardy himself was already all too familiar, Knight positively recommends her decision to abandon what might even have become a profession, in favour of the traditional female destiny of silence, obscurity, and marital submissiveness.

Knight, whose name also (be-) speaks him (as) a chess-man of sorts, had also defeated Elfride in the formalities of the great nineteenth century *Kriegspiel* itself (pp.132-7). Like Dr Johnson, who probably has something to answer for here, he also 'talked for victory', and we are told that he 'somewhat blamably, keenly enjoyed sparring with the palpitating mobile creature, whose excitable nature made any such thing a species of cruelty' (p.146). The novel's processes show Elfride subjected to what Lacan calls 'aphanisis' (Lacan describes this complete rupture with the drives as 'the "fading" of the subject's being', fascinatingly associated in the novel with the process of 'becoming a woman').[8] Masochistically loving the very torment and emotional turbulence he induces, Elfride may herself be said to 'slip up' in 'falling for' Knight even as she goes to greet Stephen's returning boat with her spy-glass (p.163). But the whole affair is in (narrative) suspense as Knight is suspended—his mind concentrated wonderfully like Dr Johnson's famous 'man about to be hanged' (or one might say 'suspended'), on this anonymous cliff (pp.166-7), which, nameless as it is, we have already seen to be symbolic of 'that which language cannot reach'. From this suspense he (and we) are rescued by Elfride, *'sans peur et sans reproche'*— reproach *for* him, that is, or reproach *to* her, despite being, or especially as being, minus the underwear with which she has made a magnificent rope for the fearfully suspended man (pp.175-6). The 'impropriety which is not one' is itself a rebuke to those who would take thoughts of feminine propriety too far. Ironically, these would certainly include the man on the slippery slope himself.

It's worth mentioning that Hardy seems to have composed the ultimate in 'cliff-hanger' narratives here, as Knight confronts his apparent destiny of imminent annihilation, uncomfortably sharing a ledge with a fossil trilobite. The extinct creature, eyes dead and turned to stone, is suggestive of Knight's own 'stony British stare',[9] as well as his petrified 'concepts without intuitions' (in Kantian phraseology). Hardy describes as if with anticipatory relish the sea far below as Knight's 'funeral pall and its edging', the implicit irony being that the very dash and pluck of Elfride's act in saving the fellow will constitute 'perdition' for *her*, as she is invariably doomed to punishment for her good qualities—her spontaneity, susceptibility and ready sympathies. She had, after all, on that occasion, merely gone out to watch her temporary fiancé Stephen temporarily returning from India in his ship. Initially engaged in watching the approach of her first fiancé, Elfride is then caught up in saving her second, the slipping Knight. This will prove to be a slip on her part, as, reduced to a mere slip of a girl in being divested of her underwear, she ropes him in (p.176). My phrasing tries to convey something of Hardy's happily conceited mischief here. The subsequent moment of unavowed but incontrovertible passion which Knight will refuse to consummate, will still have the effect of sealing Stephen's fate, inscribing Knight as the acceptable wooer henceforth.

Hardy, who progresses through linguistic conceits as well as narrative strategies, is also implying that her rescue of him entailed a kind of 'felix culpa', the 'happy fall' (or fault) of theological provenance—referring to (un-) fortunate events in the Garden of Eden. Elfride's first 'lover' (in Hardy's sense of 'suitor') was suggestively said to have been 'Felix' (so that her original 'culpa' was allegedly (with) 'Felix'). But Elfride was culpable here only to his mad mother Jethway (p.218). In fact it was 'Felix' who was himself culpable in his 'original sin' of attempting to kiss Elfride, if only after she had singled him out, ironically by congratulating him on the felicity of his name (p.218).

Jethway's subsequent hostility and malignant persecution will rupture Elfride's engagement to Knight. Properly speaking, Elfride may be said to have 'slipped' first with Stephen (with a more legitimate version of a 'felix culpa' this time), *not* with Jethway's son Felix, granting the young architect her first proper kiss—in this reciprocated form, those genuinely Keatsian 'slippery blisses'.[10] Through another kind of 'slippage', punitive Mrs Jethway functions as a kind of female censor for these *later* slips of the susceptible Elfride. Her (no-) slipping with Felix, for which Elfride was unfairly punished, had its own slippage—as she *was* perhaps culpable when she slipped from Stephen to Knight. (Again, this phrasing tries to give some sense of Hardy's congenial mischief here, as Knight, suspended between death and sex, finds Elfride in his arms. By a kind of embarrassing economy, she divested herself of underwear to save him from certain extinction, but now her near-nakedness will accommodate him as a lover, in antithetical moments of emotional intensity, both covered by the idea of 'dying', to which Knight is understandably inadequate.)

Yet Hardy has still not finished with this trope: there is also a conceptual rope connecting Mrs Grundy and Knight by way of Hardy mentor Leslie Stephen, himself a Knight and climber of mountains as well as an editor (and frequent quasher) of dangerously worded writings, and so himself often suspended on slippery slopes of one kind or another. To register the emotional basis of this, it should be remembered here that Hardy had originally attempted to set himself up as a poet. His initial failure in this respect was irritating, entailing the discovery that, in order to 'become' one, one requires some 'other[s]' to recognize the fact. Only then did he decline upon the novel-writing he so obviously considered *infra dig*, and as 'good little hand at a serial' was committed, but not without groaning, to providing cliff-hanger narratives for fussy metropolitan editors: and he might be said to be rather sardonically 'solving his problems' here by hanging a fussy metropolitan editor on a cliff—possibly obtaining thereby some therapeutic relief for the indignities, as he construed them, incident to his profession.

Nothing if not risqué, then, as he mingles (Leslie) Stephen with Knight's predicament, Hardy seems to want us to make something of the following sentence describing it: 'A slight superficial wetting of the soil hereabout made it far more slippery to stand on than the same soil thoroughly drenched. The inner substance was still hard, and was lubricated by the moistened film' (p.166). Knowing Hardy as we do by now, we may well suspect this. In a sense, Knight falls foul of female sexuality, slips up on its slope. His emotional intelligence is well to the rear of his theoretical lore, given his vulnerable awareness that he is no graduate of 'Cupid's college'[11]—as revealed not only in his embarrassed confession to Stephen earlier, but also in the confidences imparted to Elfride on board the boat returning the newly-enriched Swancourts and Knight from London to Cornwall (p.235). Indeed, we might say that Knight himself is almost as ashamed of, as it were, 'passing' some sort of 'virginity test' here as a Victorian lady might be of failing one. Unfortunately his own inexperience makes a similar inexperience for him on the part of any lady he should encounter mandatory, to Elfride's secret horror.

So we may describe his experience here on the cliff as already an allegory of his panic in the face of the loss of control, the necessary forfeiting of 'pluterperfect imperturbability', as Joyce might have called it, which falling in love would entail. Following his ordeal his scrupulosity occludes the passionate abandon which the scene, the occasion and Elfride invite, with a suggestive sense of a *délire de toucher* on his part. Metaphorical slipping and sliding are eked out by some painfully terminal Hardyan conceits here, in a transcendence of 'realism' which readers of this book will already have learned to expect. Such 'troping' continues to supply structuring devices throughout: things have miscarried, after all, and after her death from a miscarriage Elfride is put on the carriage which joins the train which is carrying (and now miscarrying, as things are, by this token, miscarrying for them) Harry Knight and Stephen Smith (pp.295-6). The latter has indeed been enriched by his architectural practice in India (p.280), the former somewhat impoverished by a Flaubertian 'no progress pilgrimage'[12] of sorts in Europe (pp.281-2), in an attempt to get over Elfride.

Indeed, this train itself nearly miscarries near Chippenham, the funeral carriage almost not being reattached, occasioning the comment by a bystander—'what fools there are in the world' (p.296). This also forms a cruel, if inadvertent, gloss on the way in which Knight and Stephen are being virtually derailed by this turn of events. The 'up train to Paddington' with Elfride and Stephen had earlier allegorized the death of desire, while this final, 'down' train seems to allegorize a 'desire "of" death'. Hardy tests even 'theory' here in his narrative cunning: the apparently significant moment of mutual 'anagnorisis' (or 'recognition') on the part of Knight and Stephen as they poke their heads out of the window to see what is afoot seemed to be final narrative 'kernel' here[13] ('each was *troubled* by the other's presence'). (Each of these former friends had pretended his indifference to Elfride as they discussed their former relationship to her, though Stephen in particular had been frustratedly agog to know why Knight had not married her [he himself proved to be the reason].)

But Stephen's and Knight's intense rivalry has become an irrelevance, as the following sentence will prove to have revealed. Its apparent insignificance introduces the final narrative effect as Elfride's impressive railway bier is added to the narrative chain: 'At Chippenham there was a little waiting, and some loosening and attaching of carriages' (p.296). This sounds like a simple piece of incidental 'reality-effecting' (in Roland Barthes' idiom). But the object itself will prove, shatteringly, to be the bier of once 'so living' Elfride, decisive and desolating for the two men—no less than for the reader who has surely taken Elfride to his heart. So Elfride's miscarriage is itself troping on this particular train of events. Successful Stephen and Knight may be, but Elfride is dead, and, although it is not formally either Stephen or Knight who have killed her, it may be felt that she has not merely lived 'a life of allegory' but died a death of one also. Her overdeterminedly womanly fate was that of being 'cabined, cribbed confined' (*Macbeth*, 3.4.24)—and finally 'coffined', as she is. Indeed, miscarrying, her own body became a kind of coffin for her own child. Ironically, then, the Elfride who showed herself to be 'too motherly by half' in responding to Lord Luxellian's little daughters, known to have been neglected by their (un-) natural mother (e.g., p.29), herself died in the act of attempting to 'become one'. Her womb became a tomb.

A Pair of Blue Eyes, then, might be described as a study in narrative miscarriages ended by Elfride's own. In an account of the servant Unity to a Knight and Stephen apprized of (and devastated by) the news of her death while still ignorant of its cause and of her 'career' subsequent to her rejection by Knight, we learn that Elfride has ironically 'declined' upon Lord Luxellian after the defection of Knight (pp.306-7). Luxellian was obviously a 'clever courter' (as Dick was described in *Under the Greenwood Tree*): as 'little mother' Elfride had qualified as a kind of glorified 'au pair' in the full-blown sense of an equal, as already of Luxellian extraction. He was subsequently able to make use of her alienation from Christopher Swancourt and his new wife, scandalized by Elfride's self-abandoned flightiness in running away to Bede's Chambers (pp.274-5). This self-abandoned knocking on Knight's door entailed a complex act of abjection in which Elfride seemed to plead to be retained even as servant (au pair in the diminished sense, as it were), an act which was to 'impair' her status in the recently-enriched Swancourt home. Stephen's own power here had ironically derived from Knight's lack of knowledge of who had had previous 'knowledge of' Elfride: he becomes almost snortingly aware that the 'lover' of Elfride was 'only' Stephen, to whom his attitude is that of patronage towards the mere 'cherry-cheeked' (p.104) boy he was as he first knew him (p.293). Knight then hastens to renew one of those ironically 'posthumous suits' Hardy will prove to be particularly expert in contriving. Indeed, it might be observed that Knight's agonized attempts to 'police' Elfride are highly 'homosocial'.[14] It is strongly insinuated that he already almost conforms to the 'confirmed bachelor' stereotype. And what he precisely imagines with pain in relation to Elfride is the possibility of his blushing wife's encounter with her former 'lover' (p.151, p.256). In other words, it is idea of *male* presence (and power) which disturbs him here, in a suggestive final 'explication' of his 'phallogocentric imperative'.

Indeed, the narrator speculates openly as to whether he was, in fact, the marrying kind (p.260), and we learn not only that he drew towards Stephen as cherry-cheeked lad, but that Stephen himself has a kind of boy's crush on Knight, thanks to his intellectual superiority, breathily imparted to an initially irritated Elfride. But Elfride herself will, in due course, ironically 'replicate' the crush for the same reason, partly of course as a result of Stephen's enthusiastic rehearsal of Knight's virtues. But, equally ironically, the point is also made that the love of *Elfride and Stephen* was *itself* one of what might be called 'homos' ('likes'), as she reports Stephen to 'Papa' as having a 'face [which] is pretty, like mine' (p.8). We are also told that Stephen's 'constitution' was 'after a feminine rather than a male model' (p.286), and final interest might be invested in the '(no-) *ménage* à *trois* itself, with an emotional current running back and forth through all three parties. By a supreme irony, the presumed, but dubiously 'heterosexual' relation is developed here as a secondary 'version' of two primary 'homo-sexual' models.

Hardy likes narrative 'feinting', and his account of this 'triangulated' relationship makes it look as if Stephen's prosperous ventures in India, which conferred a new, improved status, may in time make a difference to his suit as the balance of power tilts towards him and revelations of Knight's emotional weakness make his relationship with Elfride more problematic.   Stephen neither ''rose from the ranks of the aristocracy' nor was 'born to the purple of commerce', in Wilde's amusing paradigm of Victorian eligibility. But as the 'born-again self-made man'[15] also dear to the Victorian imagination (p.294), his ascent was amusingly relayed, and hence ironized, through the exaggerated parochial sycophancy suddenly shown to master mason (sc. 'rural builder'[p.212]) John Smith and his wife Jane. They are the more bemused as the cause of all this deference (Stephen's imperial prosperity) is as yet unrevealed to them (ch.36). The alteration in Stephen's status was used to illustrate the idea that 'change of status is change of identity', and, in the mayor's speech to the St. Launce's 'Every Man His Own Maker' club, this alteration even conferred on Stephen the blue blood which Christopher Swancourt had required earlier (p.294), in yet another of those late-flowering ironies which constitute such a large part of Hardy's 'cultural capital'.

Another such case, also revealing a sophisticated grasp of the process of representation itself, is shown in the result of Knight's eventual knowledge that it was 'only Stephen' who has previously 'had knowledge of' Elfride. This knowledge was itself derived from *representations* of her, accidentally conveyed by the well-known female profile Stephen repeatedly sketched in architectural doodlings in India—when, ironically, he 'did not know what he was doing'. These were subsequently (and innocently) perused by Knight as 'mere details' of Stephen's architectural sketches, and only recognized *by Stephen himself* as *representations* of Elfride when Knight pointed them out as conveying her likeness (p.288) —though, interestingly, Knight in turn had to question just who the representations were, as it were, 'intended for'.

Hardy's artistic production seems once more to be controlled by conceits as well as the pursuit of 'narrative outcomes': Stephen's 'reproductions' of Elfride then led to their pursuit of her, but Elfride has already died in an attempt to 'reproduce'. Indeed, Knight himself had also already re-produced an Elfridean route from (virtual) 'stunt' woman to 'stunted' woman, lavishly illustrating De Beauvoir's point that one is not born a woman but becomes one.[16] After Knight's refashionings, Elfride's literal death allegorized the results of process he initiated. In the sketches, Knight recognizes Elfride 'as represented' and as a result a final, if futile, chase is on to propose to the once 'so living' girl (p.19), now dead – and so, ironically, 'beyond representation[s]'. Elfride's 'physical' death itself provides an allegory of the more deliberate deconstruction of the truly feminine identity which her spontaneity produced. This is not to say that Hardy is unalert to the implications of physiology itself: with reference to her physical dissolution, Freud's claim that 'anatomy is destiny'[17] is sustained here, as Elfride's death *was* due to her anatomy, which 'overdetermined' her maternal role in the first (as well as last) place. Pronounced guilty of conduct unbecoming a woman by the magisterial Knight, Elfride is reconstructed as the doll – a 'rale waxwork', as one of the rustics employed by Stephen Smith's father puts it. Elfride unwillingly, and unwittingly, became part of Joan Rivière's 'masquerade' of 'femininity'[18] – but in a form not selected by the 'subject' in question. Elfride, then, became a 'mimic' woman as Stephen, thanks to his autodidacticism and 'low' formation was a kind of 're-class-ified' 'mimic man'.[19] But *A Pair of Blue Eyes* is not only a study in 'mimic men' (and women), but other 'forms of substitution' which patriarchy induces — 'forms more real than living man'[20]— but in an unhappy, decidedly *un*Shelleyan sense. A modern theoretical critic might wish to pursue notions of the simulacral here, but the novel itself would obviously prefer you to think in terms of the fogey, or the fossil.

Chapter 4

How not to be (a) Tess: The Hand of Ethelberta

It is not exactly Hardy's fault that people are mainly aware of Tess (described at one point as *soft and silent*) as his primary embodiment of femininity. This famous heroine of his also came from a humble and rustic background. After her sexual betrayal she was specifically shown avoiding sophisticated society. By contrast, Ethelberta, his earlier embodiment of heroic femininity, although she describes herself as of a 'tribe of thralls',[1] has a foothold in what is known, however ironically, as 'good society'—thanks to a youthful elopement with a quickly-expiring scion of the House of Petherwin.

And Ethelberta, unlike Tess, quickly senses the trouble which will arise from her being 'soft', while, equally far from silence, her ready tongue will prove to be her source of income as well as her defence against what we might call 'patriarchal initiatives'. Tess' passivity led to her being seduced and abandoned, later deserted, and finally hanged—which makes slightly sinister the insistence throughout 'her' novel that she was 'all woman (ly)'. Conversely, Ethelberta triumphs through the exercise of imperious will. The trouble here is that this is felt, dismayingly, to put ideas of *her* womanliness 'under erasure'.

As a young widow and protegée of Lady Petherwin the early death of whose son sparks the incidents of the novel, Ethelberta's patronage is on the condition of her not 'owning' her poor relations. This condition makes her profession of *story-telling*, fictions, themselves perhaps 'Poor Relations', which '[mis-] represent' her relation to the economic base, an apposite one. Particularly significant here is the poem 'Cancelled Words', the concluding one of her early collection, which she sent to Christopher Julian (p.26), bespeaking pressures she is subject to which he knew nothing of, and at once commemorating and quashing their love. As Christopher explains to his sister Faith, she was a governess and 'jilted me, and married the son' (of the noble house of Petherwin), although at this point he does not know that she is already a widow, left only the lease on the house in London, not Lady Petherwin's capital, when she dies (p.104)—thanks to that Lady's (regretted) caprice (pp.88-9).

As in Ethelberta's case, Hardy advances here through conceits, allusions, and the ploys of an appropriated language.[2] If this novel does fail (as its relegation to the status of 'non-essential [Hardy] work' implies), it may do so from an excess of cleverness, which might itself be a source of interest—given the nostalgic, faintly anti-intellectual 'image' given to Hardy by traditional critics. Here the 'subversive, Mephistophelian endowment, brains' (p.241), which produce fictions more potent even than those of genealogists, unites Hardy and Ethelberta as secret sharers of 'cancelled words'.

The Hand of Ethelberta has the wealth of implication and the suitable quotient of 'entertainment' to number it among Hardy novels loosely referred to as 'major'. Admittedly, there is a touch here of that 'Hardy with a Baedeker' later to be found 'wandering around' *A Laodicean* (1881) ('Valognes, Carentan, Isigny, Bayeux, were passed, and the train drew up at Caen'[p.260]). And the courtship of Ethelberta is a little long-drawn-out. For example, like an Elizabeth Bennet reversed, she is correctly *alienated* by her visit to the peremptory Alfred Neigh's desolate estate at Harefield, itself a kind of 'Pemberley *renversé*'—bespeaking the owner's meanness, not greatness, of spirit (pp.186-8). Subsequently Neigh offends her by over-familiarity during the group visit to Milton's grave in Cripplegate. Yet Neigh still seems in the running during the visit to Normandy, with the star of Ethelberta's eventual husband, Lord Mountclere, already in the ascendant (although Mountclere's bodily decrepitude combined with his dubious familiarities appear to offer Neigh the ghost of a chance).

And the 'lower orders' are less 'picturesquely' represented in this novel, which might have been alienating for those who liked Hardy's 'investment' in rustic charm(s). But Hardy refuses to be sentimental about those who struggle on the lower tiers of society here. The central ideological contrast is between Ethelberta's father, Chickerel, who knows his place as a kind of 'Admirable Crichton' figure and *refuses* the pathos with which Ethelberta seeks to invest him in his 'below stairs' position (p.215), and Ethelberta's angry brother Sol, branded in the hand by his carpentry trade (p.376), who violently *resents* Ethelberta's marrying into the aristocracy—quite apart from the fact that her alliance is with one widely regarded as a *roué*.

Neither character is particularly charming, nor are they 'comic turns', though there is much humour in the lacerating interchanges between Sol and the Honourable Edgar Mountclere, the brother of Ethelberta's husband-to-be, Lord Mountclere, throughout the novel's frantic (and frustrated) coach-chase *dénouement* (or rather, '*first dénouement*', as Hardy generously provides a second with Ethelberta's attempt to escape her self-determined fate on learning of Mountclere's reputation). The sleekly aristocratic, self-seeking Edgar bears a strong psychic resemblance to Louis Glanville, the cynical brother of Viviette in *Two on a Tower* (1882), described as an 'unbeliever in human virtue'—inclining the reader towards 'the wisdom of "Sol-man"' here. Once more one suspects that Hardy critics, traditionalists in their social views, were alienated by the mischief the novel secretes; or in their equally traditional requirements for works of art: its refusal to be easily categorized is set to trouble the reader who already 'knows what to expect' from him. In particular, Hardy is trying for a note of 'Restoration' drama here, and the book is full of a kind of 'stage-craft', with reassuring 'versions of pastoral' largely absent, although the oscillation between London and Wessex is present (if in a less sentimental 'register').

If *The Hand of Ethelberta* is something of a 'version' of *Pride and Prejudice* with a new Elizabeth Bennet facing more untoward circumstances, it proves to be a chastening 're-write' of Austen's work. *Pride and Prejudice* does, after all, provide fantasy-gratifications, textual and sexual, which will perhaps not bear too much close scrutiny: so reading *The Hand of Ethelberta* could be a useful exercise for students of Jane Austen. However, the greater family and social pressures on Ethelberta make its greater realism in this respect disconcerting. In her case, although one in which her gender is crucial, it also allegorizes other forms of dispossession and marginality. In following what Samuel Johnson called 'the choice of life', in *Rasselas* (1759), a work Hardy knew well[3] and thought about deeply, Ethelberta charts her own 'progress' from 'Romanticism to distorted Benthamism', asking 'was the moral incline up or down?' (p.297). In this matter, she is asking, in terms provided by the early *Bildungsroman*-like poem of Wallace Stevens, 'The Comedian as the Letter C', whether his hero's progress entails an 'anabasis or slump, ascent or chute?'[4] Like *The Hand of Ethelberta*, the poem asks the reader to decide how to interpret the fate of ingenuous Crispin in relation to what (if anything) is 'gained' by a quest combining artistic aspiration with experience's long wandering, and a prosaic 'closure' in domesticity.

Hardy puts this back into a context of 'family values' and the implied need for a 'science of [social] climbing', but this is still a question for the poetic temperament: Ethelberta, a Hardy-substitute, is last glimpsed writing an epic poem in the grand library at Lychworth (p.404), which sounds a little like Hardy's own poem, *The Dynasts*, itself undertaken only when he himself had achieved financial security. But this is a highly germane subject here, as Ethelberta is nothing if not a Dynast herself, and the novel, 'containing' the poem of Napoleonic ambition, provides a moving allegory of the pressures and predicaments afflicting Hardy himself. In fact, soon after her marriage to Mountclere, Ethelberta will have renewed the fortunes of the decadent aristocrat (p.400), set her brothers Sol and Dan up with a hospital-building project (p.404), installed her parents in respectable-sounding 'Firtop Villa', *and* united her early love, the genteel musician Christopher Julian, with her bashful younger sister Picotee—very much against the grain of *her own* long-lived predilection for the rather 'difficult' fellow (p.406).

Ethelberta is clearly responsive to the attitudes of Clym Yeobright's mother (in *The Return of the Native* (1878), Hardy's next, and much better-known, novel)—with her desire for social success—as she also is to those of Clym himself. But she has nevertheless 'bracketed' Clym's anguished question—'Mother, what *is* doing well?' Ethelberta ends up 'doing well' in a sense we cannot fail to understand. We may, however, still balk at a 'final solution' which rejects so imperiously the idea of 'life as an emotion'. Here Ethelberta declares for that more dignified form of 'utilitarianism' developed by J.S. Mill, against a solipsistic version of Romanticism (pp.287-8): basically, she can help people [especially 'her people'] by marrying Mountclere, or 'help herself to' Christopher Julian, the young musician who loves her but who has no inherited wealth and partakes of the unworldliness of his sister Faith.

But Ethelberta is still swayed, as Sol angrily points out, by the romance of 'caste' (p.376), so that the 'content' of her 'choice' of life is still challenging its form. Herself a poet, in the phrasing of another she finds (bourgeois) 'safety' for her lowly kinfolk in the specifically 'dangerous' alliance with the decadent aristocrat—much to *their* initial distress. For example her father bitterly asserts, on finding they have failed to prevent the wedding [p.367], that 'I believe he will ruin her happiness'. So the results of her triumph rather undercut her own premise of family solidarity and the subsuming of rank in kinship. Indeed, 'Desperate Remedies', had he not used it for his first title, would apply to *The Hand of Ethelberta* (1876).

As an initially unattractive alternative, Ethelberta's final solution of marriage with leering old Lord Mountclere is a savagely parodic version of Jane Austen's Elizabeth

Bennet saving her family at the altar of marriage ('his staircase alone is worth my *hand*' [p.304], she observes, in an ironic glance at the novel's title). Hence the outcome of the novel is 'positively undecidable', if in what may be felt to be an 'aporetic' situation: though many things have been, so to speak, 'sorted', the physically crumbling Lord Mountclere is no Mr Darcy, nor do the family actually visit Lychworth as Elizabeth's do Pemberley.

The alternative course of Ethleberta's alter ego Christopher Julian, partly 'determined' by the 'determined' Ethelberta herself (e.g., p. 174), explains much: his is the lot of the 'artist' figure divorced from the world of action (pp.319-20). Christopher is close to another version of a Hardy self-concept, with a hint of Freudian Family Romance—his *genealogy* is genteel even if he is only a cash-strapped 'garreteer' with vaguely artistic ambitions [pp.46-8]—a description of the young Hardy's own early situation.[5] In fact Christopher is also a bit like a (Blakean) emanation of Ethelberta with a gender role-reversal ('putting femininity first' here attests to a feminism of sorts in Hardy, but also to his imbrication of ideas of the artist with those of 'the feminine').

As Ethelberta and Christopher are an allegory, of 'life as a science of climbing' and 'life as an emotion', it may not be part of the logic of this allegory for them to unite—indeed, Ethelberta, the 'sacrificial mother' (who is not one) is finally as determined that her shy and retiring sister Picotee, infatuated with Julian, shall have him, as she is in other matters. Yet, though in appearance a kind of 'simulacral' Ethelberta, Picotee is disconcertingly *unlike* her in the child-like dependence Ethelberta herself is so responsive to, and the novel ends with Picotee's acceptance of Christopher in a delightful comment to the effect that ''Berta' herself will be 'glad' (p.406)—apparently establishing that *she* is doing this to please the elder sister who relinquished Julian for *her*.

Yet it is difficult to believe that if Christopher's desire was for Ethelberta herself he could possibly be responsive to Picotee—unless we accept the depressing Miltonic conclusion that 'a woman' is, as he quaintly puts it, 'an outside' (*PL* 8.568), and that her resemblance to Ethelberta will itself make Julian entranced with her: indeed, it looks as if Christopher's desire has to be awakened by appreciative remarks by a middle-aged churchwarden, when the various parties converge in failure to prevent Ethelberta's wedding to Lord Mountclere (p.365). He claims, with 'nominal' appositeness, that Picotee was the 'chicken' (i.e., Chickerel) 'to my taste' (p.368). The reader is informed that she was coming to resemble Ethelberta even more greatly (p.403). But it still looks as if Picotee's and Christopher's bed-chamber may be one of those fantasy-scenes in which the 'other' is present, as in Yeats' poems of unhappy love followed by 'second-best' marital arrangements, although Lacan thought this sort of thing was inevitable in any case.[6]

By contrast, Ethelberta, ruling with a *rod* of iron, passes over into a state of 'masculinity': her 'gender troubling' is combined with class antagonism. Her very name is interesting, as Ethelbert was the first (male) ruler of all the Anglo-Saxons, and her (unique?) female appropriation of the name[7] establishes her sex by the 'little a' alone, the extra which signals a lack. Yet Ethelberta really does end up 'wearing the trousers', or the phallus, establishing that her 'little a' really is an 'other'. Through her refusal to 'have a heart' in the conventional sense, or to 'become "a woman"' in De

Beauvoir's formula,[8] we may even conclude that Ethelberta has become something of a 'cyborg' in the terms announced by Donna Haraway's 'Cyborg Manifesto',[9] as 'a hybrid of machine and organism, *a creature of social reality as well as a creature of fiction'*. Ethelberta also suggests the 'Irigaray' version of gender transvaluations. As Julie Rivkin and Michael Ryan summarize Irigaray here: 'stop being the mirror of men, she urges; stop pretending to be "feminine"', and in this exercise Ethelberta has succeeded, perhaps only too well.[10] However, she is justified, not just from the necessity to control both Mountclere and his overmanned estate (p.400), but also as a response to the bleak picture presented in the novel of relations between the sexes in the context of the '(cash) nexus'.[11] This involves the rows between Christopher Julian and Ethelberta herself, and the suffering imposed by Picotee's infatuation with a fairly indifferent Christopher still in love with Ethelberta, but also the more 'Nietzschean' notations of deadly war between the sexes as the austerely 'bourgeois' Neigh and young artist Ladywell as well as Mountclere court Ethelberta. This is particularly obvious in the case of Neigh's possession by naked anger at being enslaved by a passion which violates his patriarchal sense of superiority: '"Oh, lord that I should come to this! But I shall never be such a fool as to marry her! What a flat that young devil [Ladywell] was not to discover that we were tarred with the same brush! Oh the deuce, the deuce", he continued, walking about the room as if passionately stamping, but not quite doing it because another man had rooms below' (p.150).

Ladywell, comparing notes with the Neigh whom he does not know to be equally attached to Ethelberta, pursues the argument that 'if she would only care for me a little, I might get to trouble less about her'; Neigh, pursuing this logic, announces '"tis to be hoped she won't hate you outright, or then you would absolutely die of idolising her' (p.148). 'Restoration Comedy' is the genre Hardy has in mind here, and its depictions of relations between the sexes are not exactly funny: 'love', as dissected there, is often not so far from its opposite. The characters' petty-mindedness in these matters helps explain Ethelberta's 'hardness', which, as socially induced, is not quite that – rather, a 'necessary vice' in a context in which traditional female virtue(s) will be exploited. As she points out to that embodiment of susceptible sensibility Picotee: 'Don't you go believing in sayings, Picotee: they are all made by men, and for their own advantages. Women who use public proverbs as a guide through events are those who have not ingenuity enough to make private ones as each event occurs' (p.145). In showing how such ideas are 'in ideology', Ethelberta is in her way a feminist intellectual, although one who finally betrays her cause—or does she?

Her brother Sol (his name suggesting that he has some wisdom even if he is also 'on the ground floor' in the class sense) refers to Ethelberta as a 'deserter of your own lot' (p.376), where 'lot' seems suspended between the senses: 'your own kind', and 'your own fate'. But this is an unkind comment when his 'lot' (people of his type) have determined her 'lot' (fate): she is doing what she does in order that they will be the beneficiaries of her talents. However, ironically, the male relatives at least are (like most dependants), fiercely independent, and Ethelberta's father Chickerel in particular has no wish to be 'rescued' (p.215). Again, Hardy 'ambiguates' here, displaying Ethelberta's Paula Power-like fascination (in *A Laodicean*) with the romance of caste, as if unaware that 'historical' families are this only as history is seen as Walter Benjamin's 'history of the victors', and commemorates only those who were present and correct enough in the *ancien régime* to be the 'lottery winners': however, the narrator points out that this was not necessarily meritorious: the *lack* of a 'genealogy' might be *positively* presented as signifying that one had ancestors 'none of [whom] had ever pandered to a court, lost an army, taken a bribe, oppressed a community, or broken a bank' (p.210), remembering the 'savage indignation' of a Jonathan Swift here. In this sense he is keenly interested in *reversing* the history of the victors and rehearsing the history of the victims. Ethelberta herself negotiates the point that though humble antecedents in one's background *might* be piquant to a gentleman, a 'foreground' of relatives who still worked for their bread would lead to social ostracism (p.210). In particular, neither Neigh nor Ladywell could be imagined as accepting such a situation.

Pursuing such lines of social inquiry, *The Hand of Ethelberta* does offer something of a 'history lesson', still ironic enough to describe Ethelberta's concessions to conventionality as she confesses herself one of a 'tribe of thralls'—as Hardy himself was. Indeed, this book is a more honest examination of his affiliations than his speciously authoritative *Life*. It also reveals a Hardy adroitly distancing himself from conventional assumptions about society. For example, the depiction of the quarrelling of Sol and Edgar Mountclere, as they enter on a chase across South Dorset in very bad weather and very bad temper in an attempt to prevent Ethelberta's match, is masterly. Edgar, never referred to by his Christian name on its own, is the morally unattractive brother of Lord Mountclere. Sol, understandably something of a 'surly and acrimonious Republican',[12] as fiercely despises Edgar as the nobleman does him (e.g., p.355). Their 'cat and dog friendship' (p.342) 'suspends' ideological issues Hardy is often taken to have resolved (in favour of wealth and rank).

The narrative here is embroiled with 'the political'. As odious Mrs Doncastle, who wants to dismiss Chickerel merely for being Ethelberta's father puts it, 'the times have taken a strange turn when the angry parent of the comedy, who goes post-haste to prevent the undutiful daughter's rash marriage, is a gentleman from below stairs, and the unworthy lover a peer of the realm' (p.338). Equally 'political' is Ethelberta's controlled pragmatism. As we saw, in choosing dissolute Lord Mountclere over forceful Neigh, artistic Ladywell and childhood sweetheart Christopher, she triumphs over a Romanticism she obviously sees as fundamentally an ego-centricity which cannot dictate things for someone in her delicately poised social situation.

This makes the novel an interesting source of insights into Hardy's sense of his own destiny (although one of 'life's little ironies' is that he married someone who greatly insisted on her status as 'a Lady', the better to patronize him, some said; but brought no money into the marriage). As it happens, Ethelberta's ambiguously 'sacrificial' quest is also ironized: although she surrounds him always with a sense of regret over *his* choice of life, and the idea of what he has to endure makes her tearful (p.215), her father doesn't want her help, and is merely irritated by what he considers the 'useless pathos' with which she surrounds her sense of his fate (p.225). But Ethelberta *is* finally vindicated here when the secret of her coming marriage to Mountclere is announced at a dinner, and her father's distress is treated with shameful harshness ('if you are ill you had better go and rest yourself, Chickerel' [p.336], says peremptory Lady Doncastle, ready to dismiss him on the spot until restrained by a sensible husband, who considers it an honour to have the well-read father of the gifted Mrs Petherwin on the premises).

Hardy obviously has some rapport with Sol's republicanism, but a more nuanced dislike than Sol has for Edgar, a version of Lady Constantine's brother in *Two on a Tower* requiring 'a milch cow for his sustenance'. This, as we saw, is dramatized in their pursuit of Mountclere and Ethelberta in a shared (if antithetical) intention to stop the wedding: the idea that he is 'too good for her' (rank) is crossed by the idea that she is 'too good for him' (talents and ethics). So the virtuous poor among Ethelberta's relations disapprove of the match as much as the aristocratic brother does, which makes the advance on the *dénouement* delightfully (distressingly?) ironic, as she does all this *for* them as they hotly pursue her in order to prevent her from doing so. For Sol, the chase is in the interests of chastity—because, with his puritan radicalism he has Mountclere down as a blackguard (p.330), and Mountclere's brother because he has Ethelberta down as a fortune-hunter (p.331) (and fears he may lose his inheritance, as Sol correctly intuits [p.331]).

Hardy thus makes the chase to prevent the marriage a kind of historico-political allegory: the lower orders are, rightly, as outraged as their betters over it, but the pursuing puritans fail to allow for Lord Mountclere's personal kindness. And angry Sol's harping on the upper crust as 'useless lumber' (p.376) as he anticipates a possible revolution is not shared by his own father, whose acceptance of his position impels him to gentle conservatism. Edgar and Sol themselves, of course, share nothing else except the mutual contempt of each for the other 'both in family and in person' (p.362). Sol is the reverse of a forelock-tugging rustic, the 'other voice' Jane Austen could not be expected to allow for in her novels—socially 'dialogic' in their own way but affiliated to a genteel tradition which, Hardy suggests, can't see straight when it sees society—can't 'see life steadily and see it whole', in the formula by Matthew Arnold which exceeds his uses for it. If Hardy is 're-writing' *Pride and Prejudice* here, one of his not-so-little ironies is that his 'work-folk' have more pride (if possibly also more prejudice) than the 'peers' who turn out, in terms of their quality as human beings, to be not quite their equals. And his heroine's attitude to the marriage is finally less like that of an Elizabeth Bennet than of the pragmatic Charlotte Lucas, to judge from attempts to reassure Picotee at Knollsea on the eve of the ceremony: ' . . . then why should I be afraid to make a plunge when chance is as trustworthy as calculation?' (p.350). Yet Ethelberta argues against Sol's contesting of her notion of 'romantic' or 'grandly historical' families, so this may still be her form of 'romanticism', however muted: and she herself evinces an acute sense of social exposure. This creates her need for the 'social security' which qualified even Elizabeth Bennet's spirited independence.[13] An alternative title for the novel would indeed be 'Exposure', especially as Ethelberta, as entertainer, is revealed as a performer but concealed by her performance. (Her greatest 'performance' is finally the 'form' she stamps on her own life.)

Hardy rather suggestively dramatizes Ethelberta's social self-exposure: the transport she presses into service as she approaches Knollsea (significantly near Lord Mountclere's demesnes [pp.246-7] as his possible importance to her is becoming evident) is a humble 'ass'. She is visiting Knollsea ostensibly, and somewhat implausibly, to check the baptismal records of her Rouen-based aunt Charlotte, but aware of gentry-folk assembling in the castle ruins under Mountclere's aegis as a meeting of the (faintly comic) 'Imperial Archaeological Association' (p.230). At this 'hinge' in the novel her other suitors—Neigh, Ladywell and Christopher Julian—have already been found wanting, and not merely in terms of class and cash (though we have already registered Ethelberta's fierce determination not to let the younger members of the family sink in the scale). Her motivation is comparable to that of Tess in her novel, but Ethelberta's capacities and her *success* make a fascinating contrast with the later work everyone 'knows' as the 'typical' example of 'the Hardy of the Feminine Victim'. Ethelberta's inability to achieve 'meaningful' communication with her uneducated older sisters Gwendoline and Cornelia (pp.165-6) with their banal observations, strengthens her resolve with respect to the younger children who will require an education to give them greater scope – and there are ten Chickerel children in all (p.127). When D.H. Lawrence referred to *Ethelberta* as 'his one almost cynical comedy',[14] the word 'cynical' applies to the 'love interest' (his area of interest), but not to the fact that the love interest is subordinate to the interests of family she loves – which is not an affair of cynicism.

Suitors offer an escape route (though she hopes to flourish artistically on her own account thereby), and Ladywell the artist and Christopher Julian the musician have youthfulness and talent but insufficient ambition and capital. In addition, young Ladywell is somewhat effete and Ethelberta is aware of Picotee's love for Julian, now assistant organist at Melchester (Salisbury)—not *too* far from Knollsea itself (Swanage), as Picotee excitedly notes. So Neigh becomes the final front-runner of the unsuccessful suitors. But, as his name suggests, Neigh is a spirit who says 'no' like Goethe's Mephistopheles, 'in denial' in relation to his own susceptibilities, so that where he loves he also hates (a startling insight).

Neigh is also, despite his name, an abuser of horses on his neglected estate, and his bleak censoriousness is equally unencouraging. However, Neigh fell at the last hurdle as Picotee herself destroyed his chances by retailing to Ethelberta the story—retailed to her by the ill-wishing servant Louisa Menlove (pp.227-8)—of Neigh's careless talk about the girls' secret visit to his property—which he treats as a joke and a confirmation of his 'right' to misogyny. This is notably ironic as Picotee, all for youthful ardour, had initially been horrified that Ethelberta might throw herself away on an 'old man' like Mountclere (p. 230). But she herself renders Ethelberta's engagement to him inevitable.

With things tilted against the only other 'serious' suitor here, Ethelberta is in a critical position as she approaches Knollsea on the ass. On this occasion the assembled gentryfolk were addressed amid the picturesque ruins by 'Dr. Yore' (pp.242-3)[15]— reminding us that Hardy often combines levity with seriousness here, as well as reminding us of that History of England which the castle offers the opportunity to recapitulate. The stylish 'historicism' which Yore 'represents' summons the long perspectives of the English past to help incline Ethelberta to the 'grandly historical' Mountclere (even his decrepitude can be converted to a plus in the context of this discourse *à l'ancienne*).

Hardy makes his own empathy with Ethelberta clear, yet he also imbibes something of the spirit of Mountclere himself at this point. And the spectacle of Ethelberta approaching on her suggestive mode of transport provides an 'uncancelled word'[16] too outrageous when considered as a leering double-entendre for editors to dally with—but leering is just what the reader seems to be invited to do here: the original illustrator Du Maurier, choosing to illustrate this point, contrives a mildly pornographic emphasis on Ethelberta's own rear (p.208)[17] as she sits on the animal in question. Yet even if this does sound *risqué*, Hardy seems definitely to be joining in, letting the beau monde gather round to admire the 'phenomenal' ass which she would have blushed to acknowledge as a 'low' mode of transport (p.239).

The beast, phenomenal in suggestiveness also, hints at dangers inherent in Ethelberta's public exhibitions of herself, a 'reversed' image of Shakespeare's 'Bottom' – the *Midsummer Night's Dream* character transformed into the creature, with whom someone even more queenly than Ethelberta made a fool of herself (and, as the narrative climax nears, everyone except Ethelberta seems to know that Mountclere is something of a 'sex fiend'). Indeed, as he announces himself with his characteristic 'Hee! Hee! Hee!' the (ig-) noble lord sounds more than a little asinine himself. And as the assembled gentryfolk consider just how the 'ass' could possibly have got there, Ethelberta's reluctance to 'own' him (which inspires guilt) also parodies the close (and closeted) relationship she has with her own humble family (p.241).

So the 'ass' as 'image' also hints at dangers of exposure and accusations of impropriety as well as her exploitation as an elevated 'sex object' for Mountclere himself. And he does turn out to have been a master of mistresses and peruser of magazines with naughty ladies depicted therein, fetched by a servant 'as duteous to the vices of his [master]/ As badness would desire' (*King Lear* [4.6.248-9]). Mountclere, through the malice of Lady Petherwin's sinister servant Menlove, also discovered Ethelberta's humble social position much earlier than she intended, and she notes Mountclere's sudden overfamiliarity on her jaunt to Normandy (p.259). Later, nothing will more plainly signal his need for 'reconstruction' than the intimations of a secret(ed) mistress, a Miss Gruchette, still available to be re-installed in a boudoir in the grounds of Lychworth (p.379) even *after* Mountclere and Ethelberta have exchanged marriage vows (p.380). A shade overspreads Ethelberta's world as the indispensably garrulous housekeeper reveals all to her, as she wanders in the grounds of Lychworth (p.380)—following her marriage earlier that day.

So the final battle Ethelberta has on her hands results from the fact that Mountclere's behaviour towards her depends on his awareness of her 'exposed social position'. Even before the discovery of the boudoir in the grounds of Lychworth entailed the inference that married Mountclere intended to carry on as before, there had been an intuition on Ethelberta's part that Mountclere's increase in familiarity towards her might be interpreted as contempt, on their apparently coincidental visit to Normandy. This behaviour revealed how ways in which 'gender is always imbricated with other [social] categories' was indeed a 'feminist issue' here (pp.259-60).

Although Ethelberta had told the truth about her own life (dressed as fiction) to the company she had entertained at Lychworth after the Knollsea lecture, Mountclere, already apprized of her humble origins, is later startlingly said to be 'secreted in the very rear of her position' (p.300). Mountclere had in fact learned through the servant, Tipman, in touch with Menlove, just after the lecture at Knollsea, that Ethelberta was no real kin to a coach (p.251). The great lord does seem encouragingly clear that 'modern developments have shaken up the classes like the peas in a hopper' (p.301). However, as this can hardly be an impression derived from his estate at Lychworth, his infatuation with Ethelberta may be leading him to invent 'politically correct' postures on the hoof—a cloven one, naturally. But this also reveals that Mountclere as a peer of the realm would *not* share the insecurity which Ethelberta's other suitors would experience in learning of her 'lineage'. And this confirmation of her intuition about this facilitates Ethelberta's acceptance of him. But Hardy's final irony is that it is *Mountclere* who has the more discreditable 'side, and this has its objective [architectural] correlative' in the false-fronted brickwork of Lychworth which passes for marble(d) (pp.296-7).

So, *also* implied by the journey to Knollsea which made her involvement with Mountclere inevitable, is that the ass, with its religious associations, strongly suggests the idea of Ethelberta as a sacrifice on the altar of family. In social terms, Mountclere is left as the only plausible partner, and the final chase is initiated on several 'fronts': firstly, by *Edgar* Mountclere's indignant disclosure of the wedding's imminence to Sol (p.329), then by the servant Menlove's disclosure of its imminence to Mrs Doncastle—after Mountclere's valet Louis, Menlove's suitor, revealed it to Menlove in a letter offering her his own 'hand'. Then Doncastle's butler, Ethelberta's father, overhears the matter being discussed at dinner by the family whose guests include their nephew Alfred Neigh, and, devastated by the disclosure (p.335), reveals her paternity and initiates his own vain 'chase' to reason her out of matrimony with a cad. In due course he joins up with Christopher Julian, who identified Ethelberta's successful suitor as the notoriously disreputable Mountclere buying a wedding ring in Melchester, vowing vainly as he does so that the marriage 'must never be' (p.324).

Menlove's very name suggests an ambiance of Restoration comedy intrigues. And, despite her enmity to Ethelberta, she is actually Ethelberta's (dark) 'verso', a *declassée* version of her—alert to opportunities, and prone to invent fantasies of sexual imbroglios involving fierce competition among suitors for her hand, of which she then retails the narrative(s). She is a kind of figure for Ethelberta's 'lowest depths of possibility' (Lowell) as one who also knows 'the ins and outs of contriving' (p.400)—as the Anglebury landlord puts it of Ethelberta herself. The wiles of the 'below stairs' Menlove, her cynical techniques of exploitation, depict a 'black magic' version of Ethelberta's fundamentally well-intentioned plotting. As a result of her contrivings, Mountclere finds that despite his cunning he has met his match in a more emphatic sense than he bargained for. Hardy finds a wicked piece of Biblical knowledge to define the new regime at Lychworth in asserting that Ethelberta's 'little finger' has become 'thicker' than Mountclere's 'loins' (p.403) (1 *Chronicles* 10.10). The image is phallic in Lacan's sense in conveying Ethelberta's winning of the symbolic initiative, and Chaucer's idea of the desire for 'maistrye' (mastery)[18] as the ruling idea of marital partners, intimating that Ethelberta is now 'wearing the trousers'—a great set-down for one with such a capacity for sexual initiatives as Mountclere. Indeed, in the eyes of the orders below him, Mountclere is the stereotypically wicked lord whose sexual impropriety attracts even more opprobrium than his social rapacity.

But, finally, they need not have worried, apparently: Ethelberta, despite a plea to 'compromise matters' (p.395) on his foiling of her complex plan of escape, *herself* soon becomes a Shelleyan 'Ozymandias', highly capable of 'cold command'[19] *and* the extirpation of those many 'parasites' to be found on her indulgent lord's estate (p.400). This point was predicted by an earlier citation of the Shelley poem about the arrogance of power just as matters between herself and Mountclere were about to become serious (p.237). For brother Sol, an extirpation of 'corruption' would have to *include the lord himself* as part of the 'useless lumber' (p.376) which will be first to 'finish in that flare'[20] if a social conflagration should occur, and it is interesting that he thinks this likely to happen. As an extrapolation of *Mansfield Park* (1814) as well as *Pride and Prejudice* (1813), the novel sets Ethelberta to reform the old *roué* here as Fanny Price might have reformed her suitor Henry Crawford (and his estate). Initiating all this, at a catalytic moment in the novel, Ethelberta broke down when she dropped her costume of fiction and gave her audience 'the actuality' in the form of the story of her life in the 'entertainment' at Lychworth (p.299). Mountclere 'entered her story' in a double sense here (a 'double sense' including a well-known prurient innuendo in Mallarmé) by suspending it—already aware of its foundation in truth. And this truth bartered as fiction by Etheleberta was very like a fiction bartered by Hardy which came close to the truth about his own life.

Finally, however, Ethelberta seems to have extirpated, not merely corruption (pp.399-403), but 'the sexual relation' itself. She has brought the puritan spirit briefly victorious with Cromwell to bear on the debaucheries of Lychworth, with a forcefulness which contrasts with the behaviour of the heiress Paula Power in *A Laodicean* (1881). The first hint of her battles to follow arises from the inadvertent revelation about Mountclere's (apparently ongoing) affair of the 'French mistress' (pp. 379-80). In the penultimate 'movement' of the novel Ethelberta attempts to flee, initially with a reluctant Sol—now an ironic advocate of the absoluteness of marriage preaching the immorality of deserting an actual husband, however *louche* (p.384): Christopher Julian was excitingly substituted in an attempt to help her escape (p.387), but Mountclere substituted himself for Julian when he got wind of the scheme, and all this contriving guarantees a good deal of 'in-flight entertainment'. Hardy, as often using 'mere realism' as a stalking-horse, finds a wonderful image for the trapped Ethelberta herself as Christopher theatrically waits for her in pitch darkness with a 'brougham' to fetch her off:

> . . the large trees on either hand became interspersed by a low
> brushwood of varied sorts, from which a large bird occasionally
> flew, in its affright at their presence beating its wings recklessly
> against the hard stems with force enough to cripple the delicate
> quills (p.391).

Apparently outwitted by the wicked lord, Ethelberta recovers gamely enough to offer to 'compromize matters'. But finally no such compromize is made available – *to him*. Gone with the wind for Mountclere are the days of the French mistress installed in a boudoir, and of naughty ladies depicted in French magazines. Indeed, as last glimpsed by Christopher himself, Mountclere and Ethelberta are like the 'pale unsatisfied ones'[21] of Yeats' poem. They have notably failed to find 'the uncontrollable mystery on the bestial floor'. 'Berta' is finally a mistress of estate management and 'the ins and outs of contriving' (p.400) rather than a sex object, a slave become *master*—one can hardly say 'mistress'. Indeed, she provides a gloss for the idea that '*mistress*', the female equivalent of 'master', sounds like a perennial name for a '*slave*' in the Mountclere context. But Ethelberta, referred to at the point of discovery of Mountclere's mistress as '*lady* of all she surveyed' (p.378), has indeed become 'mistress' in the emphatic sense of 'master'.

Far from being a 'kept' woman, Ethelberta makes Mountclere a 'kept' man, lucky to be retained for his 'services', which can hardly be imagined as including 'sexual' ones. We can only speculate—and not only as textual people have only a virtual reality: the story of 'Berta's' marriage is told only two and a half years on, firstly by the landlord of the 'Old Fox Inn' to Christopher Julian, now wintering in Italy on a small legacy with sister Faith, and then by Ethelberta's family themselves, living nearby in 'Firtop Villa' (p.401). Thus Hardy slyly conveys the privacy of even a public marriage, and the fact that her own family are held aloof, or hold themselves aloof. Or, in Bersani's words, we 'know the object itself—in its unchanging uniqueness . . . as a phenomenon of *distance*'.[22] Distance lends disenchantment to Ethelberta's case, as, finally established as true kin to a coach, her kith and kin seem, as a result of her very efforts on their behalf, somewhat estranged.

But, looking ahead to *Tess* (1891), Ethelberta also seems estranged from *the body itself*, while for Tess 'the semantic' was all too fatally involved with 'the somatic' (i.e., with her body as sign of 'the real Tess'). Ethelberta, like Tess, was Hardy's idea of a 'splendid woman' (actually a phrase he assigns to Eustacia Vye of his next novel, *The Return of the Native* [1876])—but as one who 'wins through', unlike Tess, or Eustacia herself. In a sense, though, it seems, 'a woman can't win' without ceasing to 'be one'. Critics have concentrated on the Hardy who fashioned 'woman' as signed by the body in *Tess*, but it is hardly his fault that they have chosen to pay little attention to this 'other' 'woman of his' who transcended received notions of femininity altogether in a fascinating study of 'gender' in relation to its social and historical matrix.[23]

Chapter 5

'Home Truths': *The Return of the Native* and 'the Ache of Modernism'

Hardy is interested in 'modernism' here (the word is in his large lexicon, but surfaces in *Tess*)—largely as the name for a psychological condition. In much recent discussion the writing practices of 'modernism' are called up as the 'other' of 'realism',[1] but Hardy makes 'realism' an inadequate sign for his own practice, not through 'practising modernism' in this sense but through the insights provided by the folk-wisdom (or folk-folly), the 'rough magic' speaking through the sophistications of his latter-day genre.

Hardy in his capacity as something of a literary theorist would himself sustain this idea, but we can hardly expect of him that he should provide an adequate critical convoy for his own quite startling practice(s) here. His interest in the 'primitivism' (of 'the native English') seems to be privy to the intimations of 'modernism' in raising sophisticated issues about 'the subject' and 'ideology', openly asking 'what speaks' when we speak 'in propria persona'—nowhere more clearly, perhaps, than in *The Return of the Native*. In this novel Hardy is a connoisseur of 'faultlines' which indicate divisions in society, and between persons, but also within them. The term would also of course cover the *faults* they impute to each other in confrontations in which people may find that they, like Yeats' parrot, are 'raging at their own image[s]'.[2]

This is especially clear in the deadly quarrel which erupts between Mrs Yeobright and Eustacia Vye on her home ground of Mistover over the 'spade-guineas' for her son Clym which she thinks Wildeve, Eustacia's former lover, may have misappropriated. Her 'Don't rage at me madam'[3] is addressed to a Eustacia who shares her imperiousness and quick resentments. Hence her words might easily be imagined as provoking a sharp reply to similar effect, sharp replies being something of the order of the day here (*The Return of the Native* is nothing if not a rather *frightening* book.)

Hardy is examining how characters who seem like 'opposites' both in the sense of their characteristics and in the sense of being 'rivals' have unexpected areas of common ground, form psychological 'Venn diagrams' with each other which transcend conventional representations of character(s) as studies in pure 'difference(s)' or 'otherness(es)'. Never more of a literary *bricoleur* than in this novel, Hardy is a dealer in phrases and philosophies which 'govern a life', in what he calls the cultural 'raw material[s]' (p.81)—we might refer to them as 'ideologemes'-- which fashion character(s). People are nothing if not dramatis *personae* in this novel. Indeed, they appear to 'mediate' history. They are symbolized by the mummers who perform their immemorial play at the Yeobrights' home at 'Bloom's End'. The mummers are apparently an artless lot speaking like 'automata' (Hardy's word), their authenticity spoken for by their being spoken through.

As so often, suggestive at the level of verbal conceits, Hardy tells us that the 'mummers' may speak like 'men possessed', but will number among them a *woman* who will in due course 'possess' Clym and 'divorce' him from his 'mum'. Matters do not end there, however: later, Eustacia will be 'divorced' from a Clym who will be posthumously repossessed by a 'mummy' who will speak through him, as *himself* now a 'mummer' of sorts and also a kind of 'automaton' unable to 'see terribly clearly' at this point. Clym's predicament seems highly 'Freudian'; indeed, Freud himself, as the analyst of 'Civilisation and its Discontents' seems to share an intellectual area with Clym. Yeatsian phrasing seems to provide the combination of recondite thinking and Oedipal drama which occupies the centre stage with Clym here: Yeobright, who seems to have returned with some 'home truths' to tell 'mummy', will finally appear on Egdon at Rainbarrow as a high-toned preacher with 'mummy truths to tell',[4] while the surrounding rustics—quite rightly, it seems—fail to pay much attention.

Although Mrs Yeobright died on the Heath, apparently after suffering several bitter and decisive emotional 'defeats', it finally (and eerily) seems that through her son Clym, 'The Quiet Woman' is still talking. ('The Quiet Woman', the name of the 'inn' kept by Damon Wildeve, the local 'lady-killer', perhaps bespeaks a certain misogyny here.) Incidentally, Clym, who would have little but contempt for the volatile mores of Wildeve, is still very like him, at least to the rustics, in being 'one of those professional men who have failed', as well as in his depression (p.147)—in what Damon (or 'Daemon'?) will describe as his *blue Demons*.

Both Clym and Wildeve may also be bracketed ('paired') as embryonic Bartlebys who, like Melville's celebrated scrivener, 'would prefer not' [sc. 'to accept the conditions capitalism wishes to lay on them'].[5] And rusticity is not quite fine-tuned enough to tell the difference between Clym's high-mindedness and Damon's high-handedness in their quitting of the spheres they qualified themselves for—as, respectively, diamond merchant and engineer. Highly alert to the ways in which divisions in individuals relate to social divisions, Hardy also seems to be examining the theme of 'dissociation of sensibility',[6]—in T.S. Eliot's once-celebrated phrase, which was always intended to provide a kind of 'history lesson': its 'message' was one of a 'fall' into modernity which *The Return of the Native* is already examining.

In particular, we are told that Clym's *mind* plays on his *body* in an unbalanced and puritanical way, with an effect of ageing, as one of the paradoxical effects of modernity itself (pp.140-1). Clym's very flesh is imprinted with the *mental* pressures which mark his modernity (alienation). His wife-to-be, Eustacia, however (the ultimate in 'romantic leads'), seems to be made of 'fleshly' wants. Even her *mind* seems a mere 'epi-phenomenon' of her *body*, as a 'mind which is also flesh', as Robert Lowell suggestively puts it.[7] 'Her reality' (in both senses) is somatic.

Indeed, Hardy tries out the idea that a woman in a 'special' way 'is' her body with rhetoric about Eustacia of the kind he will later and more famously deploy in depicting Tess: 'the sun shone into her mouth as into a tulip, and lent it a similar scarlet fire' (bk.1, ch.10, p.101). This flickeringly somatic sense of being will draw the fascinated Clym into its flame and unite him with a deeply unsuitable partner. In contrast to Clym once more, Eustacia seems specifically to fashion herself out of what Althusser might have called an 'imaginary relation to real existence'. Unfortunately again, Clym's need seems to be precisely the opposite one, that of 'abolishing' the imaginary in order to live *dans le vrai* ('in the true'). Suggestively, this is a positive condition which Flaubert identified with the lot of peasants:[8] Clym, when stricken with ophthalmia and unable to pursue intellectual tasks, has such an experience of being '*dans le vrai*' when he finds the fulfilment in furze-cutting which he signally failed to find in diamond-cutting ('The monotony of his occupation soothed him, and was itself a pleasure' [237]).

Indeed, although Clym came with a plan to 'improve' rusticity, there is an equally real sense in which he feels himself to be improved *by* it. And what Eustacia calls 'shameful labour' (p.239) during their overextended honeymoon at Alderworth is something we imagine he himself has always been vaguely ashamed of not having had to perform. The couple's 'differences without positive terms' will converge on the double sign of Paris, at once a 'rookery of pomp and vanity' (p.112) and a nest of regicides and reformers. A *pharmakon* of sorts, as a poison for some but cure for others, Eustacia's Paris will lift the depression the *Heath* induced, while, for Clym, the Heath will lift the depression *Paris* induced. Clym is heading back for (the) base, Eustacia aspires to the 'superstructural': even the sartorial may sustain their 'faithful quarrel' here, with Clym merging with the heath in dun clothing (p.237). The rustics are praised for this 'habit' in *Two on a Tower* (1882), but this can hardly be what Eustacia has in mind as she anticipates life as a 'stunning' *boulevardière*.

Clym is also Eustacia's 'opposite' in his experience of a kind of 'over-parenting'. He has drawn sustenance from his closeness both to his Mother, and to the Heath, itself an ancestral or quasi-parental presence teaching Clym 'the ghostly language of the ancient earth'.[9] Indeed, it seems as if both Mother and the Heath were, as it were, 'vying' for his attention before Eustacia arrived to 'Vye' with them. The novel seems to veer in Lévi-Straussian directions in seeming to ask, through Clym, if we are 'autochthonous', rising from the earth, or do we forge an identity through an 'Oedipal' drama?

Although close to his mother, Clym, returning from the Paris in which Mrs Yeobright reposed her hopes for him, seems to have wagered a good deal on the idea that Mother does *not* know best. And in terms of their actual *effects* it looks as if Eustacia, with whom Clym managed temporarily to escape from Mother, at considerable emotional cost, in certain respects turns out to be little more than an 'other' version of her, making points about the charms of Paris and profitable careers which Clym must find fairly familiar. (By contrast, the Heath, with more experience in 'parenting', perhaps, simply accepts you as you are—in life or death.) Eustacia, unlike Clym in this respect also, seems unfortunate in her evident lack of rapport with her (father-substitute) grandfather, the grog-soaked old naval fantasiser, 'Captain' Vye.

This helps explain Eustacia's alienation and discontent, making her more sympathetic. For example, Vye speaks sharply and insensitively of her loss of Damon Wildeve's inherited ('lottery') money after his grand-daughter's marriage to Clym and Damon's marriage to Thomasin ('what a snipe you were in that business, Eustacia'), and his vulgar way of referring to her wild trysts with Wildeve as he observes that he has heard that there was 'some sniffing between ye' (p.275) seems almost hateful.

We may accept that heath-bound Eustacia's memories of Budmouth and 'romantic recollections of sunny afternoons on an esplanade, with military bands, officers, and gallants around' (p.83) compose what John Lucas calls 'a vulgar dream, and one that might seem to bring her perilously close to [Henry James'] Millicent Henning'[10] (the bolting (anti-)heroine in *Roderick Hudson* [1857]).

This suggests that we might add to such parallels with clarifying results: in 'forming' Eustacia Hardy perhaps had Lydia Bennet, the regimentals-intoxicated young tearaway of *Pride and Prejudice* (1813) in mind. Indeed, Diggory Venn is so alert to Eustacia's 'psychology' here that we might almost think he has a copy of the Austen novel secreted in his van. As if needlessly depicting the charms of Brighton to Lydia, he alluringly describes the racy atmosphere of Budmouth to Eustacia in his attempt to get her off the heath and precipitate the marriage of Eustacia's original lover Wildeve and the compromized Thomasin Yeobright – a girl whom he himself still forlornly loves. But Eustacia proves more self-righteous and pretentious than Lydia, with more than a hint of the formidable side of Elizabeth Bennet. Unfortunately, though, what she conspicuously lacks is Elizabeth's sense of humour. Hardy speaks of his rustic character Olly Dowden as 'a woman noisily constructed', and Eustacia also seems to be visibly 'constructed', made out of ideological materials to hand by Hardy's *bricolage*. She seems to be a bulwark against English puritanism and narrow-mindedness as the exponent of a Continental 'sophistication'. The pursuit of such notions on Egdon Heath seems faintly comic, but may also prove to be somewhat provocative. For example, unable to engage in 'conspicuous consumption', she cultivates a little 'conspicuous idleness' while the rustics are working (p.85). (Interestingly, this strange yet familiar way of exemplifying a 'structure of feeling' specifically contradicts Wittgenstein's angry refusal to approach or pass near toiling rustics in Ireland while he himself was on holiday.)[11]

So Eustacia might be defined as, in a special way, the *effect* of *causes*. They would appear to be those which oppose the 'Roundhead' side of 'Englishness'. In Hardy's time this would suggest, more strongly than for us, emphatically *ethical, flesh-subduing* and '*levelling*' components (which her husband Clym will prove to embody). Her beribboned 'slow dying' (p.139) as 'Turkish Knight' in the mummer's play neatly suggests both a 'love-adept', in Shelley's idiom, and a peculiarly English Christendom's 'other' (fighting St. George) and a gender 'other' 'figuring in breeches' (p.149) (as, presumably, the first female mummer).

Suggestively, it is in this male guise that she succeeds in her desire to fascinate a Clym who, with such an upbringing and such a mother (and father), might even be imagined as being a (severely repressed) homosexual. This is not a necessary hypothesis, although it may be an instructive one. No lady in Paris, of all places, has turned his head, apparently. His affection for a wholesome Thomasin, said to have been 'designed' for him, is surprisingly weak. After Eustacia's death at Shadwater, his capacity for love is 'exhausted' by his short and troubled marriage to her (p.348). Indeed, as we may assume that most of Eustacia's grandfather's advice is bad, his injunction to her 'never to go figuring in breeches again' may also be dubious. A Eustacia who might say with Jessica in *The Merchant of Venice* that 'Cupid himself would blush/ To see me thus transfigured to a boy' (2.6.38-9) might have seen 'affections' consumed at Alderworth at a less 'prodigal' rate (p.227), and a Clym possessed by a less *'icy* fury' at his wife's apparent unreliability.

Eustacia's own predilections include Byron's fascination with Napoleon as well as Byron's own, final anti-*Victorian* opposition to the cluster of discourses which would sustain the Victorian order of things (Hardy's ms plainly states that 'her chief priest was Byron').[12] Whatever the merits of her pose, her repertoire of attitudes might easily decline into mere swaggering, play-acting or sartorial sumptuousness ('dressing up'). So Eustacia might even be likened to the empty-headed 'votary of fashion' who forms her 'lowest depths of possibility'[13]—Gertie McDowell of Joyce's *Ulysses*—a 'Eustacia' seen from a less romantic, or rather less than romantic perspective.[14] Such a comparison might be descried as intertextuality with a vengeance, but the reader may find it helpful.

It was of course Gertie who, without knowing it, incited (Leopold) Bloom to masturbation in *Ulysses*. This might be described as a kind of 'Bloom's End'— accidentally also the birthplace of Clym, and suggestive of him as an over-cerebral or unsensual type. Hardy's narrator expends eloquence on how Eustacia's desire is *'to be loved to madnes*s' (p.84), and Bloom's reaction to Gertie may be seen as a dismaying *reductio ad absurdum* of the idea. And in the scheme for *Ulysses*, Gertie 'is' Nausikaa, a Greek maiden in the *Odyssey*, and Tamsin Yeobright, with unintended humour, thinks of her *maternal* grandfather, Captain Vye, as 'a sort of Greek Ulysses' (it was Eustacia's father who was, in fact, a Corfiot bandmaster). If Eustacia, then, is a dreamer of dreams of which the core is to be loved to distraction, Bloom's unsavoury moments spent contemplating Gertie suggest the lowest possible version of the idea, which may be paraphrased as assuming that 'desire' is always 'imaging' its object.

And this will prove to be Eustacia's final theme, with specific reference to the inadequacy of *her* love-object, Wildeve ('He's not *great* enough for me to give myself to – he does not suffice for my desire' [p.321]). These words are spoken in her last despairing moments, as much-promising Damon, enriched with a Canadian legacy of 'eleven thousand pounds' (pp.276-7), proposes elopement to a miserable Eustacia cast off by her husband Clym. (Misunderstanding as usual, Clym seems to think he has merely cleared the air with his explosion of anger over his discovery that Wildeve has visited their cottage at Alderworth and Mrs Yeobright was apparently turned away, and has taken up residence at 'Bloom's End' to await Eustacia's return to him. The fact that he has chosen the residence of his mother, Eustacia's formidable enemy, in which to do so, shows his basic lack of imaginative empathy—with her, at any rate.)

In trying, like Clym, to find 'what will suffice', Eustacia will find only that her desire 'is too difficult to tell from despair',[15] as a Lacanian *avant la lettre* who finally sees that desire achieves only chimerical objectifications. So a verdict of 'suicide while of sound mind' as she hurls herself into Shadwater weir on the stormy night of her failed elopement itself seems fairly sound. Her romantic desire to be elsewhere becomes a Baudelairean desire to be 'anywhere, so long as [it is] out of this world'. In a sense, then, finally Eustacia died of a kind of aporia, of not knowing quite 'what she wanted'. She would have despised Diggory Venn's statement to the Thomasin he hoped to marry after Wildeve's death by water, that 'money is all my dream' (p.352) (an idea which would of course constitute Clym's ultimate nightmare).

Yet, finally, Eustacia's dream too is, if not 'made of', at least mediated by, money. Clym, by contrast, feels, with Hopkins, 'long live the weeds and the wilderness yet',[16] rendering the wild heath (as) capitalism's 'other', noting with pleasure how attempts at 'reclamation' for profitable farming have failed, but also failing to note a possible parallel with the efforts he proposes to make at social and intellectual 'reclamation' for which he has sacrificed a career which must have entailed familial sacrifices. As we saw, Eustacia's idea of the Heath as a place to escape from is opposed to that of Clym's Heath as one to escape to. Indeed, it is precisely because he seems armed (on his 'English' side) with a clear distinction between wealth and well-being and a desire to indulge an ascetic Wordsworthian philosophy of 'plain living and high thinking' that Clym's personal quest as an educator of sorts with a mission to 'raise a class' (bk.2, ch.2, p.171) also seems aporetic, self-cancelling. 'Thinking through Wordsworth', he seems already to have 'conceded', without quite realising it, that 'humble and rustic life' is superior *as it is*. Eustacia quite clearly revealed her head-tossing contempt for what she called a 'parcel of cottagers' (p.103). But the narrator is perhaps also in touch with Clym's 'other' side (and his tone can be patronising) in describing his insistence on seeking (out) 'brotherliness with clowns' (p.171).

Clym is pleased that the heath (nature) has not been improved into a state of (agri-)cultural capital, yet wishes to bring 'cultural capital' to unimproved rusticity which may also turn out to be 'unimprovable'—in the sense of being all right as it is rather than merely lumpen. For example, the surprise present of an enormous goose-feather bed by the heath-folk for newly-wed Diggory and Thomasin in the last section (bk. 6, 'Aftercourses', ch.4, p.357) underlines the communal sense informing traditional country life, bringing tears to the eyes of Clym's newly-married cousin Thomasin as she acknowledges 'these kind neighbours' (p.360). And Humphrey is an example of shrewd and well-intentioned rusticity, which Hardy likes to 'project'. Yet, whether to prevent the idealising of their way of life or present a sense of its decadence or contamination, Hardy makes the sentimental 'investments' in rusticity which he made possible (or even encouraged) in *Far from the Madding Crowd* (1874), much more difficult. In propria persona, indeed, the most prominent of the rustics seem to parody the preoccupations of the central characters.

Their tone is set by the idiotic 'Grandfer' Cantle, a kind of *reductio ad absurdum* of self-absorbed romanticism, apparently fixated on his long-gone smartness as a soldier in the 'bang-up' locals of 'four' (=1804) (e.g., bk.1, ch.4, p.46) (a sort of 'grandad's army' anticipating a Napoleonic invasion): this, presumably, satirizes those whose pursuits entail vanity and self-display, those concerned with the figures they cut and readily humiliated. The perennially juvenile 'Grandfer' Cantle is ironically contrasted with his prematurely 'aged' grandson, the equally idiotic and suggestively 'eunochoid' *Christian Cantle*, whose very name suggests the unkindest possible estimate of blind Clym's final role as a preacher on Rainbarrow.

Christian, gambling on as well as with those '*magical machines*' (p.214) the dice, has produced a phrase which also suggests the apparently 'aleatoric' procedures of a Hardy novel itself—the dice themselves seem, alarmingly, to 'have an opinion' as to 'what should happen' here. In *Christian*'s hands, they also suggest a savage parody of Pascal's famous attempt to describe Christianity as a paradoxically sure-fire wager. Christian, after winning a prize in 'The Quiet Woman', discovered, as Mallarmé puts it, that *'un coup de dés jamais n'abolira le hasard'* ['a throw of the dice will never abolish chance'].[17] He continued his gambling on Egdon Heath with a 'Damon' full of resentment that they should have been entrusted to Christian by Mrs Yeobright in the first place. Christian then lost the guineas to Wildeve, who in turn lost them to Venn (p.221).

However, as it happened, righteous Venn's appropriation of the spade-guineas on Thomasin's behalf, apparently a sign that 'God's in his heaven/ All's right with the world',[18] and that things have been, more or less, 'sorted', had in fact terrible, not happy, results. His mistake in giving *all* of them to Thomasin (half were owing to Clym), precipitated the quarrel of Eustacia and Mrs Yeobright, her death on the heath, the dismissal of Eustacia by Clym, and all that followed—culminating in the deaths of Wildeve and Eustacia at Shadwater weir on a wild and stormy Autumn night (pp.333-4). Christian's gullibility in this area contrasts with his role in attempting to restrain his grandfather in his proneness to romantic fantasizing about his role and his status.

Fantasies about roles and status are very much the subject of the novel's 'investigations'. The families of the central couple here are unhappily united in a social liminality which encourages a comparable tendency to fantasy and self-deception. When Eustacia's grandfather describes Clym's father as having been 'as rough as a hedge', he seems unaware that, by easy analogy, he is also describing a state which he himself is not too far from, despite the contemptuous relish with which he refers to the Yeobrights' humbly sanded floor and unpretentious elderberry wine (bk.2, ch.3, p.124).

And indeed Mrs Yeobright is savagely 'deconstructive' of the Vyes' pretensions, particularly Eustacia's, in 'moves' which might also encompass her own: 'she hasn't a penny' is one desperately direct lunge in response to Clym's unbearably painful revelations—not merely that he has irrevocably abandoned his career, but also his intention of marrying the 'idle' Eustacia. And, as for 'Captain' Vye, Mrs Yeobright's 'no doubt he has been to sea in some tub or other' (p.196) forms a particularly sardonic dismissal of the 'grog'-inspired fantasizer. But Captain Vye, with his insensitive manner and rough tongue, sounds more than a little like Clym's father himself (ironically, in Vye's own account of him), just as Mrs Yeobright's 'rubbishing' of the Vyes' social pretensions and claims to notice might be described by others as an unintentionally apt description of her own.

Again, Hardy points out that '[Eustacia's] maternal grandfather *had had* a cousin in the peerage' (bk.1, ch.7, p.84), making her connection with the aristocracy somewhat remote, conjectural, even faintly comic—'had had' certainly seems to add to the sense of a precarious link or tenure. Presumably it is precisely the tenuousness of the link which 'overdetermines' and makes almost absurd the stateliness, or queenliness, he works hard to associate with Eustacia (and Eustacia works equally hard to have associated with herself). Unfortunately, as we saw, this is most emphatically expressed in Eustacia's *refusal to work.*

As if inverting a 'Painite' scorn for the parasitical 'puppet shows' of aristocracy and the 'hereditary principle'[19] (a scorn which Clym, if in a gentler idiom, obviously shares), Eustacia would obviously opt for being just such a puppet in the motions of 'greatness'. But in a novel in which character(s) are shown as controlled by more abstract assumptions than 'individuality' confers it is not clear that anyone is escaping from some kind of 'puppet show' here: 'mumming', with its ironically authentic 'automaton-like' responses, provides the central metaphor for how it is for all of us, including Clym himself.

Given her appearance as mummer and her fame as the beauty of Egdon, as 'the cynosure of neighbouring eyes', Eustacia already seems something of a 'living doll'. Susan *Nunsuch*, whose very name seems to be telling her home truths about witches as nothing other than the result of the sort of 'representations' she makes of them, created a (wax) doll of the Eustacia Nunsuch had already identified as one (pp.322-33)—when she stabbed her with a needle in church (p.175). Yet 'thinking of witches', it seems clear that Susan is indeed en route to confirming *herself* as one—and in this way she may ironically evade the idea that *her name* describes a state of affairs with regard to them (i.e., that there *are no witches*).

Indeed, *The Return of the Native*, while formally discouraging the idea that there 'are' witches, seems to see to it that the reader fashions a few of her own. For example, confirming the idea that the plot of *The Return of the Native* is in its way 'hexed', composed of what Robert Lowell calls 'witchery-bitchery',[20] is the fact that it was Mrs Yeobright, *not* Eustacia, who 'caused' little Johnny Nunsuch's 'final' illness, although Eustacia had conscripted him for her earlier love-campaigns with (and against) Wildeve. Indeed, Susan's moulding of the 'wrong image' seems suggestive for a novel in which people may seem vaguely congruent even when formally 'opposites'. And each of the 'be-witching' candidates here act from insecurity in relation to notions of social class (or class fractions) they entertain. Their stubborn conviction which each woman entertains, that their family 'condescended' in marrying into the other's, leaves them possessed by the rage and bitterness 'becoming a witch'. (In a sense the 'states they are in' seem more important than what Lawrence would later call 'the old stable ego of character'.)

But this is precisely because in the world of *The Return of the Native*, class fractions seem rather 'friable'. Gentility itself is grounded on, or in, semantic instability, the sheer vagueness of what might be called relevant criteria.[21] So even intimations of the 'magical' or 'the uncanny' are socially grounded. Indeed, both the canny and the uncanny are quite clearly involved with ideas of 'having power over' persons or circumstance. For example, Mrs Yeobright's outburst to the effect that 'you are blinded, Clym', apparently a response (p.188) to his declared desire to marry 'idle' Eustacia, also appears to have the effect of an extremely nasty 'performative': he is stricken with ophthalmia soon after and never recovers.

As she visits 'Bloom's End' as one of the 'mummers', themselves clearly puppets of sorts, speaking their parts like 'automata', Eustacia is herself already possessed by a kind of erotic enchantment, but Clym himself will shortly, as a result, be its 'doll' also. Wallace Stevens provides a necessary 'link' here in pronouncing that 'if sex were all, then every trembling hand/ Could make us squeak, like dolls, the wished-for words'.[22] Eustacia, who, in however elevated a way, did indeed wish that 'sex' were 'all', and whose fate was to be re-fashioned as a doll, undoubtedly 'had influence' in such matters, practised her craft in this sphere. A semantic 'pin' seems to be stuck through dolls, automata, mumm[y]ing, witchcraft, and sex—in what we might describe as a 'bewitching' novel.

Eustacia's 'Death by Water' immediately followed Susan Nunsuch's apparent attempt to condemn her to 'Death by Fire' by melting the wax image she made of her (p.322). According to the Buddha in the 'Fire Sermon', the senses are all on fire, and (consequently) we should turn away from or quench (drown) desire. Eustacia was made of desire, or of her relation to desire, and the discovery that Wildeve does not form an adequate object for hers precipitates her despair. After this desolating discovery it seems that she did hurl herself into, did not merely accidentally tumble into, the waters of Shadwater weir, which, suggestively referred to as a 'boiling cauldron' (bk.6, ch.1, p.344), does seem to have become something of a 'witch's brew' after all.

The last section and end of the episode, 'Aftercourses', was apparently an afterthought, but feels like a necessary supplement to what has preceded it. Clym was depicted as finding a kind of imaginative freedom in 'the ghostly language of the ancient earth' (pp.344-5), and in a way he seems to become a 'voice of the heath', as he does all his preaching alfresco on sites like Rainbarrow, where the novel began. But although *on* the heath he is very far from being the expression *of* the heath. The etymology of *pagan* is 'heath-en'. But Clym appears to seek forms of appeasement for the mother who haunts him in *Biblical* contexts, in the pathos of posthumous obedience.

Like the de-reddled Diggory greeted by the widowed Thomasin's shriek of surprise here, Clym may be said (with considerably more justice) to have become 'the ghost of himself' (p.345), just as he is, in his actual effects, rather more of a 'Mephistophelian visitant' (p.91) than the Diggory originally saddled with the description. 'I am other I now' is the Stephen Dedalus claim (in *Ulysses*) with which prospering Diggory implicitly confronts Thomasin. The proposition will be used to suggest that the snobbish Mrs Yeobright would have conceded that Venn was socially elevated enough to aspire to a niece eloquent on the subject of her Egdon unpretentiousness.

Clym himself is also much possessed by the need to construct a hypothetical maternal approbation *d'outre-tombe*. But Clym's mother, after all, wanted him to be a diamond merchant, and no more a preacher than a teacher. She was nothing if not socially ambitious, partly because her own father, despite the airs she gives herself, was a mere curate whose lot in life no doubt furnished many opportunities to observe that that particular destiny was a bit of a 'curate's egg'. And the final scripture citation Clym is shown as offering his hearers, which apparently shows a mother being pleased, in fact shows a mother being thwarted (and, in due course, a son being executed).[24] Yet, in an inconsistent attempt to placate her, Clym's Shelleyan defiance of the social system seems to have been replaced by issues raised by the Matthew Arnold of *Culture and Anarchy* (1859), as Clym seems to be combing through 'Hebraic' texts looking for 'Hellenic' significances, substituting the 'sweetness and light' of the one for the 'strictness of conscience' of the other.[24] (The latter would of course correspond to Mrs Yeobright's ferociously 'judgemental' perspectives.)

Stefan Collini points out that formally, as a historical thinker, Arnold himself was literally 'faithless' but remained deeply responsive to 'certain kinds of religious emotion',[25] and the sheer vagueness of the idea seems right for Clym's overwhelmingly 'Oedipal' need for appeasement(s). Hence the specific inattention of his audience seems not only relevant but appropriate—Clym's original ability to see beyond himself and his originally acquisitive purposes has been replaced by Freudian preoccupations which leave him 'eyeless' for the conditions he originally addressed.

As we have seen, Clym is a very 'English' figure: but we also heard that he had been studying 'reforming' political thought in Paris, so perhaps he had been thinking along the lines of the Fourier who made one with those Utopian socialists who protested the exploitation of nature more clearly than did Marx.[26] It seems to be just such an 'ecological communism' which formed Clym's original vision as returning native. That he returns to find himself gone is partly because his vision is already sophisticated, antithetical, conceived in opposition to the 'commodity fetishism' he presumably found all about him in his 'other' existence in France, one in which 'the ache of modernism' got the better of him.

Chapter 6

The Art(s) of Misrepresentation:
A Laodicean

The heroine of *A Laodicean*, Paula Power, is a strong woman made to look weak at 'pressure-points' brought to bear by (mis-) representations on her apparently privileged position. An heiress of Puritan temperament but romantic aspiration, she is 'made' by her late father, John Power, a railway magnate. As such, he is a kind of personification of the forces of modernity, and the [dis-] respected profession of engineer. Engineering excellence was central to Victorian enterprise and prestige, yet figures little in literary discussions of the period. So it looks as if the most relevant book one might consult here would be less a critical work on Hardy himself than Martin J. Wiener's *English Culture and the Decline of the Industrial Spirit 1850-1980*, with its telling observation on the silent crowds which lined the streets on the death of the great steam engineer Stephenson in 1859: 'never again would the profession stand so high' (p.30). Equally germane, one thinks, might be Wiener's equally telling observation of the problems brought by the whole repertoire of cultural attitudes which make Wiener's chapter title '"Modernisation": Un-English?' a sadly apposite one.[1]

A Laodicean looks initially to be set to restore the balance, its title suggesting a personal hesitation between ancient and modern modes of existence, or between different cultural repertoires over a range of subjects and practices. But perhaps the sovereign irony of the book is that as a result of the fact that her father John Power's *praxis* has 'set Paula up', his duty seems to have been to get, but hers merely to spend, wisely. Power 'executed commissions', but Paula's duty is merely to 'commission executives' like her rival architects, James Havill and young George Somerset, for the supply of modern appendages to her Ancient Monument, De Stancy Castle, reduced to a ruin by her Puritan forebears. And finally she has the 'task' of 'arbitrating' between suitors—in this case, Somerset again (a kind of heir to an apostolic succession of talent), and Captain De Stancy (the suitably decadent embodiment of 'hoary' genealogies who is, with prosaic suggestiveness, much older than Somerset himself).

Again, we learn that John Power built railways throughout Europe, but his daughter Paula's role is merely to travel on them, as she does—ironically at the forceful suggestion of his surviving brother, Abner, who was very much at odds with him. For related reasons, Abner Power deprecates the advances of Somerset, embodiment of modernity and 'the youthful way of looking at things', in favour of the ancient line of De Stancy. So Abner Power uses modernity in transport to get Paula away from her modern suitor and in tow with her 'ancient' one, De Stancy. Ironically, however, De Stancy cared nothing for his *ancien régime* genealogy until incited to aspire to Paula.

By contrast, George Somerset is first glimpsed copying old ecclesiastical architecture, as an 'aesthete' whose imagination is solicited by tradition(s). Shortly thereafter Somerset will be found wincing at 'raw and red-bricked modernism at worship' in the form of the dissenting chapel established by John Power himself, but George, by no means imaginatively 'one-sided', is alert to the energies the chapel sets free, the consolation it offers to those in hard and lowly employments, its happily ironic retention of ancient psalm-forms which his Established Church has suppressed, the fiery unworldliness of its puritan minister, Mr Woodwell, and (finally) the piquancy of the incongruously rich and beautiful Paula offering herself there for adult baptism at the behest of her late father. Unfortunately she demurred at this point, incurring the accusation, in fiercely comminatory rhetoric (before the assembled congregation) by Woodwell, of being '*A Laodicean*'—lukewarm in religious matters. The novel's intention is to set the reader wondering whether this apparent trait of 'velleity', or hesitation between alternatives, might 'carry over' into other areas of Paula's existence.

The irony here is that Paula is like George, and suited to him, not in being what Hardy calls 'an indifferentist', but through not being intellectually sectarian. The 'key-word' here is by way of being *prédilection*, indicating the various spheres of *aesthetic* choice. But what secretly unites Paula and Somerset and *also* defines *nobility* without reference to the aesthetic contexts which insistently offer themselves here, is the *ethical*, as puritans have always intuited. In a quiet but tell-tale moment (bk.1, ch.9), it is shown that Paula decisively 'fell for' George himself through his nobility *of disposition* in refusing to take unfair advantage of his older rival (in architecture) James Havill, an unfair advantage which the scions of the 'nobility', Captain De Stancy and Willie Dare, would subsequently take of Somerset (in courtship). (De Stancy himself has constant scruples but his illegitimate son Dare constantly dissolves them for him.) But as Paula's patrimony makes her in person something like the embodiment of modernity, the weight given by her imagination to prejudicial feelings deriving from traditional 'representations' tilts the book towards conservative attitudes it seemed to be putting under erasure. For example, Somerset himself notes the way an arrow slit in Paula's castle is penetrated by the telegraph wire, an alien worm,[2] in a startling example of what might be called 'the word made *flèche*', and a 'sort of optical' (p.184) demonstration that the sign is mightier than the sword. The presence of the wire is felt to be an outrage, but is also a reminder of a modern world whose amenities finally preclude over-indulgence of cultural nostalgia.

The reader might still claim that the book enters a little too enthusiastically into Paula's callow fantasies, which constitute a historicism whose adherents, as Benjamin puts it, 'empathize . . . with the victor'.[3] But a telling interpolation occurs during the chase Paula has initiated for her dismissed but blameless suitor George: an authentic sense of '*the* mediaeval' is amusingly evoked in passing—just when Paula has decisively lost interest in the idea—*not* by grand families or ecclesiastical traditions, *but* by the *low tradespeople* thronging the evocatively ancient thoroughfares of Lisieux (bk.6, ch.1). And the De Stancys, although bespeaking antiquity, are not formidable. Rather, they attract pathos, represented by the brain-softened oldster Sir William, who gambled away his ancestral property. (Hardy would have been amusingly aware that Tennyson attributed 'power of brain' to the 'warrior-kings of old' in his début as Poet Laureate with 'To the Queen' [1851].)[4]

Sir William is living out his garrulous days in a banal modern dwelling ('Myrtle Cottage') in Markton (the town adjacent to the 'De Stancy' castle). In a typical Hardy conceit, Sir William's only physical contact with his distinguished past lies in his possession of the ponderous keys to the ancient gate of De Stancy Castle (long since replaced) so now literally 'the keys to nothing'. And Sir William's conversation offers an apt parallel to this idea in an incessant rattle of wise precepts which he is utterly unable to exemplify. Then follows Sir William's emotionally chaotic son, Captain De Stancy, with his frighteningly unscrupulous and manipulative progeny in tow. This son, Dare, was unacknowledged, but, as if in compensation, the De Stancy name was inscribed on his chest ('the flesh made word', as it were, this time). As a son of De Stancy's flesh, Dare is granted the appellation 'De Stancy' in a 'literal(ly)' fleshly sense denied *by convention* to him in person—another interesting 'conceit' with a typically unexplained origin here. In fact, the disclosure of the mystery of Dare's identity to Paula will rightly dissolve the De Stancy engagement to her on the spot. All in all, the De Stancys illustrate the novel's implied maxim to the effect that *the origins of genealogy are lost in representation(s)*. Ancestral portraits lining the walls of Paula's 'De Stancy Castle' bespeak a nobility 'absent' in a double sense, apparently.

The novel investigates power relations in 'history' in relation to a 'herstory' less often represented. In Jane Austen's fiction, her heroines are 'made' by marriage, but Paula has already outsoared their particular problem—a sense of the exposure incurred by penury, suggesting marital solutions: but she shares their need to listen to 'the true voice of feeling' in marriage-choices—choosing between suitors will prove problematic in an obverse way as Paula looks to *their* motives. She is also an 'enriched' version of the heroine of *The Hand of Ethelberta* (1876), whose own apparent hesitancy was actually 'the exquisite balance of the logan-stone'. Paula, tough-minded (if tender-hearted) causes both her serious suitors much suffering, although this *was* largely a result of *misrepresentation(s)*, a theme finally seen to be the subject of a novel itself toying with them throughout. Paula's final pursuit of Somerset through Normandy, with multiple misunderstandings en route, entails a form of ritual humiliation for her which helps keep the reader on-side. 'A Laodicean', apparently indicating one of lukewarm emotions, must be registered as an ironic title: at the level of love-interest. Paula's 'Power-ful' feelings are clearly evoked as she tracks down her temporarily 'deselected' architectural admirer. The *terminus ad quem* is Étretat, in which, by alarming report, George was said to be seeking fleshly consolation for the emotional turmoil her (mistakenly reported) marriage with De Stancy had induced. Further atoning for her off-hand treatment of her suitor, she also marries him 'off-hand' before returning to England (bk.6, ch.3). (A typical blemish here is that the form of marriage is not specified, a point Hardy made important in having Paula initially attentive to the punctilious theocentric hair-splitting of the Baptist minister Woodwell.)

Only a pseudo-Laodicean to George, then, Paula revealed her true Laodicean-ism only when she permitted De Stancy to court her after George had been depicted as a gamester and a drunkard (an ironically apt characterisation of Dare and De Stancy themselves), and so was summarily dismissed on his joining the party in Carlsruhe—

and, near-tragically, was too proud to expostulate and demand an explanation for his mistreatment. But Paula's subsequent resistance to her older suitor De Stancy is sustained, *despite* the temptations to be swayed in his favour by the abstract theme of genealogy as an adjunct to wealth, by her affection for De Stancy's sister Charlotte and consequent desire to make amends to the historically routed clan, as well as by the power invested in her father's scapegrace brother Abner to influence the proceedings in the De Stancy interest. So she (temporarily) succumbed to De Stancy's pressure to marry him only through a kind of 'catalytic overdetermination': a sense of 'the long perspectives' induced by the ritualistic atmosphere of Amiens Cathedral, where things came to a head (bk.5, ch.10); the illness of Charlotte, which united her and De Stancy in tenderness towards her; the death of old Sir William, announced by telegram, which induced the immediate departure of De Stancy and an enhanced sense of the pathos surrounding the hapless officer; the prospect of becoming Lady De Stancy; the slightly provocative *discouragement* given to the idea of marriage with De Stancy suggested by her well-meaning Aunt Mrs Goodman on the grounds of De Stancy's age; and, finally, and equally 'perversely', the sudden *forbidding* of the match by erstwhile enthusiast Abner Power, who has begun to smell a rat in the form of intuitions about the Dare-De Stancy connection. Obviously Paula, following her father in her very altered circumstances, rather enjoys a challenge.

Ironically, Charlotte was herself said to be in love with George, and after Somerset in an accidental meeting on a train journey strenuously denied he had attempted to extort money (actually a telegram request faked by Dare [bk.5, ch.12]), it falls to Charlotte's lot to reveal to Paula that Somerset is blameless. She had also subsequently checked up on consequently suspected possibilities of further traducing through photographic misrepresentation with the local photographic agent, the facetiously-named Mr *Ray*, who happens to have samples of such work by Dare himself on the premises. Unfortunately, the exoneration of Somerset which Charlotte initiates, sufficient to abrogate Paula's marriage with Charlotte's brother at the eleventh hour, puts Somerset decisively out of her reach. Charlotte's self-sacrifice precipitates her final 'choice of life [or death?]' as a member of an unspecified order of (Protestant) 'sisters'.

The novel hinged initially on Paula's reluctance to immerse herself at the point of adult baptism, which disappointed Minister Woodwell but also broke her promise to a father whose posthumous influence has proved insufficient to get her into cold water (p.45), but, given the result, quite sufficient to get her into hot water (p.47). So Paula consented to adult baptism in the place of 'modernism at worship' only because of the ('ancestral') hest of her thoroughly modern parent. In finally refusing to go through with this, she at once traduces and embodies his spirit. But this theme is recessive in a book which gives ground, not so much to *anciens régimes* as to the effete lifestyle of those to whom the acquisition of wealth has ceased to be a problem (particularly when Paula's party alights at Monte Carlo, described as 'the negative pole of industry' (Bk.4, ch.4), a concept odious to Mr Woodwell no less than the spirit of the archetypal industrialist John Power himself. The original church contretemps did, however, and however improbably, initiate the love affair of Somerset and Paula, since on hearing Minister Woodwell's beratings of her over her public tergiversation (pp.80-81), the young architect George Somerset is, in some very odd wooing, inadvertently seducing Paula through expertise in the Church Fathers.

In a different sense, Somerset is, like Angelo in *Measure for Measure,* 'baiting his hook with saints' (2.2.181) as she murmurs her 'admiration for . . . your studies in divinity' (p.84). The eloquent Mr *Woodwell's* equally eloquent name is intended to suggest an urbanely sophisticated tone Hardy doesn't quite sustain here. Homologous with Angel's father in serious *Tess* (1891), the dissenting preacher also reproduces, in his attitude to Paula, that of the Rector Mr Raunham to Cytherea in *Desperate Remedies* (1871). (Woodwell's Puritan opposition to aristocracy makes ecclesiastical squabbles a 'mediated' version of *class* conflict as precipitated by the 'too-early' English Revolution.[5] But Hardy, possibly placating his amanuensis Emma here, deserts this aspect of his official theme.)

Also 'recessive' here is the theme of 'heterosexuality' vs. 'lesbianism' in the novel's insistent thematic binarizings. Those tender squeezings of aristocratic but impoverished Charlotte De Stancy by Paula, whom she virtually keeps on her (i.e. Charlotte's) ancestral premises, show almost too warm a regard for 'family values'. As we saw, Charlotte finally retires to an Anglican nunnery (pp.404-5), and we may speculate on whether this was indeed because she was deprived of George Somerset (what the text claims), or because she was deprived of Paula (what the text may be implying). But *A Laodicean* had to get past not only Mrs Grundy but also Mrs Hardy, whose voice and presence affected Hardy's writing here. The 'incipiently homosexual'[6] relationship with Charlotte is gradually effaced by the 'Victorian' strait-lacings of the author himself: yet moments like 'after which she clasped her fingers *behind Charlotte's neck,* and smiled in her face' (p.105) do, with other intermittent sentences, make Charlotte and Paula seem 'more like lovers than maid and maid', as the landlord of the local Inn at 'Sleeping Green' observes (p.75) with startling frankness. At a more abstract level, Charlotte De Stancy's fate can be presented as simply 'resuming' the major theme in her renunciation of the (modern) world (p.382) just as Paula embraces it, not only in the person of her young architect, but in the form of the 'young architecture' which will be needed to replace that of her finally 'arsonized' castle (p.408).

Charlotte's final 'step' also orchestrates the terminally 'vestigial' state of the De Stancy family itself. The decline and fall of the De Stancys (the name perhaps the fruit of idioms like 'at a stand' and 'standing [idly] by' in a world where 'there's work to be done'—and thus perhaps also 'S[a]tan-cy')—is contrasted with the grin-inducing idea of a 'Rise of Power'. Indeed, in his attempt to graft himself to 'Power' with the help of a (character called) 'Dare', Captain De Stancy seems to be leading what Keats might have called 'a life of Allegory'. Insufficiently on her guard, Paula has forgotten that 'the Prince of Darkness is a gentleman', and Captain De Stancy takes flight when dusk has fallen on the family fortunes, homing in on the forfeited ancestral home. His personal innocuousness is needed to give plausibility to a suit which culminated successfully through the hoodwinking of Paula and Somerset by *misrepresentation,* through a process which Captain De Stancy would not himself have countenanced (p.310). Himself no Satan, De Stancy seems to need one who will serve his interests 'behind him'. It is Captain De Stancy's unacknowledged son, the Machiavellian 'Willy Dare', who supplies the penumbral tones of sinister machination needed for De

Stancy to press his suit. The deception of Paula will demonstrate the role of ideology in the construction of 'social imaginaries', particularly those entailing the temporal distance which permits things to be 'strangely misrepresented'. As he stands posing within the frame of an ancestral portrait (bk. 3, ch.2), Captain De Stancy becomes a kind of 'sign of himself' as he appears to Paula and Charlotte almost at one with it (p.197), as if himself always-already 'a form of representation'. Paula confessed to Somerset that she wanted to *be* a De Stancy (bk.1, ch.14), but, paradoxically, De Stancy himself needs to assume an 'always-already-represented' form, needs to be rather more than himself to 'suit' Paula, and Dare, with willing hands, does everything to refashion De Stancy here almost as 'his piece of work', the result of his artistry, so that Captain De Stancy is never really 'quite as he represents himself'.

Continuing the theme of De Stancy as a 'new creation', as a kind of 'composite' 'supplemented' by Dare, almost a kind of 'replicant',[7] De Stancy will also practise a bit of *textual* 'grafting' here, putting a sliver of *Romeo and Juliet* into a production of *Love's Labour's Lost* to allow him to appear to kiss Paula on stage with what Hardy describes as the *sound* of a 'a very sweet and long-drawn osculation' (p.238). This gives the impression that he is already compromisingly close to Paula to an audience consisting largely of the local gentry, and initiates the seduction of Paula herself through a process of *impersonation* which provides another clue to what he is up to, performatively simulating the grafting of himself on to Paula's allegedly wilder stock (*Winter's Tale* 4.4.93). Yet traditional history writing, preoccupied with that history of the victors Benjamin so memorably pinpointed, would have transferred its scribely allegiance without effort to the side of 'Power' in any case. These historians would be confident that to be 'born to the purple of commerce', would merit scholarly consideration more than 'rising from the ranks of the aristocracy'[8] could. Indeed, Wilde's brilliantly ironic phrasing seems to summarize much of the tone and substance of *A Laodicean* itself here.

Indeed, it is said that alliance with a De Stancy would strengthen Paula's hand with the local gentry, and another definite weakness in the novel is that the collective voice of the local gentry is not much more than a pipsqueak here (e.g., p.236). It's clear, whatever she herself thinks, that she can do very well indeed without them (and not so clear that they can do without her). Also part of the text's little, if self-subverting, irony here is that parvenue Paula outdoes De Stancy in social poise, and his louche lifestyle and needy adventurer status leave him on the verge as the scarcely respectable member of society. *Generously*, that's to say, nobly (if naively), Paula wishes to restore the Castle de Stancy as a descendant of those puritans who 'dis-figured' it, and if she does choose De Stancy (influenced by her personal affection for his sister, Charlotte), she will *also* restore the family which figures so largely in its story, 'told in pictures'. Introduced to their story as she has been, they will be introduced to hers, and, as told in French, the phrase will also accommodate De Stancy's sexual approach here.[9]

Those ancestral portraits which possess Paula as much as she possesses them (pp.196-200), representing absence, recording what's gone, are working too hard to sustain the idea that painted lineaments may be more than native talent. *A Laodicean* is a staging (or fixture) of 'capital' versus 'cultural capital' with an implicit claim that, unpossessed by what they possess, the heirs of steam power magnates acquire a lust for the patina which is the only gift not in the power of wealth (or, in this case, the wealth of Power). As we saw, De Stancy, in a sense, 'made out of' ancestral portraits, in a version of the Pygmalion theme, seems himself to step from canvas, at once representing the historical and represented by it. The two girls, Paula and Charlotte, who confront him are mesmerized by his trick of becoming a figure of art here. And if Paula is herself a historical Victor, she is paradoxically without a history to attest to that victory or representation to seal it as such. With De Stancy introduced to her story, she will be introduced to 'his(-)story'. Yet De Stancy was in fact 'mis-re-presented' by ancestral portraits, which frame his 'sterling insignificance'.

Similarly, Somerset—the 'modernist'—is misrepresented by the photography of Willy Dare, the 'Mephistophelian visitant' himself not merely represented by, but as if genetically engineered by, *his own name*. 'Willy Dare' is indeed a particularly outrageous naming of parts by daring Hardy here. Dare, it seems, is 'Oedipally related' to his father in an inverse way. It was to the 'daring' of De Stancy's 'willy' that he owes his being, so that, in Ben Jonson's idiom, 'his name speaks him'[10] in a particularly intimate way. His name also transfers the 'phallic' momentum to Dare here, making him the 'evil' superego to his *roué father*. ('But, Willy, it seems to me that, of us two, it is you who exercise paternal authority' [p.172].) 'Will' combines with 'Dare'-ing (this is part of Hardy's own sustained facetiousness here) to enable De Stancy to effect an entry to Paula's 'story' through 'stories of the De Stancys'. He will do so by 'conning' genealogies and memoirs in order to 'con' Paula (p.198) here. The 'sad captain', full of remorse for his past conduct to Dare's mother, has abjured liquor and ladies. Of course Dare himself owes his very being to the emotionally chaotic and sexually susceptible version of De Stancy, before he had abjured such delights—and 'able was he ere he saw Paula', as Joyce might put it,[11] so Dare already has an emotional investment in a rebirth of the De Stancy who begot him. So by 'Machiavellian' arrangements, perhaps also as part of an attempt to make his father more paternal in being more like 'the De Stancy who begot him', as well as fit to besiege an heiress in her castle in order to provide 'a milch cow for his sustenance',[12] Dare arranges that Paula is glimpsed as 'a sort of optical poem' (p.184) as she cavorts in her gymnasium, peeped on, initially with a grumbling unwillingness, by a De Stancy surreptitiously plied with strong drink by Dare (bk.2, ch.7). De Stancy will assume the complexly perverse position of one who may be said to be 'formerly reformed', but now successfully deconstructed again into 'a sort of bowdlerized roué'[13] by his son.

Dare's name also contains the banally-ludic 'will he dare?' on the assumption that he will indeed dare anything—he has thoughts, for example, of murdering Somerset to get him out of the way (p.215). Somerset was originally 'misrepresented' (pp.292-3) as a gambling debtor by Dare (p.285), the misrepresenter who would *himself* be correctly represented as one, so that his misrepresentation of Somerset is, tellingly, a kind of Dare self-portrait. And as one of De Stancy's former weaknesses was strong drink, and a doctored photograph showed *Somerset* in a state of intoxication, we may also say that Dare dares to *mis*represent Somerset in terms accurately representing aspects of his father as well as himself. So it was by an accident which hell provided that Dare let fall a photograph tampered with to show Somerset in a state of intoxication, horrifying the puritanical Paula, whose modernity, it seems, is not up to the technical means of misrepresentation deployed here (pp.310-11). And we are told, in an important moment, that the 'scientific' misrepresentation of Somerset had for Charlotte and Paula 'all the cogency of direct vision' (bk. 5, ch.4), which bespeaks an almost culpable naiveté on their part over acts of 're-presentation' in general. This is an implicit critique of Paula's penchant for conservative imaginings which implies that *'her lack of scepticism towards the misrepresentation of Somerset as drunkard, by Dare, in photography, is "as" her lack of scepticism towards representations of historical 'victors' in portraits, effigies, etc.'*

Yet, ironically, Dare's 'master'-piece was the destruction of masterpieces which themselves misrepresent his (ig-) noble line. His final *ressentiment*-ful burning down of Paula's castle (p.406) with its ancestral portraits followed her marriage to the George Somerset she had previously 'feinted' over to preserve her female Power. Itself a 'desperate exercise of failing power', Dare's feat became a tell-tale exercise in self-destruction. We learn that the new-married Paula, safely ensconced in the Markton hotel with Somerset as the ancient pile with its precious portraits goes up in flames, had just proposed to pass the paintings to Charlotte De Stancy, and thus, if she had chosen, to Sir William De Stancy – he whom his illegitimate son Dare has, for his own purposes, been trying to enrich throughout (bk.6, ch.5). Dare thus destroys the props which would, through his father, have guaranteed him the more-than-sufficiency he craved. Hardy is also hinting that Paula's modern marriage itself puts 'the aesthetic' itself under erasure, as Tennyson's 'The Palace of Art' (1842) (destroyed in the interests of 'the ethical' by Tennyson's protagonist)[14] is made out of just such cultural nostalgia. (And Paula's castle with its works of art is a version of Tennyson's palace.) As Dare unwittingly sees his own aspirations go up in flames, Paula's equivalent is that, as she is also under the Sign 'Woman' as well as that of 'Heiress', she is designed to 'Miss Power' in any case. Or perhaps, happy with Somerset as she is, in ceasing to be named 'Miss Power' she will 'lose Power' without exactly missing it. Dare's destruction of artistic representations of aristocratic 'features' make one wonder just which side he might be said to be on. As a collective sign of power the portraits misrepresent 'his lot' (both senses). As 'signs of Power', they 'misrepresent' hers (Paula's). But there is a question as to whether Dare isn't, despite his *illegitimacy*, the *legitimate* heir to less flattering aristocratic *features* which might be characterized as *brigandage*, as Hazlitt noted. These are perhaps as 'characteristic' of the class as those 'gentle' qualities with which originally marauding warriors, metamorphosed to quaintness by time, are now identified.

In this respect *A Laodicean* is also in part about the capacity for semantic reversability of signs and representations. By contrast, in a 'significant' moment, the 'soul-less' railway of (sc.) Ruskinian perception is itself transfigured by its context:

> Somerset looked down at the tunnel. The popular commonplace
> that science, steam, and travel must always be unromantic and
> hideous, was not proven at this spot. On either slope of the deep
> cutting, green with long grass, grew drooping young trees of ash,
> beech, and other flexible varieties, their foliage almost
> concealing the actual railway which ran along the bottom, its thin
> rails gleaming like silver threads in the depths. The vertical front

of the tunnel, faced with brick that had once been red, was now weather-stained, lichened, and mossed over in harmonious rusty-browns, pearly greys, and neutral greens, at the very base appearing a little blue-black spot like a mouse-hole—the tunnel's mouth (p.114).

This is all highly suggestive, including the suggestion that this form of modernity may figure 'Desire' as potently as any castellated relic: the 'sweet especial rural scene' (Hopkins, 'Binsey Poplars' ['felled 1879']) is happily involved with the results of 'engineering'.

This 'cross-gartered' approach to representation finds an obverse in Hardy's own portrait of side-crossing Abner Power. He originally put in an appearance as a supporter of the 'hereditary principle' in the person of Captain De Stancy (p.215) as a member of the audience for the Shakespeare play with which Paula entertained the local gentry, a 'production' which perhaps suggested that she might acquire a new name and identity which would better please them. (As Homi Bhabha claims, with startling relevance to her appearance in it 'opposite' De Stancy *and* De Stancy's posing in the ancestral portrait: 'the problem of identity returns as a persistent questioning of the frame, the space of representation, where the image . . . is confronted with its difference, its Other'.)[15] *Love's Labour's Lost* is also relevant to Captain De Stancy's broken vow of celibacy (p.173), as Shakespeare's play is based on such a vow, and on its basic absurdity. The contamination of the less-performed play with lines from *Romeo and Juliet* also bespeaks Willy Dare's successful 'reconstruction' of his father as an ardent suitor of Paula.

As a less literal 'bend sinister' in the *Power* family, his role corresponding to that of the destabilising Dare in De Stancy's, Abner Power himself also bespeaks a semiotic 'confusion'. Although originally a laodicean in political matters, his expertise in explosives had led to his being co-opted by a revolutionary society meeting in the back-streets of Geneva (p.355). As a group dedicated to 'the extermination of tyrants and despots and the overthrow of established religions' they actually sound Shelleyan in a way Hardy could sympathize with (p.355). Attempting to abjure his art like a 'terrorist' Prospero, Abner Power is blown up by his own explosives, 'hoist with his own petard', and literally scarred by his experiences (pp.356-7). So we may say that, playing with the theme of representation again, Abner Power's appearance at once re-presents and misrepresents him. A supporter of the hereditary principle in consequence of the coercion practised on him by the revolutionaries, Abner Power will nevertheless desert the De Stancy cause on learning of Dare's lack of probity, traducing of Somerset, and parasitic power over his hapless father (pp.353-4). Power's desertion of Dare also begins to look positively allegorical. But Power is himself a wanted man in several states (p.357), who has not been 'picked up', as his scars 'dis-figure' (while in a sense bespeaking) him. So there is another 'doubling' of the 'representation and appearance' theme here. And Hardy will confirm that Dare and Abner Power are 'counterparts' in a scene of rankest melodrama in which Power confronts Dare with the facts of his deviousness and unscrupulousness. Neutralising this narrative, Dare produces a rival account of Power's own 'wanted criminal' status, and a revolver of his own to counter the revolver drawn on him by Power. They agree the marriage of Paula and De Stancy should proceed, and Power, now a big cheese in the '*guano* trade', immediately returns to Peru (bk.5, ch.11).

Although it may be a weaker novel than most of the others, *A Laodicean* also secretes qualities found nowhere else in the Hardy *oeuvre*, 'visibly ideological' as it is. Major weakness resides less in stylistic infelicities and penurious plotting than in the under-representation of those forces with which it wished to assert its affiliation. It is inappropriate that George Somerset, the *jeune premier* temporarily ousted on account of his unromantic origins, should be 'cushioned' with a fairly aristocratic pedigree, with an 'Admiral' and a 'Royal Academician' in the family, spoiling the idea of 'the commoner as gifted parvenu' (p.118). The argument from a conservative view of what is '*grandly* historical' does not find a sufficiently emphasized counter-argument for an apostolic succession of talent in the 'practicable arts' adduced by Somerset (p.130), and the voices of rustic commentary, with their dialectal 'supplements', are also under-represented. This may be because Emma was reported as saying that *The Hand of Ethelberta* (1876), *A Laodicean*'s complement, had 'too much about servants in it'.[16] By way of compensation, *A Laodicean* (1881), some of which was 'written' by her, if only to a prostrate Hardy's dictation, has barely enough. The rustic voices themselves return only in the novel's penultimate chapter in the Inn—one of them, 'Dairyman Jinks', voicing the theory that Paula might solve her problems by having her paintings 'touched up' to resemble *her own* '*gaffers and gammers*', suggesting a final, healthily insouciant, approach to 'problems of representation'.

And indeed Hardy himself misrepresented things when he claimed that *A Laodicean* 'represented' his own background.[17] He was much 'closer' to humble Stephen Smith of *A Pair of Blue Eyes* (1873) than to the almost too 'perfectly genteel' George Somerset. First seen virtually 'Copying Architecture in an Old Minster',[18] George himself seems as *ancien régime* as any. But Hardy is still playing games in reporting on a 'metaphysician' in the family (p.118): perhaps 'metaphysicians' teach us, among other things, that there is something insubstantial about purely 'physical' 'affiliation'. This is one sign that he does find ways at once to indulge and 'deconstruct' the snobbism he handles here. The novel is thus finally 'about' historical (mis-) representations and/as (mis-) representations of history. And although *A Laodicean* is not, if you will, a 'good novel', it should not simply be given a critical drubbing: this would correspond rather closely to 'kicking a man while he's down' (i.e., a Hardy flat on his back on [possibly bad] medical advice): and it is still highly interesting as an ingeniously conceited inquiry into the forces that shaped the Victorian age and the Victorian psyche, and ours.

Chapter 7

The Transit of Venus: or, *Two on a Tower*?

Not quite a novella, not quite a novel, *Two on a Tower* also seems to wobble between its theme(s) of a passion for the stars and the passions traditionally announced by them (hence, 'Heavenly Bodies', catching its slightly mischievous tone, might be an alternative title here). Indeed, the book seems to be 'made out of' many such not-quitenesses--for example, a rustic rather 'Saussure-ishly' notes that Lady Constantine, the heroine virtually deserted by her abusive husband, Sir Blount, is in a decidedly interesting condition as 'neither maid, wife nor widow', and so made of 'differences without positive terms'. Viviette's interestingly 'liminal' social position is one from which the novella itself embarks. Indeed, young Swithin St Cleeve, its astronomer-hero, is himself suspended between the estate of peasant and patron as the offspring of an intelligent lapsed clergyman and a local maiden. And finally the rustics themselves seem to 'double up' as malapropistic yet shrewd analysts of the proclivities and predicaments of their 'betters'. The closing words of Swithin's despairing ejaculation—'perhaps I shall be dead and gone before the next *transit of Venus*' is a phrase as much recycled as the recurring heavenly body itself. It too seems to enunciate another 'ruling ambiguity' here, suggesting itself as an all-too-appropriate title for a novel which, in this sense, dared not speak its name: indeed, Hardy's dissatisfaction with his official title[1] seems to confirm the idea that *The Transit of Venus* was *his* original choice—over which he got (understandable) cold feet—revealing, once more, a certain penchant for 'mischief making'.

Ruling *linguistic* ambiguities suggest a certain doubt about just how *things* are 'to be taken' here, in another brilliant Hardyan illustration of the Victorian mind in crisis. T.S. Eliot, a towering coiner of phrases delivered *de haut en bas*, observes in *Four Quartets* that 'here' 'the impossible union/ Of spheres of existence is actual', an accidentally powerful description of *Two on a Tower*. And in another way 'spheres of existence' may suggest each other quite powerfully here. For example, for its young astronomer-hero 'Venus was in a favourable aspect for observation that afternoon',[2] most innocently. But there were other afternoons, in their way not less innocent, as the couple believed themselves to be married, when 'Venus' was 'observed' in a different sense. The cold heaven of the astronomers is weighed against 'the better heaven beneath' (p.98) in the form of the charm(s) of Lady Constantine for Swithin. Making up a probable trinity here is the other 'cold heaven', that of churchmen and theologians.

Such 'techniques of trouble' generate Hardy's literary effects here. We can easily imagine Mrs Grundy's displeasure in responding to this work, at once enchanting (as a formal performance) and disenchanting (as a 'performative'). At a more abstract level the novella is partly about passionate intellectual and emotional propensities which the prism of society refracts in different ways; but also about the specific indeterminacy of those more creaturely feelings (including generous ones) released in the deserted and unhappy Lady Constantine by Swithin.

In this sense *Two on a Tower* is not at all the D.H. Lawrence work *avant la lettre* you might well take it to be. But, to the extent that it might seem that, there are reasons for preferring it to the work of a Lawrence who will later offer to do better for Hardy what Hardy, it may be felt, is already doing perfectly well for himself.[3] Feminists, at least, one feels, might rejoice to concur (in Johnson's idiom) with this. Indeed, a true precursor-text of *Two on a Tower* might be something like Wordsworth's 'To a Highland Girl'. In this poem the point is not for the narrator to 'pick up' the girl, but rather to relish the feelings of tenderness and protectiveness which her presence releases. So the most significant lines in the poem are perhaps

> What joy to hear thee, and to see!
> Thy elder brother I would be,
> Thy Father—anything to thee!

'Anything to thee!'[4] Hardy, quite typically, assigns this idea to the woman (Lady Constantine) about the man. He had already announced that he was about to explore something surprising in dramatising the narrator's embarrassment over a description of Swithin as 'a youth who might have been characterized by a word the judicious chronicler would not readily use in such a connection, preferring to reserve it for raising images of the opposite sex' (p.5). He means 'beautiful'.

Indeed Swithin, for all his imperiousness, is something of a mere 'boy' (corresponding to Wordsworth's 'Highland Girl' in effect). He almost killed himself, and almost wilfully, by the overnight drenching he received as he lay out of doors in despair after his discovery that his initial astronomical discovery had been forestalled by a few short weeks (pp.74-5). He then suffers a kind of 'deferred action'[5] reinterpretation of 'what should cause one to live'. He had originally been 'revived' by news of a comet rather than by the passionate kiss which the anguished Lady Constantine bestowed on him in her distress over his placidly predicted decease (pp.77, 79).

Hardy suggestively describes the comet as a mere fiery 'tadpole' (p.81) at this point. This anticipates both the passion of the pair and the progeny resulting from it as the passion for comets is superseded by romantic passion. So despite the ironic emphasis on the 'indifference' of the heavens, the comet seems positively to *adumbrate* the passion of Lady Constantine and Swithin (just as the hurricane which took the new dome off the Ring's Hill tower ironically orchestrated the overpowering feelings of Swithin and Viviette in their resolution to marry in untoward circumstances: 'the apocalyptic effect of the scene surrounding her was, indeed, not inharmonious, and afforded an appropriate background to her intentions' [p.122]). As the novella, mediating the intellectual crisis of the Victorians, seems to be saying: 'if a contingent, post-romantic universe cannot offer a genuinely symbolic concordance with human emotions, it is still an interesting repository of (metonymic) effects which we still, however arbitrarily, associate with them'.

Hardy is at his most brilliantly ironic in showing how the onset of the lovers' passion, which the rustics intuitively describe in terms of the traditional '(non-) science' of astrology, is actually induced by their shared emotional investment in the austerely scientific pursuit of astronomy. Yet, even more piquantly, its immediate *cause* was the actual prediction of the rustics as overheard by Swithin chatting at the base of the tower (in the light of Sir Blount's reported demise 'on the banks of the Zouga' [p.86] in South Africa), to the effect that if the attractive young pair get up in the tower 'ruling plannards together much longer, their plannards will soon rule them together' (p.97). Hardy makes a very 'relishable compound' (his phrase) here out of the rustics' combination of illiteracy and insight, which draws its strength from their 'earth(l)y' position.

This humble prophecy thus serves as a 'performative' of sorts, inducing in Swithin the feelings cannily foretold as they continue to observe that the abused, deserted and apparently widowed Lady Constantine, with her 'comely carcass' (p.97), has earned her pleasure(s). And as Swithin is 'planned, cut out, and finished for the delight of woman' (p.97), this makes a point reminiscent of the vicarious eroticism with which the poet (more pointedly) addresses the lovely youth in Shakespeare's Sonnet to the effect that 'she pricked thee out for woman's pleasure'.[6] Hardy definitely has the Shakespeare sonnet in mind here, but he also has the good taste not to smother the physicalities of a love affair with the degrading [and meretricious] vulgarity with which we are all too familiar. He draws on a sense of the fastidious temperaments of both lovers, which would not countenance an irregular union. This very scrupulousness turns an apparently legitimate marriage into a delightfully clandestine version of pastoral, one in which the couple *conceal from society the 'fact' that they are married*—although it was based on a mistake. It is also a version of Hardy's own Freudian Family Romance, initiated textually by his 'lost' novel, with its instructive title, *The Poor Man and the Lady*. The 'heaven' of ecclesiastical rhetoric and the 'heaven' of astronomerly inquisition are replaced by the 'heaven' of gratified desire — and so also 'of the earth, earthy', though no one actually says so. All three might be described as rival 'constructs'. With 'kindly mischievousness' Hardy draws together the 'allotropic' structures involved in pursuing 'forbidden knowledge': a Church seen as offering a kind of 'self-involved freemasonry', the astronomers' inquiry into the 'heavenly bodies', and romantic entanglements.

Indeed, the cold abstractions of the astronomers' heavens and that produced by a clerical *apartheid* seem to have a certain icy congruence. They are also suggestively masculine spheres which only a feminine voice and presence will thaw out a little, apparently. Indeed, when Mr Torkingham, the local Rector in Welland, encouraged the astoundingly pompous Bishop of Melchester ('Cuthbert Helmsdale, D.D., ninety-fourth occupant of the episcopal throne of the diocese'), to talk eternally of the Diocesan Synod, itself a kind of ecclesiastical 'stellar region', this clerical *conversazzione* was itself conducted by the 'kindly light' (p.184)[7] of Lady Constantine's lambent charm and the 'Christian contentment' (p.180) they confidently impute.

This 'kindly light' (the phrase itself fetched—not at all kindly—from Cardinal Newman), is actually a product of her 'recently gratified' (p.180) affection with Swithin. This had the ironic effect of engendering inappropriate thoughts in the Bishop himself (that is to say, thoughts 'warmer than Christianity requires' as one rustic voice put it of an earlier clerical infatuation in *Under the Greenwood Tree*). According to F.E. Halliday, Hardy is not satirising the Church in this novel,[8] but then Hardy has always had a comet-tail of 'not always terribly perceptive' critics. The Bishop, warmly seconded by Lady Constantine's cynical and acquisitive brother Louis Glanville, will subsequently propose, be rejected, but will finally prove to be a refuge in time of trouble for Viviette after all. She will sacrifice herself on the altar of the sublimely self-absorbed cleric in order to protect her unborn child and Swithin's professional freedom (p.291). Men may be the professional bearers of spiritual counsel, but Viviette shows the way through what Keats called the 'vale of soul-making'.[9]

Keats is keen here on the idea of 'schooling' an intelligence to make an 'identity'. But Hardy's point here (as elsewhere, but hardly ever so convincingly), seems to be that social 'identities' tend to be formed of acts of 'interpellation', in Althusser's terminology[10] rather than the spiritual self-determinings we like to envisage. These 'hail' (or 'hale') people into often untoward or unrewarding roles or identities. But Hardy is interested in the negations or 'differences' in the social formation which indicate withdrawal from such social fixities and definites.

As we saw, in what looks like a rigidly hierarchical world the young astronomer Swithin is in an interestingly 'liminal' or undecidable situation, as the son of a highly intelligent and independent-minded clergyman who married a 'peasant', was socially ostracized, and quit a church which, he implied, specialized in snobbism (pp.11-12), and required ingratiation. So the initiation of the novella's concerns (not to mention Swithin himself) was based on this private act of anti-ecclesiastical 'rebellion', tacitly approved of—just as the highly intelligent Swithin seems in person to vindicate the idea that the fruit of such 'queer unions', as Hardy puts it elsewhere, is 'naturally good'.

Not everyone quite appreciates this, apparently: as one basically kindly rustic, 'Haymoss' Fry, puts it to Lady Constantine, in a wonderful confusion of the social and the natural, that, as an alleged result of his *'having two stations of life in his blood'* Swithin 'mopes about' and is 'good for nothing' (p.12). He is being brought up by 'Granny' Martin in a roomy cottage (p.13), his mother having pre-deceased her. Neither she, nor the ageing servant Hannah, appreciates his astronomical avocation either. (Hence Lady Constantine's feelings for him are intensified or 'over-determined': her love for him appropriately partakes of the 'maternal' as well as the passionate [although she is only nine years older than he], and they are *also* confederate in an exciting intellectual pursuit which few in the village of Welland appreciate.)

Swithin is, then, socially speaking, neither fish, flesh nor good red herring (made out of social 'differences without positive terms' like his 'partner' [the term is apposite as they were never married]), and the result is a sense of marginalizing which corresponds in some measure to the anomalies of Viviette's case. And *her* condition depended on, or from, the prolonged absence of Sir Blount (himself 'a gentleman who is not one'). As a fanatical big game hunter he was a 'notoriously unkind husband' (p.240) (who also 'was not one' as we learn he has now, typically without compunction, 'married a native princess' according to the 'local rites of the tribe' [p.236])—and indeed astronomy itself, something of a ruling passion here, supports the sense of a certain relativity in such matters.

This is itself a significant irony, given the 'technically invalid' marriage of Viviette and Swithin themselves—Sir Blount lived on for a time after his reported decease. Indeed, the ultimate decisiveness of these footling ecclesiastical arrangements is doubly ironized given the obviously 'relativised' status ascribed to them: they are underscored by the particularly 'sorry clerical specimen', a kind of *locum*, who united the pair (or rather failed to do so, as if in confirmation of his ineptitude although not caused by it), amid the decaying splendours of Bath (the month appropriately that of October). The pathos of this (non-) event is heightened by the obvious genuineness of the attraction and solicitude that the young pair show for each other. Viviette has had an intuition that the marriage will not take place, which is both true and false, as the ceremony occurs, but is invalid as Sir Blount yet lived at that point and had died only in an idle report. It was complete in itself as a performance, but in J.L. Austin's terms, it was a '"failed" performative'—but one which, taken in good faith, did not prevent Lady Constantine and Swithin 'performing' 'acts of union'.

Increasing this empathy for Viviette is our growing knowledge of the specific qualities of the absent Sir Blount, a 'notoriously unkind' husband with a passion for those field sports to which Hardy himself was so passionately opposed. And Lady Constantine's almost over-scrupulous observance of the proprieties (she has agreed not to go into society for the duration of his absence) inevitably increases her isolation, vulnerability, and, consequently, her susceptibility. In fact even her secret 'marriage' was contracted at the behest of Swithin, and assented to by Lady Constantine, mainly as a remedy for the interruption to his studies caused by the emotional turmoil of his newly-awakened love for her: her own gratification is secondary. Her moral fastidiousness *also* shines brightly by contrast with the behaviour of her manipulative brother Louis Glanville. Indeed, Louis proves to be a kind of upper bourgeois 'resumé' of Sir Blount himself. Like Sir Blount, but in a more prudential register, he is what Blake would describe as a 'Devourer', arriving from Rio de Janeiro at the worst possible moment seeking 'a milch cow for his sustenance' (p.125), and afflicting the young couple with his detective-like ardour in establishing 'the precise nature of their relationship'. As it happens, this 'precise nature' was ironically concealed from the young couple themselves, happily coupling when not actually married—'happily' only in the light of their faith that they were so.

Glanville lacks the playfully destructive manner of Sir Blount himself, said to have whispered to a naive rustic to recite 'women and wine' as 'the articles of his belief' (p.165) at a service of Confirmation, to that rustic's disgrace and discomfiture. Indeed, Glanville's 'softly softly' approach, though concealing cynicism, may bring him closer to the Bishop. In fact Sir Blount, Louis Glanville and the Bishop of Melchester bring an unholy trinity of patriarchal impingements on Viviette herself. The Bishop seems to follow Sir Blount in making Viviette's married life all but intolerable. The effects of her acquisitive and worldly-minded brother Louis are symbolized by the cut from his whip accidentally inflicted (from behind) to Lady Constantine's face as he disciplines his horse near Warborne. He is accidentally encountering the young pair making their cautious way back from Bath, 'just (un-) married', while on his own way to Welland House, just back from Rio de Janeiro (pp.144-5), where he has thrown up his job, apparently as diplomatic attaché. (The accident happily allows Swithin temporarily to secrete his Lady in the hut he installed on 'Ring's Hill Speer', temporarily releasing them from the social masquerade and the pressures of this virtually 'caste' society [ch.20].)[11]

Yet not only are Louis, the Bishop, and Sir Blount each 'versions' of the other in their actual *effects* on Viviette: in a further insinuation of the 'simulacral',[12] *Swithin himself* is caught up in the relay of patriarchal cruelty. As he dons Sir Blount's stinking great-coat to keep the rain off as Louis arrives *à l'imprévu* at Welland House, his sudden appearance in it tells of the abuse Viviette has suffered at the hands of Sir Blount. But her shriek of terror at this point also anticipates her death-shriek on the occasion of Swithin's final return from the Southern Hemisphere, when he insists on claiming her despite his initial flinching in the face of her physical decay. The shriek which greeted Swithin as a 'version' of the abusive Sir Blount, would *also* finally identify Swithin himself as the ultimate male inflictor of pain. Swithin as 'character' may seem the *opposite* of Sir Blount and the Bishop (though absolutely at one with them in pursuing his hobby-horse *à outrance*), but his return will create a moment of agony like that which would have greeted Sir Blount's return, when his initial expression shows that he no longer loves her as of old.

The ways of patriarchy, callowly estimating women in terms of appearance only, bring suffering from every quarter for the noble lady here. Hardy's brilliantly ironic reversal here is that it is, in effect, the almost sinister *Glanville* and '*the bad Bishop*' who rescue her from her impossible predicament. This seems to entail a Hardyan rule of '*Reversibility of signs at the level of individual (male) characters, stability of sign(s) at the level of patriarchal effects*'.

It is noteworthy that Lady Constantine's definition or character-siting is 'gender-specific'. Her femininity entails the effect that the cachet of rank is slightly undercut by her shortage of cash. This is due to her absent husband's profligacy and the fact that she will not inherit the glories of Welland House, and her financial pressures greatly increase with (inaccurate) news of Sir Blount's death (p.89) (and the accurate calibrations of the financial results of his profligacy). It is this misinformation which indirectly precipitates the passion of Viviette and Swithin, their 'marriage' (p.143), and the subsequent entanglements induced by the offer of the legacy of £600 per annum to explore the stars of the Southern Hemisphere. This was initially an irrelevance, produced by the misogynistic uncle, Dr Jocelyn St. Cleeve, virtually on his deathbed, on the understanding that Swithin remained unmarried (pp.135-8) (as, unwittingly, he did). In fact even the legacy-letter was itself less this than an excruciating anti-feminine polemic, specifically targeting Lady Constantine herself, which Swithin did badly in letting Viviette see (pp.250-1)—even if this was partly the result of an unlucky accident.

Hardy pits a sense of the instability of social 'register', of the potential penalties for losing one's social moorings in a Victorian world in which—estates no less than 'long-haired comets'[13] having been 'ordered' by the Deity—to be made out of social 'differences without positive terms' comes nigh to ('ontological') blasphemy. But, as we saw, one class in particular can feel that they are not living a wholly imaginary relation to real existence[14]—the rustics, who are the more enchanting for not being sentimentalized here, and the condition of *their* estate is feelingly registered as they discourse on their ruined constitutions: 'I assure 'ee, Pa'son Tarkingham, that in the clitch o' my knees where the rain used to come through when I was cutting clots for the new lawn in old my lady's time, 'tis as if rats wez gnawing every now and then' (p.19) (Haymoss Fry). This does not prevent their evolution of their own kind of 'deconstructive' wisdom, as, for example that 'losing' Sir Blount in (or to) Africa is like losing 'a rat in a barley-mow . . . he's lost, though you know where he is' (Hezzy Biles, p.18). J. Hillis Miller would surely relish the aporetic quality of that observation,[15] and indeed, the 'rat' image, Sir Blount being what he is, is itself an apposite addition. Innocent yet shrewd, Hardy's rustics here, less patronised than in *Far from the Madding Crowd*, are as clearly *dans le vrai* as Flaubert's peasants.

In a sense one hidden irony of the book is genealogical: despite his father's rejection of established religion, Swithin merely replaces one 'cold heaven' with another. It is the warm heart of Lady Constantine (fantasizing a heaven, or haven, of desire itself) which forms the connecting rainbow between heaven and (h)earth here, while her aristocratic position makes her kindly union with Swithin the inverse of his educated father's marriage with a local girl, as if to form another kind of 'compensation'.

Indeed, in a double sense, the novella constitutes 'a blow for feminism', as she triumphs as a character in generosity and self-sacrifice, but is treated abusively in effect, if not intention, by all of 'her' men, as we saw: not only the Bishop of Melchester, and Sir Blount Constantine, as well as brother Louis, convincingly depicted as an 'unbeliever in human virtue' (p.184), but even the formally exonerated Swithin himself in his monomaniacal pursuit of his version of 'heavenly joys' for which he does indeed finally neglect the 'better heaven' of Lady Constantine 'beneath' (p.98).

Despite the narrator's special pleading for him here, we intuit Yeats' point in 'The Song of the Happy Shepherd' that 'there is no sooth/Saving in thine own heart':[16] in the context of the novella itself the starry heavens are indeed 'symbolic', and Swithin, despite special pleading by the narrator, is imbued with something of their coldness, although the idea is never formally acknowledged. And he does go off, if only at Viviette's insistence, to enjoy the benefits of a legacy whose condition was he should not marry before the age of twenty-five, induced to disappear into the southern hemisphere, where prospects were brighter for star-gazers (p.269).

Unfortunately this was not without his having unwittingly made her pregnant in a last night of passion (p.266), which seems like the height of imprudence. However, Swithin initially imagined he had persuaded Viviette that he should neither leave, nor accept the legacy, as she had begged him to do with self-sacrificial ardour. This is their first (and last) 'act of union' performed in the knowledge that they are not married. Their premise at that point was that the astronomical adventure was to be suspended and the marriage, made in Bath but not, as it were, in heaven, be made not merely legal, but also public. It was through the 'hero(in)ism' of Viviette that Swithin's exploration with the legacy due to 'celibacy' (an extra irony here) *was* in fact pursued in spite of these decisions when she then refused to see him. But on his departure she found she had conceived a child as well as an idea.

Subsequently, licensed to observe the observatories of the earth in no particular order, Swithin was, ironically according to the very hests of Lady Constantine herself, 'nowhere to be found' (p.150). This is the famously laconic note on the idyllic 'morning after' their honeymoon night in the hut erected by the tower (as a 'pine-clad protuberance' an eminently 'phallic' property). The sentence neatly presages the fact that he will indeed be 'nowhere to be found' when the fact that there is 'fruit of their union' is discovered by desperate Viviette in a condensation-enactment of their first and last acts of (sexual) union. (This, again, is amusingly adumbrated by psalm-lines the rustics recall intoning to the embarrassment of one young bride: 'His wife like a fair fertile vine/ Her lovely fruit shall bring'.) Driven to the brink of suicide (she notes in her desperation that the tower itself would facilitate this step), she only then abandons the 'marriage which was not one', and accepts the desperate remedy of Louis' duplicitous marriage-brokering with the Bishop of Melchester. His conceited self-regard is fatal to any compunction which even Louis might have practised as he enters the Melchester Deanery in pursuit of his Puck-like plot (p.285). Viviette then becomes an ironic 'beneficiary' of the 'bad' Louis and the 'bad' Bishop.

Viviette has succumbed to a highly unusual form of temptation, that of marr(y)ing a Bishop to protect an unborn child and Swithin's future, a move which will prove doubly self-sacrificial. The Bishop himself, as he rushes over to Welland to declare his ecclesiastical ardour, is described as a man looking 'too good for his destiny' (p.290) and ironically congratulated on the accuracy of the presumption (given that Viviette is pregnant). And, on emerging from the actual interview at Welland House, the Bishop, literally flushed with success, pompously announces to Louis that the depressed and chastened Viviette was 'not one to refuse Heaven's gift' (p.291).

Indeed. And did the Bishop prove to be God's gift to woman, as he predicted? Apparently he was not, but turned into an ecclesiastical version of Sir Blount, associated with the cynicism of Louis, and, through his accidental 'impersonation' of him, with Swithin himself, as part of a disturbing patriarchal relay. Swithin, though 'attractive', also had 'deleterious' effects. And curiously, Louis, the primal threat to the unworldly union of Swithin and Viviette, turns, as 'actant', in Greimasian terminology, from apparent 'opponent' to 'helper'[17] in brokering the marriage between Viviette and Cuthbert. But that did indeed turn out to be a very bad deal, as Torkingham darkly hints to the returning Swithin after the Bishop's death. Indeed Hardy might be of particular interest to Greimas here, as his 'actant' is also finally 'undecidable' as he moves from 'opposing helper' of one kind to a kind of 'aiding opposer': he had been contriving an undesired marriage with the Bishop when Viviette imagined herself safely, if secretly, married to Swithin, but was subsequently permitted to effect this when she confessed her pregnancy in despair as a desperate remedy (which [again] was not one). Hardy seems to induce this application of theory: we see Louis 'differently' partly because when he effects the union of the Bishop and Viviette we don't subsequently hear of him, proving that his destiny was not one to consider, that he existed as an ancillary function, as a mere 'catalytic converter': Viviette (dying), Swithin (hero's return), Tabitha (musically trained in London, proto-feminist), the Bishop (dead of an apoplexy), the rustics (still working, still endearingly malapropistic), and Mr Torkingham (still talking) are all accounted for. But Louis seems to have vanished, quite possibly in a puff of smoke.

Swithin, his researches completed, is also attaining the age at which he may contemplate marriage without the sacrifice of his annuity when he learns of the death of the Bishop from a newspaper cutting posted by his grandmother and of the fact that Viviette has returned from Melchester to Welland with their four-year-old son. Swithin is finally a returning 'native' who finds the Viviette whom as a young man he inevitably knew as an appearance, transformed – partly as a result of the anxieties which he, however innocently, had induced. In particular her hair, tell-tale excrescence, contains a 'Via Lactea' (p.311), Hardy's narrator's feline notation of just how an astronomer would register these 'sad and stealing messengers of grey'.[18] This grim Schopenhaurian sense of the transience of female beauty and the superficiality of youthful affection had been adumbrated by an ultra-cynical phrase about young men's 'first ventures in this kind' (p.102).

Hardy makes the result harsher by pencilling in the young Tabitha Lark, now an intellectual young woman and trained church organist, as a 'natural' successor to Viviette—given that Swithin, after some animated converse with Tabitha and a pronounced reluctance to approach Viviette at all, has already engaged Tabitha as amanuensis (pp.306-7). (Indeed, in this sense he may already be said to have 'secured "the hand of Tabitha"' in yet another typically 'Hardyan' implication.) But Hardy, a gentler spirit than Schopenhauer, also complicates things in pointing out that Viviette's middle-aged beauty might have appealed to a more sophisticated male apprehension (p.311), and added the subtle supplementary point that when she died Swithin perhaps 'grew fond of her again'.

The last chapter of the novel contains Viviette's death-shriek, as a *Liebestod* of sorts induced by joy on seeing Swithin return to claim her in spite of her attempt to dismiss him (p.313) when she noted his (possibly only instantaneous) dismay at her appearance. As we saw, this shriek is a brilliant reprise of the shriek of terror which she emitted on seeing Swithin inadvertently 'disguised' as Sir Blount (p.162), now seen as a prediction of his final effect on her, and a Leo Bersani might unwittingly be drawing out its (apparently opposed) allegorical implication: 'the endless repetition of desires suppressed by guilt and angry frustration ultimately leads to the fantasy of death as the absolute pleasure'.[19]

This is the final brilliant stroke (involving what may be a stroke) in a novel which resumes the Victorian experience of 'being decentred'. The 'frosty heavens' reveal that 'nothing is made for man' (p.32) (amusingly undercut by the rustics' point that Swithin at least seems to be fashioned for [the delight of] woman). One succinct way of describing what Hardy is doing here is to say that he is recontextualising the theme of 'Dover Beach': '"Without the church to cling to, what have we?" "Each other".'[20] But Matthew Arnold himself was finally too much the 'traditional intellectual'[21] to take the form and pressure of his time undistorted by 'the effects of ideology'. Hardy takes Arnold on his own terms, agreeing with him about retreating Faith, but alert to the transience of love itself as well as the difficulty of negotiating the unpleasant side-effects of class stratifications and what his poem 'In Tenebris II' describes as 'crookedness, custom and fear'. Despite (or perhaps because of) its brevity, the 'novella' has a wealth of implication. And indeed, considering its brilliant concision, it might be said that in some respects he never wrote better.

Chapter 8

Misconstructions: *The Mayor Of Casterbridge*

The Mayor of Casterbridge is nothing if not a sombre-suited work, set in the heart of the 'dream-country' of Wessex,[1] but this time with the effect of nightmare. There seems to be a rock-hard commitment to character as an absolute given 'prior to any social formation'.[2] We are also reassured of the tone, if not the genre, of Tragedy (although Hardy includes as many actual features of one as is consistent with his own 'genre' commitments). Such traditional features present us with an 'over-determined' bid for the literary respectability Hardy in his besetting insecurity was never quite sure the novel, and the serial novel in particular, could confer. In combining a sense of 'value for money' with 'literary value', Hardy, himself 're-constructed' as a kind of literary master-mason by perceptive Proust,[3] offers sound construction, well-knit members—almost the intellectual equivalent of 'having the builders in'. Indeed 'Henchard', it seems, was originally the name for a rugged old Dorchester *building* pulled down long before 'Henchard' became the name for a 'rugged old' *character* to be 'pulled down'.[4] But the very virtuosity at work in the novel's construction is employed to create an intense and unremitting sense of *in*security, a constant presentiment that things are about to fall about our ears, consistently with 'stories of builders' (and 'builders' narratives').

'Construction' is derived from the Latin *construo*, whence also 'construe', and the semantic wobble here suggests the procedures of *The Mayor of Casterbridge* itself, with its incessant narrative shuttling between sound *construction* and unsound *construing*, particularly in Henchard's case. Hence, we may say, the reader's experience is above all that of Henchard's endlessly baffled sense of just what exactly he is getting into, in a sense of just what 'his own experience' is 'of', as his position becomes ever more constricted. The 'Capability Henchard' who rises to Mayoralty as Dorchester's 'Action Man' is from the outset simultaneously distinguished by his *incapacity* as a perpetually floundering reader of (the) signs—insidious precisely on account of their own apparent 'incapacity' for any sort of ambivalence. Indeed Henchard owed his 'fall' partly to this failure, after consulting 'Conjurer Fall' (his name a kind of omen, apparently, and he himself respected as a semiologist of sorts), to take his admirable advice. 'Suspending' ideas of the canny and the uncanny here, Hardy shows each 'secreting' its 'other'. Canny Scots may be the unwitting or even unwilling bearers of the latter, while the uncanny, Henchard's doom, is finally traced to its 'canny' source in his 'cursed pride and mortification at being *poor*' (p.197), perhaps qualifying the text's own ruling idea of 'character' as a stable signifier ('the story of a man of character'), by foregrounding the idea of 'social conditions which produce [the] character[s]'.[5]

The reader is also involved in the difficulties of putting a 'sound construction' on things here. Yet, for those who imagine they like 'the plain sense of things' and feel they can keep them that way, the signs appear initially to be favourable. Blake speaks of 'the cunning of weak and tame minds which have the power to resist energy'.[6] Hardy's large-framed and bull-like Henchard is said to have deployed his 'one talent of energy' (p.197) in such a way as to dominate and domineeer in Casterbridge as the slave become master by being masterful rather than cunning, who conquers by power of voice and presence rather than the 'remote control' techniques of modernity; by speech (not to say bellowing), not writing. Putting brute power in place of knowledge or simple *savoir-faire*, he specializes in personal (or physical) contact (rather than mere contacts)—as poor Abel Whittle learned to his cost when he was 'bullied' to work without breeches (p.102). Bull(y)ing is the portmanteau word for these activities of Henchard's, and on that account he should, in a way, be odious, but Hardy works to create empathy rather than estrangement, paradoxically based on Henchard's own self-estrangement, describing him as 'the self-alienated man' (p.282): typically, even when Henchard is trying to kill his supplanter Farfrae, the narrator qualifies a description of this 'infuriated Prince of Darkness' with 'as he might have been called from his appearance just now' (p.238), attenuating the apparent commitment to adverse judgement. The reader is involved in this, made to invest narrative interest in speculation as to whether Henchard is a 'positive' or 'negative' quantity, and his feelings about Farfrae and Henchard in particular come to compose a kind of counterpoint. Henchard seems to represent whatever is culturally vestigial, is emotionally affiliated to that which is going 'out of mind' or being 'silently destroyed',[7] in Wordsworth's phrasing. Indeed, the very phrase 'out of mind' seems to be echoed by the terms of Henchard's own last will and testament as a kind of 'special request' that he should be put 'out of mind' by everyone concerned.

As we saw, Henchard, originally the name of an old mansion-house in Dorchester, represents 'rugged olde Casterbridge'. Apparently, then, you know almost by definition where you are with both it and Henchard, by contrast with what threatens them. But, in what constitutes the first 'turn for the worse' for those who like easy-to-follow paths through Wessex (itself not exactly in atlases, and perhaps even offering 'a map of misreading' here), Casterbridge, however charming as 'built environment', is humanly speaking a place of petty resentments and sly malevolence, representing that 'old England which would do for you if it could' as Ronald Blyth puts it.[8] Casterbridge seems to be peopled by embittered and malevolent Joshua Jopps and Nance Mockridges, by a collectively formidable but characterless bourgeoisie and less than wholly appealing rustics like Christopher Coney—who digs up the four pennies the former Mrs Henchard had placed on her eyes to spend in the 'Three Mariners' (p.119).[9] Its whispering denizens even bear some resemblance to the 'damned compact majority' which tormented Dr Stockman in Ibsen's *An Enemy of the People* (1882).

Hardy, almost 'giddies' the reader with 'paralogical' procedures and double(d) signs here. For example, if the adversary, Farfrae, might be deemed a 'Mephistophelian visitant', he is, paradoxically, one of irresistible charm and talent, while Henchard, if a native, fails to be reassuring on that account. It is he himself who is much more obviously 'Mephistophelian': indeed he is described at one point with Carlylean rhetoric which links him specifically to *Faust*, as 'a vehement gloomy being who had quitted the ways of vulgar men without light to guide him on a better way' (p. 114)—with, as a bystander puts it on the occasion of his remarriage to Susan Henchard, 'a *bluebeardy* look about 'en' (p.91). By contrast, one has the impression that some politely expressed prejudice has gone into critical discussion of Farfrae.[10] Kevin Z. Moore, more considerately, thinks he arrives from an intertextual land, courtesy of Sir Walter Scott, so we might say he hails from the '"Scott"-ish' Highlands.[11] Yet Hardy, as usual, doesn't actually play it simple: he keeps calling him 'the Scotchman', then makes him attractive, so that the reader will, as usual, be 'bisected'. Yet Farfrae's mesmeric charm is finally uncanny in itself, imbricated with the mysteries of capitalism, a kind of (dubiously 'remedial') *pharmakon*[12] for farming folk. He secretes the 'uncanny' by seeming to be precisely the opposite. Shlomith Rimmon-Kenan, summarising the Freudian import, concludes that it is indeed 'the canny which is the uncanniest of all guests',[13] which sounds just right for 'the effects of Farfrae'. For example, the whole story of his relations with and estrangement from Henchard will prove that at each new turn of events Henchard himself was entirely in the wrong (just as, when he consulted the conjurer 'Fall' he was genially received, offered a delicious meal, and told the truth [p.171]), yet suggestively-named 'Fall's' effect on Henchard's life, like Farfrae's, was weirdly disastrous.

Interestingly, too, 'uncanny' in Freudian discussion is '*unheimlich*', 'unhomely', yet it is precisely Farfrae's misty-eyed nostalgia for far-off Scotland which strikes an immediate chord with the locals who accept him at once as someone who 'belongs' (p.65) with a kind of 'welcome guest' status. Henchard, it seems, is 'unhomely', not merely in the banal sense of not being a popular figure, but also un-canny in the prudential sense, and un-canny in one sense of 'canny', close to 'cosy', and reassuring in that way. But Henchard also seems to encounter his own uncanniness in the form of a '*Doppelganger*' (p.257), an apparition, construed by Henchard as heaven-sent, which 'saved' him from suicide by drowning in Casterbridge's '*Schwarzwasser*' (p.124). However, this double turns out to have been the discarded effigy from the skimmity-ride or satirical procession (pp.242-3), which guyed (and 'dolled') his improper relationship with Lucetta, thanks to the (successful) efforts of the failures of Mixen Lane. (And interestingly, the Freudian investigation of the 'uncanny' concerned the attribution of consciousness to objects such as puppets.)[14] Although it was the product of malice and pettiness, the skimmity-ride effigy thus produced an effect of benign intervention.

Again, if Henchard represents the culturally vestigial which attracts Hardy's imaginative empathy, the not-so-little irony here is that *Hardy* himself is unquestionably closer to *Farfrae*, sentimentally attached to romantic folk-culture, but prudential and business-like, committed to writing rather than speech, 'superstructural' and 'upwardly-mobile'. Even the satirical moment in which reference is made to Farfrae's 'dear native country which he loved so much as never to have revisited it' (p.278) may be related to Hardy himself, formally returned to Dorset but still slogging away at a 'science of climbing' in a new, eminently *bourgeois* incarnation symbolized in architectural terms by the highly unprepossessing

Max Gate. A more conventional novel might initially entice the reader into seeing Farfrae as the stereotypically penny-pinching, upwardly-mobile Scotchman, but Hardy will peddle the idea only towards the end of this one, just as his 'Preface'—a retrospective view—will see him muttering truculently about hyperboreans quite as if he were auditioning as Dr. Johnson (p.26). But the reader of the greater part of the text must instead come to terms with the fact that the narrator, much of the time, seems to be virtually in love with Farfrae, just as Henchard himself exudes an (ambiguously?) '*tigerish* affection' (p.95) for him, which half Casterbridge seems to share. Henchard's own waggoner describes with envy how he 'creeps into a maid's heart like the giddying worm' (p.175).

Refusing easy empathies or reliable emotional cartographies, *The Mayor of Casterbridge*, which concludes with the word 'pain' (p.286), is almost as painful for us to read as Dr Johnson found *King Lear*, and not surprisingly, as *The Mayor of Casterbridge* finds itself hugely 'invaded' by its daunting precursor text, in some respects a 'version' of it. The reader might indeed feel here that, as Keats puts it, one is 'sitting down to read *King Lear once again*'.[15] Yet Hardy, in a way we should recognise, is also up to some ironic or playful 'conceitedness' which bespeaks his own preoccupations. Here, for example, he has some sport with names, sending Henchard's former girlfriend Lucetta bounding off to 'Port Bre(e)dy' to marry (and, apparently, immediately be impregnated by) Farfrae [p.184]), while the 'Mr. Grower' to whom Henchard is suggestively in hock was the witness to Lucetta's marriage. This forced Lucetta herself to witness to it when Henchard asked her to declare herself affianced to himself to get 'Grower' 'off his back' (p.189). Unfortunately not only was this just after her 'fatal' union with Farfrae, it immediately followed the incident in which Henchard saved her life by twisting the bull's nose (pp.186-7). Proliferating irony thus shows Henchard inadvertently saving Farfrae's wife while still thinking her the very woman he himself should marry—another misreading; while the bull, that threatening 'other', is merely a version of himself, apparently formidable but easily baffled and subdued in its blind rage, 'purposiveness without purpose',[16] and easily-overcome 'strength'. Indeed, too bull-like altogether here, he has just been seen threatening Lucetta himself (but was likewise foiled) (pp.220-1). Unlike the 'Immanent *Will*' of natural impulse that 'stirs and urges everything' which Hardy found in Schopenhauer,[17] Henchard's is definitely a Nietzschean *will* to mastery, finally abrogated by his *will* (as testamentary act)—a typical Hardy touch. (It was in fact Heidegger who noticed the sharp opposition of Schopenhaurian and Nietzschean will,[18] but the distinction is not arcane.) The crowning irony, then, is that Henchard's final act of 'unwilling' through his 'will' (as testamentary act) paradoxically achieves or consummates a posthumous paternity suit to his ungovernably compliant 'daughter'.

This suit had seemed to be prematurely granted in the domestic episode of the 'seed shop' (e.g., p.260), not exactly a 'sperm bank', but surely a suggestive place for Henchard to be placed, as the text suspends questions of paternity pending the return of New*son*, the disconcerting 'nominal' father of his 'new daughter'. Henchard may find a happy interlude in the seed shop, but Farfrae also has much to disseminate. This is emphasized in his enthusiasm for the mechanical seed-drill, producing a *deus ex machina* by placing (or planting) him *in* a machine. Indeed, as he is, simultaneously, singing a Scottish love song, 'The Lass O'Gowrie', he seems something of a 'desiring machine' himself, as well as a symbol of modernity signalling a retreat from traditional agricultural ways and means providing the Parable of the Sower and the romance of the past. But Hardy, whose provision of emotional checks and balances is always adroit, also projects a sense of the menace and malice at work in 'that old England', forbidding a facile nostalgia for good old times.

And New Man Farfrae, fertile in person as well as expedient as he sings love-songs from a seed-drill, while satirized by the narrator as well as the jealous Henchard, is also serious-minded in a way Elizabeth-Jane likes. And Lucetta, as wife-to-be, is a paradoxically puzzled and excluded party here in what turns out to be something of a Society for the Propagation of Christian Knowledge, slow to pick up on references to the Parable of the Sower (or possibly 'Grower', the gentleman to whom Henchard will shortly be seen to be greatly in debt?). The Romance of the Sower, gone for good, is finally a fall from cadences, a retreat from textual grace, but as sower-substitute Farfrae seems more than adequate as an all-conquering desiring-machine. Farfrae's romantic songs no less than his seed drill have a 'phallic' function—'phallic' seems an apposite way of including his attractiveness to women and his commercial power, and Hardy sees to it that the two qualities are 'confused'. Innocently advancing on both 'fronts' Farfrae will 'cut out' Henchard in the marital as well as the commercial sphere. Yet, curiously, as we saw, it is Henchard who, later, will be set up in a little 'seed shop', a location relevant to dissemination of thoughts about paternity, gossip about 'who's who' in the genealogical sense. 'Seed shops' seem all in a day's work at Casterbridge, which, as Hardy points out in a famous passage, is emphatically 'twinned with rusticity', where things are breeding and growing ('Bees and butterflies in the cornfields at the top of the town who desired to get to the meads at the bottom, took no circuitous course, but flew straight down High Street without any apparent consciousness that they were traversing strange latitudes' [p.69]). Yet the text puts nature's paternity suit 'under erasure'. When the novel creeps close to anything 'biological', it is rather as if the narrator were in the grip of that sense of propriety which makes Elizabeth-Jane as rigid as the slightly priggish Fanny Price to whom she bears such an unmistakable resemblance, and 'sex' finds only the most indirect and attenuated expression here.

It seems particularly appropriate, then, that the beginning of Farfrae's wooing, his blowing of the seeds and chaff from Elizabeth-Jane's dress (p.99) ('there's a whhhh, just a whhhhh', as Joyce's Leopold Bloom might have put it),[19] is an act of 'spirit' (originally, of course 'breath', or 'wind'), and somehow just right for Farfrae, as the act entails a kind of 'libidinal economy', a sort of 'performative' eliding linguistic communication. With a differing evasiveness, the expurgated version of Lucetta's embarrassing former involvement with Henchard seems, in an artistically appropriate way, to possess a never quite penetrable ambiguity as to what exactly had occurred (especially as Lucetta seems to be at least as ashamed of coming from Jersey as she is of her compromising moments with Henchard). Indeed, the '*étourderie*' of Lucetta, as she calls it (p.140), might well be reflected in the reader's response to the 'affair which was not one'—or was it? However, '*étourderie*' is suggestive in being used to refer flippantly to the full-blown seduction and elopement of the married Maria Rushworth by her brother, by Mary Crawford in *Mansfield Park*—which, as we have seen, Hardy seems to have been perusing at the time. So we may assume that, for the narrator at any rate, Lucetta is as capable (or culpable) of euphemism as she is of using French here.

Later, the narrator seems to be insinuating an interesting recycling of the Farfraean economy of 'the spirit' (= 'breath, wind'), so that the mutual attraction he and Elizabeth-Jane feel is 'spiritualized' by comparison. The 'twenty minutes blow' on that rather windy highway to Budmouth which Farfrae takes 'just to winnow the seeds and chaff out of him' (p.263), enables him to encounter, not wholly by chance, the 'previously known as blown' Elizabeth-Jane. This small indication of incipient courtship already constitutes a blow to Henchard, described as 'the netted lion' (p.260), which is particularly interesting as Elizabeth-Jane has been presented as an accomplished 'seine'- [or net]-maker) (p.194), so this may be more of her work. Once 'the swaggering bully with the clumsy jest'[20] (in phrasing by W.H. Auden which may in fact be remembering Henchard here), the former Mayor is completely within the power of the increasingly empowered Elizabeth-Jane. She seems to be as remorselessly dutiful as her Austen prototype as a kind of 'Miss Grower' who will, ethically speaking, tower over Henchard in a pointed comment on the 'genealogy of morals', since it is to 'immoral conduct' that she owes her (biological) being— although her illegitimacy as 'issue of Newson' is, surprisingly, not thought to be an issue. Indeed, the emotions of the moment of her 'restoration' to Newson, who bought her mother from Henchard when (the latter was) drunk, seem appropriate to a ceremony of 'legitimation' (even her double-barrelled Christian name seems to enact a slight hesitation over 'who she is, exactly'). Here Farfrae seems to 'produce' Newson, as if from a hat (p.270), suggesting a surprising kinship between the two men themselves, possibly under the rubric of 'those who find lightness of being quite bearable', which would exclude both Elizabeth-Jane and Henchard—who thus form another disconcerting 'linkage'.

Embodiment of the proper and of propriety, Elizabeth-Jane is the opposite of Henchard in a way he finds pleasing. As 'not-him', we might say, she is his. Unfortunately, on his finding that she is 'not-his' in a natural, not merely a cultural, sense, she becomes 'not his' with what might be described as a vengeance (hers and his). This Henchard discovered through perusal of her mother Susan's posthumous note (which was *not* intended as a parting or Parthian shot *d'outre-tombe*). Unfortunately, though, it *became* that due to Henchard's typically disrespectful refusal to honour Susan's request that the note should not be opened until Elizabeth-Jane's wedding-day (p.122). As a kind of 'changeling', she proved to be New*son's* 'new' daughter. Biologically speaking, (and 'let us not speak of the biological' seems to be one of *The Mayor of Casterbridge*'s structural members), she is 'living proof' that she is 'none of his'.

Yet perusal of *The Mayor of Casterbridge* seems to reveal that 'living proof' is no proof at all. As 'his daughter (who is not one)', Elizabeth-Jane *returns* to him in *language*, in the form (to be voided and cast out) of *dialect*. Curiously, the narrator describes these dialectal idiosyncrasies as 'those terrible marks of the beast to the truly genteel' (p.125), which sounds a little like Elizabeth-Jane herself, defensively 'proper' in reaction to her chequered origin(s). 'Thy speech bewrayeth thee' is a quotation Hardy uses elsewhere for this theme, in a poem in which a Christ-betrayer is trapped by shared dialect.[21] Oddly, again, the phrase is used later in the novel itself to refer to Lucetta's tell-tale French (p.144), bespeaking Jersey and a penumbra of mysterious Continental louchenesses, apparently. Dialect, the *patois*, betrays one's origins, yet its eradication is also 'a betrayal of origins', just as Henchard was betrayed by Elizabeth-Jane's, as well as by his original thoughts of what those origins were. Discovered to be 'none of his', Elizabeth-Jane immediately 'discovers herself' to be part of him, if only as (precisely) the part to be discarded. But finally Henchard is the 'self-alienated' man, ejecting *himself* as he votes for his own expulsion from Casterbridge and the care of Elizabeth-Jane (p.268).

Yet another not-so-little irony is that the Henchard-replacing Newson *also* exiles himself from Casterbridge and from Elizabeth-Jane with jaunty (if not terminal) insouciance—in this sense most emphatically showing himself to be 'none of hers', a sea-man to the last (p.281). Newson becomes a kind of (Shakespeare's) Pericles *manqué*, rejecting his 'Marina' in favour of the merely marine, despite their sentimental re-uniting. This 'act of union' was itself apparently a positive, but already 'contained' negation—it was used to erase the very idea of Henchard, about whom, posthumously, Elizabeth-Jane so busied her thoughts, finally putting a kind of amnesty in the place of her wilful amnesia (pp.285-6). Having dispensed with his wife, Henchard seems compelled, in this respect a Flying Dutchman as much as a Wandering Cain (p.269) (accompanied by his personal Abel), to remain an eternal suitor pursuing a kind of perpetual paternity suit. His final plea, itself unheeded, is really a version of the idea that no one should tell his story (partly because in Casterbridge in particular, people will tell stories about you). However, he had admitted in court, the justice come to judgment, that the 'accused'—the 'furmity-woman' with her tell-tale narrative about his misdoings—was perfectly just, so that he was not 'in a position to judge her' (pp.182-3).

King Lear seems a mighty 'intertext' here, and dispatching Henchard to die on the heath as a tragic figure cast off by his daughter(s) (suggestively 'identified' by Lear as 'no daughters of his') is a fate already looming with the 're-interpellation'[22] of Henchard by the crone who had specialized in lacing bowls of furmity with liquor at Weydon-Priors (p.30) with unhappy results. *Lear*'s sardonic claim, 'change places and, handy-dandy, which is the justice and which the thief?' (4.6.149) is sustained in a brilliantly telling way by the furmity-woman's tale of an act of drunken turpitude on Henchard's part much more consequential than her own passing 'nuisance' (pp.181-3). Never more of a just judge than when abruptly declaring his unfitness to be one (p.183), Henchard likewise departs abruptly when accounts of him shortly to be reaching Elizabeth-Jane's ears will reconstitute him as a person unfit to plead at the bar of narrative (p.268) with his personal account. In a parallel way he was unable to settle his *accounts* as a declared bankrupt (p.196). Finally, although Elizabeth-Jane seems related to Hamlet-like urgings that she would 'in this harsh world draw [her] breath in pain' (5.2.359), well placed to 'tell his story', she is enjoined, rather, to take pains not to. Her compliance with this might exact the knowledge that it is she who has killed Henchard with a wicked invention of hers to the effect that Newson's heart was broken by the wicked invention (of Henchard's) which sent him packing (p.280),[23] if only temporarily. Indeed, the narrator's special pleading on Elizabeth-Jane's behalf, as a highly 'Victorian' figure of female serenity (enunciating a philosophy which precludes it [p.285]), might lead to a revolt of the reader. But Hardy, his narrator and Elizabeth-Jane make a kind of trinity here, with third-person narration creeping close to what is palpably *her* thought-process. Entrusted with 'mummy truths'—or at least truths which her long-suffering mother would certainly have confirmed—to the effect that happiness comprises an occasional interlude 'in a general drama of pain' (p.286), Elizabeth-Jane seems poised to add to it, as something of a Job's comforter to the poorer sort. And it seems that she herself has actually very little to 'bear', as Farfrae will presumably continue to flourish as a 'green-fingered' commercialist (himself grown a kind of 'Mr. Grower' here), as Elizabeth-Jane silently critiques him. So the reader has finally heard the story of how she was told not to tell. But Elizabeth-Jane's role in it is highly recommended by the narrator who is himself a kind of 'suture' of 'Hardy' on the one hand and 'Elizabeth-Jane' on the other. Indeed, the narrator himself sounds like a 'father-figure' of sorts, and so not entirely a man to trust with tales of fathers and daughters.

For example, we are shown how Henchard was banished on Newson's account. But Hardy later sprang a highly significant surprise in reporting that Newson, less 'Mephistophelian visitant' than Mephistophelian absconder, could not abide the landlocked rusticity of Casterbridge—no returning native he. He is last glimpsed trying to get a glimpse of the sea, over the Budmouth roofs, 'notwithstanding the society of his daughter in the other town' (p.281), which means either that he enjoyed and sought out her society but needed to live by the sea, or he needed to live by the sea so much he was prepared to forgo her company—which puts a rather different gloss on things. The latter explanation would certainly add a good deal to our sense of the pathos of Henchard's fate, enabling him to file a posthumous paternity suit after all, as 'the netted lion' (p.261)—especially given the dubious justice of her rejection of him in favour of her real (or at least biological) father, who took things as they came—and went, apparently. But, as we saw, the final point seems to be that it is precisely 'the biological' which is (or ought to be) under erasure here. Paradoxically, it was Newson's very insouciance which inspired Elizabeth-Jane's (in itself repulsive) repelling of Henchard (p.280). It is Elizabeth-Jane, made into 'a thing enskied and sainted', as the Shakespeare of *Measure for Measure* would put it, by the narrator who exacts revenge, for Henchard's original rejection of Susan as the mother (of his child, but not this child), and as a wife also 'not one' by his own willing (given his 'offer' of her to Newson at Weydon).

Paternity, as Stephen points out in Joyce's *Ulysses*, may be an inference,[24] but Hardy permits further speculation on bases for the inference. Henchard rejected his own daughter when she went off with his wife, but *this* daughter 'was not one' for the reader, who knows only the later Elizabeth-Jane, a new daughter of 'New-son'. Yet was the rejection of the daughter who was not one, but who, in a double sense, might have been, atoned for when they were briefly at one in the suggestively named 'seed shop' (p.260)? Elizabeth-Jane puts on sympathetic knowledge of Henchard with his powerlessness, but lies told to Newson by the Henchard who feared to lose her themselves lost her to him. Thus she was divorced from the 'false' father and united with the 'true' father, one she knows as 'taking things lightly'–a trait which will finally include taking *her* lightly. If Newson has indeed deserted her for the sea-view, this would mean that *he and Henchard* were finally united under the rubric 'they ceased to see her', and this does turn up the volume of sympathy for Henchard here. This sympathy also increases as a result of the refusal of pathos Henchard's 'will' intended to enact. It is also perhaps augmented by the fact that the receiver of his posthumous message was Elizabeth-Jane, described earlier as a 'discerning silent *witch*' (p.159), and we should perhaps take this seriously.

She is last seen applying a reversed version of one of Hardy's most disputable *mots*, to the effect that 'there have been triumphs of justice which have been mockeries of law', as here there have been triumphs of 'law' which have been mockeries of 'justice'.[25] We might describe this as a 'law of the mother', since her resolution, in his presence, to forget Henchard (p.272), goes with his own, 'self-alienated' (p.282) desire to be forgotten, which causes him to be remembered in his absence, and also makes the grief he forbids something of a racing certainty.[26] The elegy spoken by Mother Cuxsom over her mother, the always-already-ghostly Susan, to the effect that 'her wishes and ways will all be as nothing' (p.119), is negated in his case precisely by such powerlessness being specifically *requested* by Henchard. This will become the iron (-y) which enters into the soul of Elizabeth-Jane. In fact Henchard requested, strictly speaking, to be remembered by 'no man' (p.285), so perhaps the provisions of the will, which in other respects also proved ticklish, permit Elizabeth-Jane to remember him in a fashion the reader will recognize as a posthumously granted 'paternity suit'. Remembered as one who wished to be forgotten, he becomes her 'ghostly father' at last, as a final flourish to Hardy's thematic arabesques.

It was Elizabeth-Jane who initiated the conundrums over paternity which obsess the novel: is its status a matter of inference, legality, emotion, 'origins' (biological or non-biological)? Ironically, as we saw, it proves to be Newson who 'begets' the new daughter he, nearing the end, 'gets', and yet finally (it appears) almost 'forgets'. Newson is clearly the 'opposite' of Henchard, and, given this hint of a functional, 'inorganic' approach to character, Farfrae and Henchard also are not so much the names of individuals as of a kind of (ideological) 'binarism', alternately waxing and waning. Farfrae, a 'nice person' (if always vaguely complicit with the workings of 'capitalism'), nevertheless only becomes the stereotypical penny-pinching Scotchman in the nick of time—time, that is, for Henchard to be seen as contrastingly Lear-like, with his own Fool, his own Heath, a rejecting daughter—a Goneril or Regan even— who also turns out to be 'on double business bound' as some sort of Cordelia (p.284). Seeking Henchard after having treated him badly and cast him off, Elizabeth-Jane encounters Abel Whittle, badly treated by Henchard, who stuck like a limpet (p.284)— bearing news of Henchard's death.

Farfrae has triumphed without conspicuous villainy—and indeed as, very much an injured party narrowly escaping death at Henchard's hands in the fight in the barn-loft, set up by Henchard. Yet, contrariwise, it is Henchard's 'turn' to be 'lovable' again as he dies—if only in order to make his self-cancelling bequest stick in the throats as well as the minds he willed to forget it. His final place in the scheme of things, indeed, seems to be as a mnemonic contributor to Elizabeth-Jane's Dr Johnson-like philosophy, which also bespeaks what the reader might feel is a highly improper self-righteousness. For it was her 'abjection' of Henchard which precipitated the tragedy, led to his doom and a kind of 're-invention' of him by Elizabeth-Jane which caused his wishes, slightly chillingly, to be 'respected as far as practicable' (p.285) by this 'daughter (who was not one)'. And finally, 'piety', it seems, would entail *not* having Henchard buried in consecrated ground (see his will, p.285)—a nice touch, as is the veil the narrator draws over the nature of the proceedings Elizabeth-Jane undertook at this juncture. Her very forms of goodness ironically alienate: her 'Minerva-like' (p.282) 'serenity', her sense of good fortune combined with her determination not to be grateful for it, and her highly 'Victorian' Job's comfortings of poor folks (pp.285-6), perhaps make something of a 'witch's brew' after all.

We had been warned (p.159), although it was poor Lucetta whom the skimmity-ride seemed to 'be-witch' (and the narrator also seems to embark on something like a skimmity-ride against Lucetta, with persistently implied denigrations). Yet Elizabeth-Jane's wholesale disenchantments—even with Donald himself as she claims she will not tamper with the *outré* provisions of Henchard's will (while simultaneously doing so) 'to give her husband credit for large heartedness' (p.285)—make one doubt 'what Henchard knew', when he 'knew' that Farfrae had a 'better' wife in her than in the infatuated Lucetta (p.277). In a paralogical moment Hardy or his narrator insinuates that 'experience had been of a kind' to 'teach' Elizabeth-Jane, 'whether rightly or wrongly', that 'the doubtful honour of a brief transit through a sorry world hardly called for effusiveness' (p.286). The conditional modification 'whether rightly or wrongly' seems to destroy (not merely qualify) the argument, and we may be left with the reflection that experience may be teaching that experience does not do so—especially if what it produces is as unpredictable as it is here. That surprising sentence suggests how, in general, *The Mayor of Casterbridge* does seem to be one of Hardy's strangest 'performances', without the idea actually challenging the received opinion that it is also one of his strongest. As we saw, he was never more (so to speak) the 'monumental mason' celebrated by Proust than he is here, and Casterbridge and its Mayor seem all 'rugged trim'[27] and 'four square' dependability. We seem to know where we are with them, yet the novel seems finally to proceed under the sign: 'all signs submitted to 'processing' here are reversible (and likely to be reversed)'.[28]

Chapter 9

'Retaliatory Fiction': *The Woodlanders*

Like *The Mayor of Casterbridge*, *The Woodlanders* finds ways to announce itself as a fully 'canonic' 'Wessex' novel. Its rustic microcosm cannily placed in relation to a 'world wide web' of human interconnectedness[1]--later, as we know, to be achieved by the 'machine' of scientific advancement rather than the 'tree' of organic unity, to cite the book's dominant opposing images from Thomas Carlyle (and the Matthew Arnold of 'Balder Dead').[2] The apparently reassuringly 'organic', folk-culture implications of its title and setting are played off against a 'sort-of-Darwinian' struggle in nature reflecting an Unfulfilled Intention[3] in the cosmos, which make the natural descriptions here disturbing rather than reassuring. Similarly, its initial depiction of Little Hintock as a lonely and sequestered nook (p.41) immediately notes how the romantic locale is already 'penetrated' by a kind of 'Mephistophelean visitant' in the minor mode, in the form of Percombe the barber hotly in pursuit of Marty South's hair (p. 44ff.).

The hair, a sign of sexuality, will indeed be 'traded off', very much against what seem the initial odds, and become something of a prop in the rather stagey affair of local *chatelaine* Felice Charmond and aristocratic but impoverished Edred Fitzpiers. Lady Macbeth might cry 'unsex me here' in her famous soliloquy (1.5.41), but this would be spoken in a different tone by the peasant girl Marty, who will desire this depressing destiny and lets herself be shorn like a sheep only because the object of her affections, Giles Winterborne, does not desire her, or because, as Giles only should desire her, it is fitting that she shall no longer be subject to desire. So Marty parted with, or was parted from, her 'sex-appeal' partly because she proved to have none for Giles himself in any case (pp.37-8). Her name suggests the martyr role she will finally embrace with a vengeance. Unfortunately this role is one in which the man she mutely adores will vye with her all too successfully.

Marty's hair, then, proves to be her commodity rather than the 'gads' she is splitting (p.34, p.53) with, Hardy implies, 'artistic' hands, which scarify (p.48). The hair already has 'exchange value', and its 'use-value' will be to help Dr Edred Fitzpiers, *The Woodlanders'* anti-hero, exchange his wife Grace Melbury for the widowed Mrs Charmond herself. Hardy's emphasis here is from the outset highly 'sociological',[4] and the 'Sophoclean' drama he broaches (p.44) is already under erasure, although the idea that Sophoclean tragedies occur naturally in places like Hintock is cleverly insinuated. (But of course Sophocles didn't write about timber merchants in the first place.) Similarly, the (useless?) pathos of the 'Nordic' mythology with which he associates Marty (p.54) also seems fairly irrelevant to the theme of rustic deprivation, which had already been announced by Thomas Gray, in a poem which positively obsessed Hardy—'Elegy Written in a Country Churchyard'.[5] Gray's eruditely melancholy ponderings over the contrast between rustic forbears, have-nots who harmed no one, and those ambitious souls given opportunities for greatness who fulfilled their destinies at others' expense, supplied intellectual scaffolding for *The Woodlanders*.

As a recompense for a lack of orthodox genealogical support, Hardy tries to confer the dignity of long-view racial perspectives on Marty, but the ancestral intuition he specifies here, a sense of the 'Ginning–Gap' (p.54) more effectively and relevantly suggests the emotional void which awaits Marty herself as she will hug the (posthumous) 'idea' of a dead Giles deserted by 'his Grace'. Contrariwise, his dubious heroine Grace Melbury is herself *antithetically* fashioned of a 'shallow [or light-minded] modernity', which ironically confers superior status in this context.

The 'Elegy' reference reminds us that Marty's talents might have led her to play instruments rather than split gads (p.48), and Hardy would not have been convinced by Gray's implied argument, famously 'extracted' by William Empson,[6] that the rustics were, so to speak, 'better off poor'. Indeed, his insinuations about Marty's unfulfilled potential might be said to be well-connected with his sense of the educational mortifications of hard-working George Melbury, the local timber-merchant and the leading employer in Little Hintock. Ironically, in terms of possessions and properties Grace's father has clearly already made himself a not-so-petty bourgeois (p.68). But what he fatally lacks is 'cultural capital'.

Hardy's inquiry into the hard lives of aspiring timber merchants and downtrodden rustics is deeply serious, but *The Woodlanders* also seems ludic, if not exactly funny, in a familiar way. The plot of *The Woodlanders*, itself something of a trap in this respect, edges towards the incident of the trap set by bitter Tim Tangs (p.423). This was an expression of his marital disappointment, intended to cripple the Fitzpiers who has (antecedently) come between himself and his wife (pp.199-200).[7] Revenge, as Bacon said, is a kind of wild justice, and, wild as he is, Tim seems to have stumbled on a certain appositeness. Hardy's idea, one which he would wish us to remark as much as he must have hoped his original editors would not, is that the trap is a kind of *vagina dentata*, acting as a counterbalance to the warm welcome afforded Fitzpiers by Suke. (Confirming the idea, Fitzpiers, doctor turned dentist for the nonce, 'covered' his affair by lies [to Grace] about a need for his urgent attentions to Suke's mouth and teeth.) As so often, Hardy actually makes matters too outrageous for editors to twitch over: but it is important to note, in responding to him, how his cultural context encouraged hypocrisy and suppression, ours a vulgar and meretricious 'frankness', which he would not have liked. The trap has a resumé-like suggestiveness as at once a savage memento of the rural class war *d'antan*, a testimony to the cruelties of love, and a symbolic 'follow-through' to Grace's solemn perusal of the rubrics of the marriage service ('what God hath joined') just before she sets off for an encounter with the trap whose repercussions will see her caught (trapped) in the humiliations of her bad marriage once again, thanks to both parties' narrow escape from the (literal) trap. Tim's Unfulfilled Intention with respect to the trap combined with Grace's (and Edred's) narrow escapes cause Grace herself to conclude that 'an Eye [sic] has been watching over us tonight' (vol.3, ch.14), but the text permits ironic speculation on just what sort of 'Eye' this might turn out to be. The trap itself is lingeringly described by Hardy, and ironically commended as a memento of 'Merrie England' (p.421), a fact which should linger in the memory of anyone still inclined to think that Hardy is 'made out of' pure nostalgia. Tim's 'intervention', intended to 'part' Fitzpiers and Suke, will have the effect of restoring Grace to her promiscuous husband (pp.426-8). As a result, it will also restore the (dead) Giles to the sole custodianship of a Marty South shedding the qualities of (her) sex as she invokes him (p.438), appositely enough, as Giles had declined to interest himself in such qualities.

With alternating currents of pathos and satire, Hardy plays the light (of) irony over the theme of lost love and other major forms of 'dispossession': losing what he might call his 'grace and favour' residence (p.194) (though it was not strictly that), Giles has simultaneously lost his Grace (and her favours) as Marty's scrawl predicted (p.157): 'O Giles, you've lost your dwelling-place/ And therefore, Giles, you'll lose your Grace'. Again, typical of Hardy both in terms of his conceits and his interest in his characters' capacities for reading the signs in various senses here, is this writing on the wall of the house for which the writing *was* on the wall, thanks to Mrs Charmond's petty refusal to renew Giles's lease (p.239). (The crisis ensued as a result of the death of Marty's father John South, deranged by a tree-fixation which results in his own death when Fitzpiers has the tree felled in a typically crass attempt at a final solution to South's psychological problems [resulting from his social anxieties].)

But the actual eviction of Giles resulted from Charmond's annoyance at his refusal to cede ground with his wagons, heavily loaded with timber, and give way to her coachman, as she goes idly about her travels. (Later, a contrite Felice will reflect that her ousting of poor Giles not only destroyed his suit to Grace, but also made a 'legitimate' liaison with Fitzpiers impossible for her.) Subsquently, after losing Grace *and* his grace and favour residence, Giles seeks refuge in a hut (p.359), then evicts himself from the hut in the interests of the chastity and fidelity which Grace will finally beg him not to respect (p.375). Unfortunately, however, he will by this stage be too far gone to hear or respond to her plea. Thanks to his 'chivalry', he has declined from leasehold dwelling to shack, and thence to a kind of hastily-improvised bivouac which 'offers little protection', like the cosmos and society as Hardy depicts it here. Once poised to acquire Melbury's extensive property, Giles will inherit only (as Matthew Arnold put it) 'the vasty hall of death'.[8] Freud seems relevant to Giles' case, as he beholds in Grace 'a thing enskied and sainted', difficult to accommodate to the necessities of rough wooing in terms of the case set out in Freud's dismaying essay on 'The Universal Tendency to Debasement in the Sphere of Love'.[9] By contrast, it's clear that his rival Fitzpiers, trained to look down his nose at the locals in addition to looking down his microscope to discover a 'desacralised' view of the universe (p.181), will have all too few problems in this respect.

Giles' 'manly' respect for Grace will turn into a literally terminal problem. Their 'final' union will assume only the momentary form of a posthumous story told by Grace to Fitzpiers when Grace, driven literally to distraction by her erring husband and the death of Giles, will be induced to simulate having been 'had' by Giles (p.388) as a 'fictional' retribution for Fitzpiers having 'had' (as she puts it, p.302), Mrs Charmond (and Suke Damson). Described as having reached 'the most *extreme*' point (p.388) with Giles, this is a reference to mortality itself rather than the 'little death' of the sexual act, proving that Giles 'can die . . . if not live, by love' in Donne's phrasing (if not Donne's sense). As Fitzpiers puts it as he inspects Giles at Grace's urgent, if somewhat tardy request, 'the *extremities* are dead already' (p.387). Giles' inhibitions over Grace stem from class feeling, and he approaches the 'hypergamy' of the marriage with her which Melbury encouraged him to think of as a *fait accompli* with trepidation (p.339). The novel is 'about' desire as mediated by social liminality, with Fitzpiers 'not quite a gentleman' in either sense of the phrase, while Giles, with the sterling qualities which should fully entitle one to the name, is shown to lack social cachet. Yet even in terms of material possessions, Giles ironically sinks in the social scale only through the pettiness and false values of those, formally his betters, who either lack his qualities or fail to appreciate them in him. Giles is positively encouraged to aspire to a Grace Melbury memorably characterised as being caught 'as it were in mid-air between two storeys [or stories?] of society' (p.273). Somewhere in 'social space' she hangs suspended, apparently, and the 'suspense' of the narrative is itself fashioned from hesitations over the proprieties, social 'indeterminacies',[10] and the obsessive calibration of those class positions so frequently confused with personal worth. Indeed, Melbury's late advice to Grace, after the death of Giles, itself the result of her inveterate hesitancy, *not* to 'go shilly-shallying and playing bo-peep' (vol.3, ch.13), would have been well taken at any stage—but never was. And her final decision to re-join Edred in Sherton Abbas (en route to a new practice in the Midlands) is accompanied by regrets over 'not having a brush or comb' rather than for the apostasy from what seems to be virtually a 'Cult of Giles' initiated by herself and the stauncher Marty South.

Even Tim Tang's trap seems to agree that Grace is a little difficult to get hold of (p.426), suggestively catching only her dress. So perhaps the expensive 'finishing-school' in Sherton for which Melbury paid so dear really did finish her off after all. In fact, although she is highly educated by Little Hintock standards, a touch of 'Middle England' informs Grace's enthusiastic response to the idea that Fitzpiers should destroy his French novels and books of speculation (i.e., the signs of the intellectual interests which undoubtedly make Edred interesting), and stick to his trade (p.414). Again, it seems to be intimated that naturally, left to her own devices, she would prefer Giles (e.g., p.341), but in this sense too, it seems, she is not herself or 'identifies against herself' in attaching herself to Fitzpiers. We are left wondering whether she wasn't finally entirely fashioned of the social aspiration she learned in Little Hintock no less than Sherton Abbas.

Certainly, with George Melbury, timber merchant, as its linchpin, *The Woodlanders* deals with the fruits of snobbery no less than the production of apples by nature and cider by men. It is as if the meaning of his own life is bound up with the marital destination of the daughter who is the apple of his eye, while he in turn will, in social terms, be a kind of (woodland) beam in hers. Or rather—as he himself pleads after being disrespectfully treated by a member of the local hunt in Grace's presence—after her marriage to a 'real gentleman' she will be invisible to him and she may pass him in the street, as knowledge of her relationship to him may do damage to her social standing (p.213). This is, in its quiet way, one of Hardy's most terrible moments. The crowning glory of his daughter Grace's expensive education will be not to know the father who has sacrificed himself on that very altar, enjoined as she is to pass him by 'looking the other way'. This seems to entail a kind of inversion of Althusserian interpellation, a process of 'hailing' people in a taken-for-granted attitude which assumes their ordained social roles.[11]

But Hardy has in fact already dramatised in a particularly telling way Foucault's unsettling points about 'education', in that intellectuals tend to be the bearers of the 'hegemonic' rather than the liberating.[12] Curiously, though, Melbury's answering of the 'classic' question 'Who chased whom round the walls of what?' in terms of Little Hintock 'characters' rather than Achilles and Hector (p.68), shows that he already knows more than he thinks he does. It is perhaps in such terms that the reader will be induced to accept the idea that Greek drama 'occurs naturally', as it were, in Little Hintock, where archaic patterns also tend to repeat themselves. But finally, following a kind of Wordsworth spoor here, Grace will see that education may take differing forms, and that the dead Giles was 'naturally' affined with Marty in that, letting Nature be their teacher, they could both 'read its hieroglyphs as ordinary writing' (vol.3, ch. 11). In this sense, Grace ironically learns that both Giles and Marty are, in a vital sense, better 'readers' than she is.

While writing *The Woodlanders* Hardy wrote to George Gissing in the summer of 1886 ironically expressing a sense of what might be called an 'Unfulfilled Intention' in relation to the novel itself. Perhaps he was disconcerted to find that his Wessex Tragedy had turned out to be merely another Satire of Circumstance, and that it embodied not so much a favourable Wordsworthian sense of sublimity as an unfavourable Freudian sense of sublimation. He speaks of the 'hydraulic' (p.305) power of the sap-raising trees, and these woodland processes, if all too suggestive to the reader, remain insufficiently suggestive to Giles. Giles will become a connoisseur of the sublime through an excess of sublimation, while in purely social terms he was always a little 'sub-liminal' in the specific sense of being below the level at which he might legitimately cross the threshold with Grace herself.[13] Questions of desire and the body are fully involved with the social theme of 'class consciousness' here. Giles' desire for Grace was initially encouraged by Melbury because of the wrong Melbury had done Giles' father Jack in stealing away the lady who became the first Mrs Melbury, now dead—but the arrangement seems always to have been subject to a kind of 'subject to status' clause. Giles' noble disposition and ignoble social position both cut against him here, while Fitzpiers, simply sublime to the easily-awed Melbury (p.211), and made doubly sure of his social level through his abject deference, declined to sublimate and had no problems with the 'hydraulics' of 'rising sap'.

In this sense he may even be said to have become, in his own way, the wood-god Giles was in Grace's eyes, troubling the reader over which of her men was the true '*manqué*'. Giles steps manfully from this version of pastoral, as a hunk (or trunk) of pure woodland masculinity, but, for Grace and others, it is, paradoxically, Fitzpiers who will provide '*L'Après-Midi D'Un Faune*'. Giles, Winter-borne, borne towards Winter or born of winter, seems to explicate Lyotard's basically Kantian claim that 'the sublime might just as well be thought of in terms of melancholy and despair rather than in terms of pleasure'.[14] Curiously, again, this is derived from Kantian notions of sorrow over that 'unrealisable ideality' it is apparently for Fitzpiers, acquainted with Kant, to know intellectually and Giles to 'see feelingly'. If Giles offers, to Grace's misty-eyed imaginings, the High Romanticism of Keats' famous Ode as a vision of 'Autumn's very brother' (p.341), Fitzpiers flatters to deceive as the cash-strapped 'gentleman who is not one' and as a wooer whose love is of a quality to 'bear division and transference' (p.285), like the lyrical apostrophist of Shelley's

'Epipsychidion'.[15] In a sense 'role-playing' even as a 'man of quality', Fitzpiers qualifies for Melbury's open-mouthed acceptance of what a 'person of quality' actually is. But as one whose qualities need to be 'supplemented' by those of Giles, Fitzpiers is also so unsuccessful as a doctor as to create a curious turn on the phrase 'professional gentleman'—one which turns decidedly against him here. Indeed, Hardy seems to suggest that Fitzpiers' silver-plated background and his scientific training are mutually 'deconstructive', and his odious snobbery is 'overdetermined' by its very insecurity of tenure. Yet if Giles, Nature's gentleman, offers a 'sterling personal character' (p.403), Fitzpiers comes closer to offering what might be described as the earth(l)y passion Lawrence taught us to associate with virile underlings in his re-writings of Hardy, and perhaps *The Woodlanders* in particular.

Fitzpiers does particularly well at the Midsummer ceremonies involving divinations by village maidens, using them to 'possess' Grace by verbal assent (p.198) and Suke by more physical compliance (p.200), while Giles, about to be dispossessed of his cottage, also stands empty-handed here, deprived of his Grace, cut out by the smart young doctor. It might seem odd to imagine that Grace and Giles' grace and favour residence are 'as one'. Yet as Grace indignantly noted, even her doting father Melbury seemed to consider her as a mere 'chattel' (p.135), and the two forms of possession are closely related. Indeed, as recently-married Grace, back from her honeymoon travels, meanly calls out to toiling Giles from 'The Earl of Wessex' (p.230), his man Robert Creedle agonisingly tells Giles' loss *entirely* in terms of Melbury's 'other' possessions: 'Ye've lost a hundred load o' timber well seasoned; ye've lost five hundred pound in good money; ye've lost a stone-windered house that's big enough to hold a dozen families'—and so on (p.229).

On the other hand, these 'midsummer ceremonies' the local maidens perform do sound as if they were originally fertility (or orgy) rituals in which sexual activity (as opposed to polite enquires followed by a blazingly 'epiphanic' disclosure as to which trade one's husband would engage in [p.195]), was very much in order. In these terms, then, Fitzpiers is hardly doing anything untoward and indeed may even be said to be the only one behaving, in context, with perfect propriety. To retire to a 'haycock' with the highly compliant Suke Damson (pp.199-200), whose name suggests that she is indeed rather ripe for 'tasting', is an appropriate narrative 'climax' here. This, after all, is a traditional scene of *droit de Seigneur* (not quite one) in which light-minded sexual behaviour, however louche and reprehensible from a workaday or 'bourgeois' perspective, suggests that sexual passivity in such cases may itself be criticized—the error being, in Ezra Pound's phrasing, in 'the diffidence that faltered'.[16] Unfortunately, Giles is a past master at this kind of thing, too noble to fulfil those promptings which will apparently subvert the idea that he is that, suggesting that if his 'caste' had been higher, his 'morality' in this case might have been beneficially lower. By contrast, Edred will set about illustrating Freud's points about the necessary debasing of the object in the interest of the satisfaction(s), points of which Giles' scrupulosity towards Grace is the unhappy obverse. Indeed, by comparison with his country fun with Suke, even Fitzpiers' affair with Felice Charmond looks palely stereotypical; the participants appear to be extracting some kind of entertainment over what Hardy in the 'Satire of Circumstance' 'She Charged Me' calls a kind of 'slave and queen'[17] dialectic 'conditioned' by Mrs Charmond's velleities, in a minimalist version of a rural 'drama society'. But it was made fascinatingly clear that the younger Fitzpiers, as a penniless student in Heidelberg, was ('homologously') judged to be as unfit to pretend to Felice's hand as Giles was later deemed worthy of Grace's (p.243).

Hardy's narrator will finally pinpoint Fitzpiers as a thoroughgoing salaud as he shows him being 'finely satirical' (p.395) despite his 'generous nature' (!), over Charmond's Marty-derived hairpiece (the narrator himself being 'finely satirical' here). In similar style, Hardy points out that Fitzpiers 'almost' envied Giles his chivalrous nature (p.402) when he knew the whole story of the 'hut incident' in which Giles's delicate and deferential chivalry towards the wife Fitzpiers couldn't but despise a little cost Giles his life. We may feel, however, that this effortful blackening of Fitzpiers' features shows quite the opposite, that Hardy finds the figure of Fitzpiers so attractive that he actually needs to have his narrator spend a good deal of time abusing him. That 'solitary student' of 'subtle thought on things',[18] citing Spinoza and Shelley (p.190, p.260) would normally usher in a highly sympathetic character, and the narrator has to work too hard to establish the idea that Fitzpiers is finally too louche to like (just as he fails to convince us that the money lavished on Grace's social acquisitions doesn't pull her decisively out of Giles's reach from the outset).

Ironically, the only person apparently able to appreciate Edred's intellectual interests seems to be Giles himself. Given a casual lift by the bored young doctor, he is forced to note not only Fitzpiers' kindling interest in Grace, but its 'Spinozistic' nature, nicely caught in Giles' almost academically feline observation that 'she's only the tree your rainbow falls on sir'—hinting that he might just consider leaving the Grace he has merely glimpsed in the distance alone. (Similarly, with his mind apparently full of the young poetic pastoralist Keats here, Hardy remembers his point that 'the Imagination may be compared to Adam's dream--he awoke and found it truth', and Fitzpiers' first real encounter with Grace takes the form of a daydream vision of her as he naps after late-night studies—perhaps suggesting, in Jane Austen's phrasing, that 'his regard for her was quite imaginary'.) But the point also seems to indicate that Giles was himself eminently 'educable'. The idea might be used to challenge Fitzpiers' later assumption, enunciated in the high-class 'Earl of Wessex' Hotel to Grace, that people like Giles, 'moiling and muddling for their daily bread' (p.230) outside, seem to belong to 'a different species'. Ironically, Giles does belong to 'a different species' in the sense that, although Edred, didactically speaking, will remind Grace of the four 'cardinal virtues' as elaborated by Schleiermacher (p.142), it is Giles, not he, who will actually embody them.

And again, Fitzpiers' very snobbery is 'overdetermined' by that penury which, as Thomas Gray pointed out, repressed the talents of peasants like Giles, who, it seems, might have perused Spinoza with profit, or Marty, whose hands might have swept the lyre rather than split the gad. If Fitzpiers had been Clym of *The Return of the Native*, presumably he would have enjoyed introducing Giles not only to Spinoza, but also to Kant, also mentioned as part of his intellectual repertoire, who might then have been cited to reprove Fitzpiers' pursuit of 'chance desires'. *The Woodlanders*, then, makes shape to form a kind of 'pre-text' for a solemn occasion as a rather serious lecture on the state of the cosmos (ontology), but this seems to mask another kind of discourse on what Auden called 'the amorous effects of brass'[19] with the consequent ideological misrecognitions (sociology). Indeed, it seems to have been all too easy to miss the tone here, by no means without that levity by which seriousness may be intensified. This may even be seen in the famous remark, used of Marty's desperate lunge, her intimation by correspondence to Fitzpiers that he might find her hair on his lover's head. The narrator writes that 'her bullet had reached its billet at last' (p.395). This seems also to mean that her *billet*, rather more *aigre* than *doux*, is something like a *bullet*. As if to underline the concept, Mrs Charmond is subsequently shot in Baden shortly after by her deranged 'South Carolinian' suitor, apparently a 'stalker' who 'used to follow her everywhere' according to Mrs Lucy Melbury (Grace's stepmother). Subsequent reports hint that Felice may have been pregnant at the time, underscoring Fitzpiers' loucheness, and illustrating the idea that the Unfulfilled Intention was at least able to fulfil one of rescuing Fitzpiers from the pickles his egocentric lack of concern creates.

Fitzpiers was initially perceived as a kind of '*Il Penseroso*'s "Platonist"'[20] figure who proved not to be that, despite his initial 'romance and mystery'[21] as one whose lamp is (Miltonically) 'seen at midnight hour' in the woody recesses of Hintock. But Grace, visiting by daylight on behalf of the ageing servant Grammer Oliver terrified into granting invasive rights over her dead body to Fitzpiers, finds the doctor as a mere lodger in a suburban-like and eminently prosaic dwelling. Ironically, it is *Melbury's* ancient and 'rambling' properties which bespeak a genuine tradition, despite Melbury's cringing deference to Fitzpiers as the scion of an old county family down on his luck. Hardy makes it clear that not only was Melbury's dwelling-place the remnant of the old manor-house of the district, but that the Melbury family were the original owners, signifying the arbitrariness and transience of those class divisions Melbury *himself* ironically takes to be immutable absolutes. And it is precisely Melbury's own fawning approach to Fitzpiers which will significantly diminish the young doctor's 'valuation' of Grace herself (p.206). Hence, in the battle of 'capital' versus 'cultural capital' Melbury's crass cash and extensive properties count for little, while, on the other hand, in the battle of 'cultural capital' (the aesthetic) versus 'individual integrity' (the ethical), the former wins hands down until, at the point of Giles' death, Grace has what should be the essential moment of 'final' enlightenment in realizing 'how little acquirements and culture weigh beside sterling personal character' (vol.3 ch. 12). But the irony of this lies precisely in its *lack* of actual finality, as Grace will betray this insight in succumbing to the unappreciative Fitzpiers once again. Grace herself is 'a self which touches all edges' here, as, cultured and an heiress after her fashion, she has not lost anchor with respect to a basic sense of right and wrong. It is she who might have provided a maturer arbitrement, but, fatally touched by the Melbury insecurity her Sherton education should have enabled her to transcend (but appears to have reinforced), she respects the counsel of others until it is too late. Cowed by Fitzpiers, she becomes formidable only when dealing with women, rebuking Mrs Charmond for not 'levelling' with her about Fitzpiers (pp.297-8) and making a sharp reply to Suke Damson, found suggestively cracking nuts (p.193, p.264) with her 'lovely molars' (p.223), and in so doing destroying Fitzpiers' professional alibi, (advanced to Grace with salaud's sang-froid), for their sexual encounter. Suke's display of dental perfection is simultaneously a display of other forms of imperfection, apparently: 'So much the better for your *stomach*', comments

Grace (p.265), straying momentarily into a kind of 'Jacobean tragedy' innuendo which leaves Suke strangely untouched (if not at all intact).

Hardy's creative mischief and glancing ironies continue to the end. He sends Melbury, cued by the derelict 'bar-room' lawyer Fred Beaucock, on a fool's errand to free Grace from a Fitzpiers currently living abroad with Felice, but eventually finds the new marriage act would deem Fitzpiers's treatment of Grace insufficiently cruel to permit a divorce. A troubled idyll had ensued the first broaching of the idea by Beaucock, with Giles given encouragement as the incipient suitor, but he is doomed to be perennially 'incipient', in what seems to be a parody of Keats' delight in the eternally 'warm', if unfulfilled, lovers of his 'Grecian Urn' Ode. The narrator rebukes Giles for not seeing that Grace did not mind their going to a low pub ('The Three Tuns') in Sherton Abbas (where he paid), (p.348) instead of the high-class 'Earl of Wessex' Hotel (where Fitzpiers did not); whereas the reader irresistibly forms the mutually cancelling impressions that (a) she did mind (the incident as told); and (b) she did not mind (in terms of what we are told about the incident). This helps towards an appreciation of both Hardy's method and Grace's 'character'. It might lead you to think that an alternative title for *The Woodlanders* (1887) might be 'the story of a woman of no character' (who survived), in ironic contradiction of *The Mayor of Casterbridge* (1886), subtitled 'the story of a man of character' (who did not).

The novel ends with the tribute of Marty's (posthumous) fidelity to someone who had never been particularly interested in her as she is spotted by the returning rustics (p.438), forced to scour the countryside with the distraught Melbury—only to find Grace has been induced to bed down with Fitzpiers (p.433) in 'The Earl of Wessex' yet again, thanks to the trap, in a final move which seems to negate Mrs Charmond's earlier suggestion that *women* were 'like' mantraps (p.101). The only diversion from so desolating an ending is that the rustics, less impressed by Melbury's concern for them than his pointless solicitude over his erring daughter, quite rightly force him to entertain them in the familiar pub before the long traipse back to Little Hintock (pp.434-5). Perhaps Melbury will at least have learned to divert some of the emotional capital he invested in his daughter's welfare in the direction of his over-loyal work-folk. At any rate, he seems to have arrived at a necessary cynicism over her final destiny, and may be 'a sadder and a wiser man' as a result, but the position is one in which he can do nothing to rescue the daughter from the fate he helped to 'spin'.

And, of course, though Giles is dead, life goes on: for example, as we leave Fitzpiers and Grace in the Sherton hotel we might wonder whether he took the opportunity to discharge his debts there, or whether they continued to mount. Nor, strictly speaking, can it be known whether Edred continued (putting it as unpleasantly as possible) to 'mount' Grace—or whether, according to her father, 'the woman walks and laughs somewhere at this very moment whose neck he [Fitzpiers]'ll be coling next year as he does hers tonight' (p.435). Hardy himself, endorsing Melbury, claimed, in a parody of authorial omniscience, that Fitzpiers 'goes on in a bad way all his life'.[22] Grace, that is, has made her bed, but someone else may occasionally lie in it.

Indeed, Hardy has already, in his 'associative' way, encouraged the reader to make 'unpleasant connections'. The gentle mare called 'Darling', a 'mount' purchased for Grace by Giles (p.156), became a kind of forfeit of his failed courtship, and, as a result, it is Fitzpiers who will 'mount' his 'Darling' (p.257)—an implication Hardy seems to be secreting here as an effective way of conveying the painfulness of Giles' emotions as rejected suitor. In addition, it was ironically clear that 'Darling' saved Fitzpiers' life when Edred's state of exhaustion caused him to fall asleep in transit (pp.268-9), as Melbury's workmen point out, by gently bearing him back from his tryst with Mrs Charmond at Middleton Abbey. (She had fled there from Hintock House, in an attempt to stifle their affair which merely rendered it inevitable.) Indeed, 'Darling' seems to partake of Giles' own gentleness, which finally served to prevent Fitzpiers' not being rather justly cuckolded (p.375). But perhaps, for Hardy, this is just another example of the 'Unfulfilled Intention' (p.93).

The Unfulfilled Intention is 'in' the novel (ch.7), and expressed in the 'internecine', not Wordsworthian, nature of the forest itself in a famous passage (' . . . the lichen ate the vigour of the stalk, and the ivy slowly strangled to death the promising sapling'). This drama is also 'rehearsed' in Hardy's minor poem 'In a Wood', in which the forest confirms rather than negates the *social* struggle the speaker is attempting to flee from. 'Outside' the novel, but still inside its mind-set, is another expression of the ethos of Darwinism read off in relation to *social conditions*, never used or undersubscribed by Darwin himself—'the survival of the fittest'. 'Life-rafted' by their bourgeois training and (to Fitzpiers), that particularly convenient legacy from a 'maternal great-aunt' of his, Edred and Grace will run off to the Midlands to begin their lives anew (ch.48). As the 'to-be-forgotten' Giles sinks forever into the earth mourned only by the dispossessed Marty, *The Woodlanders* seems to be providing a particularly sardonic commentary on the idea that it is the fittest to survive who automatically do so.

Chapter 10

'Re-presenting' *Tess of the D'Urbervilles*

Tess of the D'Urbervilles is, by common consent, a quite extraordinary novel. What its extraordinariness consists in, or of, might still be seen to result from rather unusual writing practices it will be the business of this chapter to explore. Hardy's approach to representation, for example, is highly original, making some of the innovations of modernism seem less startling in retrospect. *Tess* is often described as a 'poetic' novel. In its post-Romantic pathos it does have a profoundly 'ecological' sense of how we emerge from and share the earth. Its burgeonings and seasons are interwoven with our own sensations, and emotions. We belong on and to the earth and might be happy in it, as Tess and Angel were, as something of a new 'Adam and Eve' (a kind of 'original identity') in the half-light of Talbothays dawns.[1] But things miscarry and miscue, or rather, they 'always already have', as subsequent narratives will show that both Tess and Angel may already be said to have 'fallen'.

So Tess and Angel proved to be Adam and Eve in a slightly darker sense than first postulated, in what for this novel proves to be a typical piece of 'comparative' 're-presentation'. Highly experimental after his fashion here without the slightly alienating exhibitionism of full-blown literary modernism, Hardy is particularly alert to what we might call frames of reference, 'placing' his characters in relation to an allusive relay of cultural ensembles and 'ready-mades', conferring identity through this particular form of an apparent comparative approximation which is a means of bringing the 'object' itself into being.

If a work of art rather than its peruser, as Norman Holland[2] thought, has an 'identity theme' which enables competent reading, the 'identity theme' of *Tess* is surely that of 'identity' itself—or rather, the processes by which 'one' is 'identified', which surely secretes an 'identity politics'.[3] And Chantal Mouffe has nicely indicated 'the deconstruction of essential identities'[4] as a necessary part of a commitment to feminism.

'Woman can never be defined',[5] certainly, but patriarchy will never leave off trying to do so, and finally Hardy himself seems to be establishing that 'woman can never be defined' through a paradoxical excess of 'definition' which never quite covers the case. Tess herself is, in the blurry fecundity of Hardy's 'thick' descriptions, above all, woman—or even, Woman (an idea already at odds with the singularity of Tess it seeks to pin-point). So perhaps, in terms of praise with which some men encumber their partners, she is 'all woman', the incarnation of womanliness—or, more pertinently, womanliness as incarnation.

Interestingly, the first communication Angel heard from Tess at Talbothays (not even addressed to him personally, but, in a sense, 'how he got to know her'), was precisely that she was *not* her body – that she too was, in this sense, an 'Angel' ('I know our souls can be made to go out of our bodies' [p.120]). Uttered as a generalisation independent of 'gender', the point is negated by stolid Dairyman Crick, who confesses that he has never felt his soul rise a half-inch above his shirt collar, so that Tess' counter-claim to be 'soul-full' is pathetic precisely because everyone seems happy to identify Tess as eminently corporeal. Tess' 'out of body experiences' are disconcerting to those who think she is bodily experience personified.

The dairyman's wife identifies Tess as 'pretty', and is then reprehended by the narrator as the word is not quite accurate to what strikes you about Tess. The word we are left to grope for in silence is one not quite in Hardy's large lexicon. Tess is, in a word, *sexy*—a word which might induce a wince here, yet undeniably indicating just what *Tess* is very much involved with for everyone who claims to 'know' her--one reason for Henry James' bridling at the book. However, even if Tess herself 'is' this, we are given to understand that she is so without the conscious artifice the word itself might be thought to suggest. But hints of sexiness might cover the sense of a kind of 'unspeaking eloquence' in Tess herself. *Sexy* stands poised between subjectivity and objectivity here, with a possible implication that Tess was consciously provocative, but Tess is more provocative precisely through her enchanting unawareness of her 'special effects'. Curiously, it is this paradoxicality, that of her being a kind of 'unmoved mover', which moves the plot and makes the structure of *Tess*.

We might even say Tess' final hanging in 'Wintoncester' makes a fitting climax, but not on account of her killing of Alec. This can be bracketed as an (un-) happy accident 'while the balance of her mind was, quite properly, disturbed' in Sandbourne. In terms of the logic of *the novel itself*, Tess is hanged, finally, as she was intolerably provocative precisely because she can never be accused of being so (indeed, at one point she mutilates herself slightly to divert male attention[s][p.280]). Hardy's narrative projects a plot of patriarchy to erase Tess with something of 'the moves of a chess player' (p.287), but this erasure-as-consummation itself has an erotic charge or inflection. Tess seems to recognise this herself, declaring herself 'almost glad' (p.396) when her flight with Angel after the idyll at Bramshurst Manor in the New Forest comes to an end and she is arrested: we might even read this allegorically as that finding of 'pleasure in pain'[6] cited as a possible condition of the construction of feminine identity. A 'clubbable man' is, it seems, one thing, and a 'clubbable woman' another.

Alec D'Urberville's aggressively phallocentric responses to women in general and Tess in particular are allegorised in the casually mentioned Rude Giant of Cerne Abbas (p.334, ch.48), primevally etched on 'The Slopes' with his club and phallus, or club as phallus (and vice versa). (Alec's manor in Trantridge was known as 'The Slopes', and the poet Philip Larkin projecting a cod-Gothic persona boasting about 'the women I clubbed with sex'[7] also sounds right for Alec's reckless [if perhaps not quite heartless] seductions. We understand these to be partly a fruit of 'new money' irresponsibility and partly a misogyny learned at the breast of his suggestively blind but powerful and 'bitterly fond' mother.)

Even Alec's preaching after his surprising conversion sounds oppressively ferocious and patriarchal ('In the beginning was the phallogocentric' might be his message.) His 'identity' even as 'convert' is 'cancelled and preserved'. The threshing machine as 'red tyrant' (p.325)—which Tess is forced by the bullying farmer Groby to serve until she is 'weak as a bled calf' (p.335)—itself sounds alarmingly phallic. Indeed, even the policeman who steps forward as a kind of modern emanation of sacrificial Stonehenge to arrest Tess is rather suggestive. He announces to Angel that flight or resistance is useless as 'the whole county is *reared*' (p.395, ch.58) rather as if in response to sexiness rather than criminality, or, more precisely, female 'sexiness' as 'criminality', or inducing criminality.

Tess is figured (and 'fingered') as a *body* throughout because people like her (and it) that way, pleased to think that her 'body as sign' bespeaks her. A returning Angel 'saw the red interior of her mouth as if it had been a snake's' (p.168, ch.27), in partial reminiscence of Eustacia in *The Return of the Native* (1876). Unfortunately, Angel himself will prove to be a returning version of the priggish Clym of that novel. Milton's Angel identified woman as 'an outside' (*Paradise Lost* 8.568), but for Hardy's Angel Tess is defined in terms of 'interiority' here. The narrator himself might be accused of some prurience in this presentation of Tess. Himself thinking along these lines, Alec, pursuing the deserted Tess at Flintcombe-Ash, at this point the only man to have had 'carnal knowledge' of her—of Tess as 'interiority' one might say—abruptly and sardonically exclaims that he '*knows her*'. He then odiously sneers at the idea that they are now 'strangers' (p.317). This is an insecure bit of swaggering arising from his just having been staggered to learn that Tess is married. In a suggestive contrast, her own mother, with her purer love, equally staggered to find an ineffectual Angel at the door of her suggestively desirable 'house with walled garden' in a village itself never quite identified, admits that she '*has never truly known her*' (p.375).

In *Tess*, above all the other novels the 'semantic' is 'somatic' and the 'somatic' 'semantic', with Tess's body as silent signifier. Hardy uses *Measure for Measure* adroitly here, cleverly splitting Angelo's priggishness and prurience between Alec and Angel: 'In her looks/there is a prone and speechless dialect/such as moves men' (1.2.172-4) seems a particularly relevant citation, and might be used as a more telling epigraph or introductory quotation than the sentimental one he culled from *Two Gentlemen of Verona*. 'Dialect' is particularly a word to seize on here. Shakespeare's linguistic metaphor for the sort of sexiness they find in Tess is specifically imaged as the 'oppressed linguistic equivalent' of Tess' relatively unsophisticated but genealogically interesting rusticity.[8] Later, on Tess and Angel's 'wedding night which was not one' at Wellbridge, Tess will identify herself and Angel as what we might call 'Shelleyan' counterparts ('doubles'). (Matthew Arnold identified Shelley as an ['ineffectual'] 'Angel' in a famous description,[9] and Angel is compared to Shelley and contrasted with Byron by Hardy here [p.192].) But Tess was ignoring gender differences and discriminations (and could hardly know that Angel was not merely a return of priggish, hortatory Clym in *The Return of the Native*, but also of the intellectual Henry Knight in *A Pair of Blue Eyes* [1873] with his patriarchal passion for 'untried lips').

Angel is apparently untouched (or not in the 'right way') by Tess' touching tale of how she came not to be intact, and Hardy uses imagery from the Angelic Shelley's 'Ode to the West Wind' to describe Angel's Hebraic, or Pharisaic overinsistence on the idea that Tess was wrongly identified. Originally she was 'one ("pre-narrative") person', but 'now you are another' (p.228): 'propensities, tendencies, habits, were as dead leaves upon the tyrannous wind of his imaginative ascendancy' (p.245). In a further, and typical, poetic reminiscence, of Tennyson,[10] a sleepwalking Angel will lay her body as 'dead self' (old identity) in the stone coffin near Wellbridge. Tess will passionately claim in her final desperate plea to Angel by letter that she was always 'the same person' he had originally 'fallen for' (p.336). Yet she herself had agreed earlier in a kind of anguished soliloquy, that who she was was indeed a bit of a problem ('for she you love is not my real self, but one in my image; the one I might have been' [p.214])—which seems a little hard on her self. Yet Hardy does seem to make Tess seem a little 'metamorphic' after all, problematizing representation: slightly 'out of her element', she even has the look of 'a friendly leopard at pause' when caught in the lights of that metropolitan train which announces 'the ache of modernism' (p.187) entering the pastoral region. Hardy seems to be something of a post-Romantic eco-warrior here, suggesting that Tess may allegorize everything about to be hunted out of existence as part of the 'big game' of modernity.

Tess' appearance one minute may be reminiscent of the ferocious D'Urberville features depicted in the frightening dames of the panelling at Wellbridge (p.217), but also seem to retain the soft contours of her childhood, adding immensely to the pathos of her fate (Was Alec 'something of' a paedophile as well as 'something of' a rapist? Tess certainly seems to think so: 'Angel! I was a child—a child—when it happened' [p.232]). So we see Tess as at once prematurely womanly and not old enough to be a woman. Hardy's contrapuntal methods of representation seem to be 'trying, above all, to make you *see*', as Joseph Conrad might have put it, but he is actually making it impossible for you to do so, despite the gusto with which people describe Tess—including, most eloquently, Angel's mother, who has never seen (and will never see) her.

She is enabled to do so through Angel's own verbal description (p.262, ch.39). This emphasizes how Tess is an already intensely 'mediated' verbal construction, a woman made out of words, at the very moment of rendering her 'unequivocally': 'You said the other day that she was fine in figure; roundly built; had deep lips with keen corners; dark eyelashes and brows, an immense rope of hair like a ship's cable; and large eyes violety-bluey-blackish' (p.262). Angel has failed to turn up with her, so Mrs Clare remembers Angel's description of the woman we know from other (quasi-objectifying) descriptions. The attempt at precision does several things. It shows Mrs Clare entering into and even sharing Angel's infatuated feeling (we have already seen how Hardy raises the erotic temperature here in showing how even women cannot but recognise and respond to her charms). This of course increases our sense of the pathos as well as the irony of Tess' never actually meeting the parents who are already more than half won over to her 'cause'; also, in the very attempt at linguistic precision in conveying her physical quality, or qualities, the quotation also feigns the knowledge that Tess is not 'made out of words' (which of course she is). And the hiccupy linguistic slippage of 'violety-bluey-blackish' paradoxically reveals, through the very strenuousness of its attempt to 're-present' Tess with precision that Tess, in another 'complimentary' sense, 'exceeds representation'.

Tess then unknowingly gets another 'brand(-ing) identification', through a *reading* this time, in the parsonage she never enters. This is the description from the book of Proverbs—on 'The Virtuous Wife' as conveyed, this time, by 'the words of King

Lemuel' (ch.39, p.263). Tess would in fact have been a 'virtuous wife', but Angel seems to have abolished temporality to make himself a kind of 'cuckold by [temporal] transposition' so he can feel righteous about the hurt and angry feelings which lead him to cast Tess off so cruelly at Wellbridge. Faced with all this evidence, one might feel that an alternative title for *Tess* might be *Habeas Corpus* ('You may have the body'). The legal phrase will refer at once to Tess' claim to be spirit, her appropriation by Alec, her spiritual adoption of Angel, her specific doom of 'hard, horrible work'[11] with 'stone-deaf taskmaster' Groby, and her hanging—proving that, as Jane Austen might put it, 'the whole affair was *in suspense*'. Even poor Tess' story of her 'out of body experiences' is describing a state of '*suspended* animation'.

Tess, not without spirit in either sense, assumes that Angel takes her for what she is, not what Alec has taken her for. Hardy spends a good deal of narrative time showing how very different Angel was in his approach to women from womaniser Alec, including his attitude to the infatuated Izz Hewitt, Retty Priddle and Marian of Talbothays, in love with him and thus at his mercy. And he seems particularly aware of Tess herself as a being to cherish. Angel identifies her as Artemis and Demeter (p.130, ch.20), unwittingly getting at Tess' paradoxical combination of inner chastity and hapless fertility, which will 'cash out' later in yet another 'identity parade' as he reshapes his morality in the rigours of Brazil and has come to recognise 'the virtual Faustina in the literal Cornelia, a spiritual Lucretia in a corporeal Phryne' (p.370, ch.53). (Faustina was reputedly unfaithful to Marcus Aurelius, Cornelia faithful to Gracchus; Lucretia chaste and Phryne a courtesan.)

For all that, Angel's appreciation and appropriation is merely that of Alec differently inflected: for him, too, Tess offers a body as sign. Her assumption that she will be forgiven because Angel has 'fallen' sexually as she has leads to a particularly searing introduction for her to the asymmetricality of 'sexual relations'—where 'relations' may include the notion of accounts, narratives. Mallarmé's line '*M'introduire dans ton histoire*',[12] a plea to be introduced to someone's story, includes a sexual pun as part of a sexual plea or invitation. This citation might combine with a reminiscence of dying Hamlet's plea for Horatio to tell his story, which would entail 'absence from felicity awhile', which is very much the unhappy outcome of Tess and Angel's telling theirs here. Apparently Tess and Angel were each begging to be introduced to the other's story on their wedding night (ch.34) in an incorrect translation of Mallarmé's phrase—their narratives will in fact preclude rather than precede their sexual union.

Both have lost sexual innocence, but only Tess has lost 'the hymen', and marriage is nothing if not 'hymeneal', or so Angel thinks. (Concentration on Tess obscures the fact that it is *Angel* who is failing Tess' 'no virginity' test here.) À propos, Hardy cites Browning, piquantly and perhaps a little pruriently: 'a little less, and what worlds away' (ch.35, p.235).[13] Angel, that is to say, has in fact identified her in a favourable but still 'sexist' way as a kind of 'Virginity Tess'. 'Virginity Tess' was intended as a kind of prize, but even Tess herself, it seems, was a substitute for that other prize not vouchsafed to Angel—a 'Fellowship' (ch.34). In Angel's already nostalgic identification of Tess as 'my Fellowship' we have reached perhaps the oddest moment of conferred identity, also disconcerting in that it makes Tess sound like a substitute for something which, *au fond,* he would rather have. (Angel has been denied the entrée to Cambridge reserved to his elder brothers as his evangelical father sees ordination as the only appropriate climax to tertiary education.)

It is particularly sad to reflect that Angel's identifying her in this way also forms a kind of pun, as their marriage would indeed have constituted a 'fellowship'. Angel himself enthusiastically pointed this out, both to his own parents and to Mrs Crick at Talbothays. This makes a particularly pointed contrast with Alec's purely sexual plundering and unbridled philandering, as well as with D'Urberville's odiously generic identification of Tess as merely another 'cottage girl'. But one of Hardy's most piquant points here is precisely his *elision* of Tess' story, her own account of herself and hence 'what she is *to* herself'. We are never told just what she told Angel, while being told of her narrative's terrible effects in punctilious detail. Tess' uncertain self-esteem is to consider here, and she never was eloquent in her own defence, and in that sense her confession as 'apologia' ('self-defence') probably turned all too quickly to simple apology. Her best defence would surely have entailed Hardy's claim that she was indeed *a pure woman*, which engendered outrage in reviewers and has occasioned some bafflement ever since. But Tess can claim to be 'pure' in the specific sense that it seems that until the advent of Angel *she has never given herself to a man*, although this is something the text is itself rather equivocal about: Hardy's phrasing will compare her to (Shakespeare's) Lucrece, who was indeed raped, but Tess' phrasing to Alec will imply that their subsequent relation was of some duration and continuance, partly because Hardy has a number of ideas to communicate here— which would include the claim that the exact nature of her early sexual experience, not initiated by her, didn't really matter; and that it only intensified her love for Clare to discover that 'a man' could be so different from, and preferable to, Alec D'Urberville. So the final change wrought in Tess by her experience with Alec might be said to lie in her greater appreciation of a man like Angel.

Interestingly in relation to the theme of this essay, an ingenious Deleuzian critic David Musselwhite correlates Tess' 'purity' in a recent article with an ability to 'disburden herself of identity'.[14] Unfortunately, though, at the point he uses to illustrate this the narrator's pronouncement is negated: we are specifically shown her *inability* to achieve this, although it specifically surfaces as a form of self-deception straight-facedly, and hence deceptively, 'reported' by Hardy's roving narrator describing her journey from home after her desertion by Angel and the spending of the last sovereigns, equally 'angels', committed to her in Chapter Forty-one. This journey is indeed ironically described as a 'disconnecting [of] herself from her past'—only for Tess immediately to encounter her enemy Groby, privy to the knowledge that she had been 'sexually assaulted' (and so himself 'assaulted' by Angel). Then, in quick succession, she will slowly become horrifiedly aware of the presence of the hunted and wounded pheasants she will unknowingly 'identify' with herself on the gallows as she 'tenderly' breaks their necks; and the 'convert' Alec, who will immediately initiate the process which will lead her there. He will do so by discarding *his* 'new identity' in her favour: he comes to accept Tess' own scepticism about this identity with ironic alacrity, replacing the image of his sacrificed God (in his current theory, 'on his account') with that of the to-be-sacrificed Tess (also, in a way, 'on his account').

The surprising narrator of the novel seems to position himself between Alec D'Urberville's sardonic irony over and Angel's resentment of Tess' 'fallen' condition, also finding new forms of identity for her as he identifies against as well as with her. For example, he points out the irony of Dairyman Crick's unfortunate linguistic favouritism in addressing Tess as '*maidy*' (p.135, ch.21), and pedantically and perhaps not altogether accurately claims that Angel 'little guessed that *the Magdalen* was by his side' on their Talbothays rambles (ch.20, p.130). It is clear, after all, that Tess's sexual initiation was 'against her will', or, as the mediaevalism (in a document referring to penalties for rape) quaintly puts it, '*hir unthonke*' (or, as we might say, 'no thanks').

Tess was, in fact, taken, 'appropriated' (ch.11, p.74)—a keyword for Alec's outrageous sense of a 'right to her body', reminding us that 'gender is always imbricated with other categories': as he arrogantly puts it, 'you are mighty sensitive for a cottage girl' (ch.8, p.56), another identifying mark or suspect 'fingering' of Tess which might reasonably secrete rage in the reader. In relation to one adaptation at any rate, according to a young Jane Marcus full of irritation with Polanski's filmic elision of the death of Alec, a feminist might be imagined as entering the cinema in order, as she puts it, 'to see Tess *kill* Alec D'Urberville'.[15] Hence, surely, D.H. Lawrence is also at his most irritating in his claim that, 'in a way, D'Urberville was her mate'.[16] This is technically true, but he was not a 'mate' she actually chose, which 'makes a difference', or ought to. And, with desolating irony, it was actually her worshipful sense of Angel's 'difference from' Alec which induced Tess to tell the tale about him to Angel which will divorce her from Angel and re-unite her to Alec.

So Tess told, although she had in fact already been told not to tell by her archaic mother, or rather, in her precise terms *not* to 'Trumpet her Trouble' (p.191, ch.31) (as one becoming thereby a kind of 'impudent Trumpet', her lowest identity thus far). She ignores this humble and rustic advice and gets a good deal more Trouble (not to be Trumpeted this time, when on this occasion she certainly ought to have Trumpeted it. Her journey to Emminster to plead with Angel's parents, as the narrator emphasizes, entailed her greatest mistake.) Her courage failed her and she immediately thereafter encountered Alec, turned preacher at the behest of old Mr Clare himself, almost as if Alec had been ironically substituted for the gentle Clare senior himself as part of Tess' thoroughly bad luck. Her (good) looks and Angel's (equally, 'Mr Clare's') 'infidelity' ('lack of faith'), naively relayed by Tess, ironically reconverted Alec to paganism *and* sexual pursuit of his ('Mr Clare's') wife. In pursuit of his purposes D'Urberville then identifies the absent Angel as a merely 'mythological personage', (p.331, ch.47). This was how Angel sometimes considered Tess herself, and what we as readers might consider Alec, as 'a D'Urberville who "was not one"'—with the emphasis now on the word *personage* (he is not quite the man of consequence his name suggests, being of a family of moneylenders from the North).

Angel implicitly staked a great deal on the idea that Tess was known as not having been 'known' (in the Biblical sense), and knowing that she has been will cause him to refuse to 'know her Biblically' himself. Ironically, Angel has already used the Bible to gloss or identify her, Hebraically rather than Hellenically this time, whispering 'three *Leahs* to get one *Rachel*'[referring to the story of Jacob's 'fourteen-year-itch' for Rachel in *Genesis*] as he bears the girls over the flooding Froom (p.145, ch.23).

Ironically, Angel himself seems something of a God to Tess, particularly when eloquent on such subjects as the loss of faith. This is a theme, ironically enough, used by Matthew Arnold in 'Dover Beach' to emphasize that the betrothed should be 'true to one another' [i.e., not 'faithless', the linguistic turn on which the poem itself revolves]), and this is another poem Hardy had deeply considered.

But precisely because Angel has become faithless enough to provide the reason(s) for Alec to abjure the Christianity he ironically imbibed from Clare senior he will be enabled to resume his 'courtship' and capture of Clare junior's wife (ch.46). (This will be at least partly as a result of economic pressures brought to bear on the Durbeyfields, thanks in large measure to the disreputability *Alec himself* was responsible for. It will establish Tess' identity as a kind of 'whorage' [p.67, ch.10] [her word], even: 'the eldest daughter had made queer unions' [p.352, ch.51] is the whispering voice of parochial respectability [and malice] relayed by the narrator.) Tess' reputation is diminished in the parochial imagination with unfair insinuations of a sexual immorality which the *results* of all this will ironically render inevitable.

Ironically, also, Alec, influenced by Angel's notions, confesses that without the faith that religious practices will lay up treasure in heaven he cannot be 'moral'. In complete contrast, in Angel's case the conscientious retreat from his father's doctrine merely causes him to tauten a kind of moral noose, which will in effect 'divorce him from' Tess and lead to her being hanged. The shape of the action here reminds one forcibly of Nietzsche's critique of English moralism of the George-Eliot-to-Herbert-Spencer type[17] which Angel embodies here. (Nietzsche attacked the idea that an inevitable agnosticism should be felt merely to conduct one to apply tighter moral strictures.) This is despite the fact that, wishing to propagandise for the Tess he wished to marry, Angel had approached, then fled from, the 'spiritual refrigerations' of Emminster vicarage, the pruderies of Mercy Chant (surely a softened version of what was originally 'Cant'), strait-laced 'Victorianism', and the propagation of Biblical knowledge.

Angel identified Tess, by contrast, as a kind of figurehead for the warm and happy paganism of the Var (which sounds like the local pronunciation of 'Far'), a kind of 'sappy valley' full of fecundity. Different kinds of 'Bible' knowledge, then, awaited Angel at both ends of Wessex's spiritual spectrum, in the forms of Mercy's garrulous prudery and Tess' silent susceptibility. At Emminster, Angel identified with his father's charity but was alienated by his brothers' priggery. Ironically, though, he will prove to be the bearer of the latter, not the former. Possessed by this particular form of censoriousness, he will claim that Tess' grand name merely bespeaks a genealogical want of firmness and that she is no better than a 'peasant'.

This composes a particularly momentous kind of 'identity crisis' for Tess (p.232, ch.35). Tess replies that she is a peasant by position only, not nature. Unfortunately, however, 'peasant' *is* a class term, and, your position once established, no one is particularly anxious to inquire after your nature. 'Peasant', though, is indeed, an 'identity which is not one', and it was earlier emphasized that the whole point of Angel's 'formation', as opposed to that of his mincingly bourgeoisified brothers Cuthbert and Felix, was to realise this fact, and to be at one with the narrator's blistering contempt for the idea of 'Hodge', the 'pitiful dummy' (ch.18, p.117). This is the urban impression of field folk willed into existence by metropolitan prejudice which roused Hardy's indignation in his rare foray into essay-writing, 'The Dorsetshire Labourer' [1883]). Indeed, not merely is the 'peasant' an 'identity which is not one', but, equally precisely, an excuse for the maltreatment of which Tess's fate is in part a kind of allegory.

And, as we saw, if briefly, peasants and pheasants may have more than homophonic resemblances: in a grim anticipation of her own *terminus ad quem* as a hunted creature, Tess 'tenderly breaks the necks' of the pheasants injured in the *battue* or field sports exercise Hardy so detested (p.279)[18]—so Tess might add pheasant, as well as peasant, to her collection of conferred identities—the former conferred by the reader this time. The field sportsman, nothing if not a bad sport, is a visible embodiment of the perhaps not-quite-motiveless male malignity which finally 'finished its "*sport*" with Tess' (in one of Hardy's most notorious sentences) by breaking her neck at Wintoncester. This emphatically combines thoughts of the unspeakable field sportsmen with a sexual implication—specifically from Milton's 'Lycidas' (he had alluded to this in *A Pair of Blue Eyes* [1873]). In Milton's poem the youthful poet thought 'to *sport* with Amaryllis in the shade, or with the tangles of Naeera's hair'.[19]

Already we can see a little more clearly what Hardy means in his famous last paragraph, in which the 'President of the Immortals' (p.397) is said to have 'finished his *sport* with Tess', a comment so often attacked or uncomprehendingly mused on. This 'President', apparently Aeschylean, was transposed by Shelley (a poet who obsessed Hardy) into the psychological projection of a tyrannical social dispensation, and of patriarchal power, or the power of patriarchy. So finally, we may say, in summary, in a gesture indicating that he is sick of this sporting life, Hardy will tenderly break Tess' own neck, blame it on the President of the Immortals, yet privately will be unable to suppress personal (and specifically erotic) memories of female hangings of his own 'peasant'[20] youth. *Tess of the D'Urbervilles* is a great novel partly because Hardy is so thoroughly caught up in the fantasies about Tess which render her so vulnerable.

These fantasies may raise or reduce her, but, ironically, don't establish a 'level' for Tess except as she is reflected in them. Perhaps this is, ironically, why Tess is considered as his most real and present of characters, as this is how we form impressions of real people, which may be contradictory. For example, the infatuated Angel had already laboured to explain to his parents at Emminster that Tess was no peasant, or that peasants were not quite what you take them to be, so that the later accusation that she was looks again like 'bad faith' on his part. On the other hand, he had wonderingly identified the Tess who had caused such emotional turmoil in him as a mere 'milkmaid' (ch.25, p.154). But Angel is already in the process of unlearning a certain reflex snobbery resulting from his upbringing here. Hardy even inserts an adjectival reference to a month in the Revolutionary calendar ('Thermidorean', p.149, ch.24) to refer to this inner revolution of sorts originated in him by Talbothays and Tess.

The narrator here rejoices to concur, eager to explain, with typical Hardyan 'overdetermination', not merely that stereotypicality dissolves on contact but also that Tess was indeed educated after a fashion, or that she was at least educable and was going through a kind of crash course in refinement with Angel, as a prelude to her introduction into good ecclesiastical society. This would at once confirm that she needed to be 'added to' and was being added to (new identity), and that she was perfect as she was and didn't require to be 'added to' (original identity). Both attitudes embody half-truths. Tess, in fact, and this was precisely how she was to be defined, through lack, seems to have been 'half-way educated', in what will amount to a 'difference without positive terms' way. Her 'National Standard' school training sounds suspiciously like the elementary formation Renée Balibar pin-pointed as reserved for the lower orders[21]–it is doubtful if one is, so to speak, going to 'go up into the next *class*' when the process is over. So, on the one hand, what Tess conspicuously lacks as a result of her education is the take-it-as-it-comes fatalism of her robust and rustic mother (who, amusingly, points out to Tess that she didn't tell Tess' father everything about *her own* pre-marital experience [p.191]). On the other hand, Tess didn't have the sophistication of the fine ladies who read novels—these presumably warn them plainly that there are D'Urbervilles—or perhaps 'mock D'Urbervilles' about. Ironically, these mock D'Urbervilles may themselves mock your genuine claim to be one. Tess herself *was* a D'Urberville, but book indexes may remind the reader that she was 'of the Durbeyfields', and Alec can hardly be listed there under his true name of 'Stoke' (p.39). Then again, Tess points out that her beauty actually derived from her mother (maiden name not established), who was 'only a dairymaid' (p.102), which might suit Angel's theory of old families as he swings between positive and negative valorizings of Tess' lineage. Then again, so many of the locals are the 'decrepit' remnants of the genealogically distinguished that they achieve a paradoxical 'ten-a-penny' quality (or, as one might say, that of 'no-quality' 'quality'). (This might, incidentally, be thought of as including 'the Hardys' ['so we go, down, down, down'], as Hardy commented with amusing inaccuracy as the author of [highly successful] 'decline and fall' narratives.)

In fact the Durbeyfields' ancestry was 'not credited' (or, as one might say, their 'true identity' recognised) in their home village of Marlott, as the family are unceremoniously expelled from their cottage on the death of John Durbeyfield (p.352). John finally lies, ignobly as ever, in the local churchyard at Marlott, not the 'Family Vaults' at Kingsbere he craved—and the returning Angel will have to pay for his fancy headstone. But the bereaved and evicted Durbeyfields will be forced to seek sanctuary there in desperation (their intended lodgings have been taken), and sham D'Urberville Alec ('false identity') will spring from a sarcophagus like an animated effigy to terrify Tess into thoughts that, as the poem devoted to her has it, she'd 'have her life *unbe*' (dissolved identity).[22] 'What's in a name?' it seems, can hardly be treated as a rhetorical question after all, and that other hackneyed but interesting question in the Shakespeare 'Song' from *Much Ado* set by Schubert, 'Who is Sylvia? *What* is she . . .' slides off, in a telling slippage from subject to object. This slippage is one which people particularly like to enact with a 'sex-object' like Tess.

Tess is also 'made out of' variations in what we might call nomenclature, relishing the name 'Mrs Angel Clare' (p.214), but sensing that it may already have been 'impossibilized', in Joyce's idiom, by her being, 'in a sense', 'Mrs Alexander D'Urberville' (p.235). This is, in a very real sense, nonsense, although it is nonsense which Angel will pick up on and intensify ('he being your husband in nature' [ch. 36, p.243]—which is itself not possible). Indeed, Hardy will intensify the feeling by having Alec, in his new identity as preacher, bring a marriage licence for a marriage her wedding with Angel precluded. Angel refused to 'perform' with Tess, although the marriage service itself is a kind of 'performative', but Alec had committed the sexual act with her (definitely 'the act of darkness', particularly given the description of the Chase, where it occurred [p.73]). And this 'performance' will be fateful, not only because of the subsequent birth of the quickly-expiring baby ('Sorrow'), but because the casual spoliation of Tess by Alec will be the cause of Tess's *mariage blanc* with and without Angel).

Stunned by the grandeur of Tess' lineage, just as he has just been stung by his mother's penchant for gentility, Angel will only half-mockingly address her as 'Mistress Teresa D'Urberville' (p.189), a name uneasily appropriate given that she was, if only briefly, something like a mistress. Tess was linked to Alec through a D'Urberville name he appropriated, just as he appropriated Tess herself yet refused her the name ('but Tess, no nonsense about "D'Urberville" – Durbeyfield only, you know' [ch.5, p.43]). Ironically, again, Tess claimed she 'wished for no better', which might mean that she was proud of it, or that she wasn't. But she was reminding the reader that she herself did not share the family's euphoric cackling over a new identity the name supposedly conferred, and was not herself possessed by their insistence that she should 'claim kin' (pp.47-9). (She would have preferred the social identity of [qualified] 'teacher', but the fact that 'father was not very industrious and he – drank a little', as she told Angel with gentle Victorian pathos, precluded this.)

In a sense Tess was 'accepted' by Alec, but only as an inferior, and refused as kin by someone who was, in genealogical terms, her inferior. Later Tess managed only a riddling confession to Angel to the effect that the name D'Urberville was 'all her trouble' (p.188). As Angel points out, in a sense he can't be expected to follow, if Tess does dislike it, she can as it were 'get clear off' by taking *his* name, '[Clare]-ing her name', as dialect pronunciation of his name would indeed make it identical to 'clear'. Finally, on Angel's return from Curitiba we will have a new perspective on Tess' approach to her identity and his complete misconstruing of what is going on as he attempts to locate her. With a motivation the reverse of a detective, his *tracking* of her will still be a kind of 'proleptic' or anticipatory enactment of the *pursuit* of her that the effects of his *finding* her will actually induce. (Incidentally, Tess had identified herself earlier as a species of 'murderess' [p.73] when 'Prince', the family horse— himself sporting a fair pedigree, it seems—was killed.)

This is felt by the reader to be outrageous, and so it also seems cleverly anticipatory of (and so attempting to influence?) the fact that Angel will apparently consider Tess' distraught claim that she has become 'a murderess' at Sandbourne outrageous, a much harder case to adjudicate.) Again, Angel finds she has not used the name 'Clare' at Flintcomb in order to avoid compromising the family, and he is found enquiring after a 'Durbeyfield' in Sandbourne so that she is discovered at 'The Herons' only as a result of what we might call 'a ricochet of postmen' (p.377). This 'fortunate' event is simultaneously the death of Tess, through her killing of Alec, if only after a rejection of Angel which she imagined would 'kill' him (p.381). Angel will locate her as 'Mrs D'Urberville', which composes, if Angel but knew it, a new slant on 'identity' in that Tess is not here as Durbeyfield putatively D'Urberville, but has assumed the name as it was (falsely) assumed by Alec. Of course she is only a Mrs *without* the attached name in this case. (Etymologically speaking, however 'Mrs.' is really only a 'contracted' form of 'mistress'.) Angel is inappropriately pleased in his assumption that she has merely resumed what he takes to be the proper spelling of her actual name (p.377). In fact this new attempt to gloss what Tess 'is' defines what divorces her from (as opposed to uniting her with) Angel.

In the light of its thematics and 'conceited' procedures, then, perhaps finally the saddest thing about the book is its 'optimistic' uniting of Angel and Tess' little sister Liza-Lu according to Tess' own injunction (p.394).[23] This seems to destroy what we had been given to understand was the case—roughly, that 'there is no substitute for Tess'. (It is true, however, that Angel had a cynical moment at Wellbridge in which he invited Izz Huett to join him in Brazil as a kind of [temporary] 'Mrs Angel Clare'. But that was precisely because Tess had lately revealed herself to be, as it were, 'somebody else'.) However, as Tess's identity was always traced back to her body, anyone with her genes and gender was perhaps bound to be in the running. Indeed, as we have no right to assume that Angel and Liza-Lu will not be happy together, we might be led to conclude that Angel might conclude that *Tess* had always been an inadequate substitute for *Liza-Lu*. Mary Midgley remarks (THES 6.10.00) that 'our sense of our own identity really is something complex, and the various ways in which we interpret it do affect how we live'. The various ways in which others do so are also a factor to consider, as *Tess* makes clear.

Chapter 11

'Hey Jude': *Jude The Obscure* and Interpellation

Some critics write of *Jude* as if it represented a problem, others as if it problematized representation. The novel certainly seems to be 'making representations' of one sort or another, and about 'how things are represented', and so about how literature and ideology are 'meshed'. 'Interpellation'[1] is the once-fashionable name for how one is ha(i)led into what John Bayley might describe as one's 'ordained' place[2] (in society). Describing the process does seem to be what *Jude* is 'about'. Yet some people, it seems, can never quite be persuaded to notice that Hardy is a man used to 'noticing such things'—in addition to phenomena such as hedgehogs crossing lawns,[3] 'enchanting' as the poetic results of the latter process may be.[4] Ultimately, however, there's a connection between these different forms of 'noticing'. The 'thread' which links Jude to his 'fellow-creatures' (for recognising them as such, as an inadequately scary bird-scarer, he was promptly thrashed)[5] may tacitly unite them as those '["justly"] excluded from consideration by the dominant social and political processes'. Our sense of 'Jude's rights' is sustained by his sense of 'animal rights'. This is also, as it happens, a 'thread' which will link Jude to cousin Sue. Sue is herself unhappily 'linked' at this point to a connoisseur of Romano-British antiquities (p.133) and suggestively troubled by sounds of the rabbit caught in the gin which Jude had gone out to 'mercy-kill'—as herself caught in one, apparently (pp.179-80). T.S. Eliot's idea of the 'objective correlative' might be cited here.

Hardy's initial formula for the book as a study of 'a young man who could not go to Oxford: his struggles and ultimate failure'[6] is an inadequate one because Christminster (Oxford) itself is finally 'under erasure' thanks largely to Sue. But it is also because Hardy shows himself as a 'real artist' here by developing Sue, or letting Sue develop, to the point where she becomes at least as 'interesting' as Jude himself (challenging the adequacy of his own title, for example). But perhaps the formula already offers a sort of 'self-deconstructing' *Bildungsroman* through the attempt to 'insert' what H.G.Wells calls 'the educated proletarian'[7] into a bourgeois genre—the *Bildungsroman* is generally understood as a novel of (bourgeois) formation and consequent, if temporarily thwarted 'upward mobility'. But its class character remains, for the most part, invisible. Taking this in hand, we may say, then, that Hardy 'perceives' that there is 'something wrong with our literary formulas' no less than our 'social' ones (to adapt Jude's crowd-hectoring phrasing on the occasion of his return to Christminster). Jude is recommended as one of those fine spirits 'touched to fine issues', in a citation from *Measure for Measure*. Yet the supremely Victorian spirit of

Samuel Smiles, specifically not so touched ('Samuel Smiles over all', as one might say) also smiles over Jude's tentative setting-forth here, with rather worse thoughts of how to 'better oneself'. After all, Jude, whose deprivations are material as well as maternal, can't but notice that a £5000-a-year bishopric would certainly come in handy (p.27), and in this sense the 'educated proletarian' knows his place well enough to want to quit it as soon as possible. The reader might even conclude that we look up to Jude when he looks down at his fellow-creatures more than we do when he 'looks up' his betters.

Jude himself will ultimately recognise 'worldly ambition masquerading in a surplice', become quite sincerely ecclesiastical, and painfully accuse Sue of being 'quite Voltairean' (p.126). In due course he will become 'quite Voltairean' himself, while Sue herself will become laceratingly ecclesiastical. This was of course, as a result of Jude the Younger's becoming quite a (practising) Malthusian,[8] taking the problem of child overpopulation into his own hands (p.286). In the light of these transformations in its protagonists, *Jude*, in its criss-cross no-progress to emotional crucifixion, seems to be destroying the idea, itself ideological, that 'character' is unformed or uninformed by ideology. Perhaps H.G. Wells' useful idea that Hardy has involved novel-readers with the 'educated proletarian' was actually, in retrospect, pushing it a bit for rural Jude—despite the almost 'housing estate and factory farming just around the corner' feel to Fawley, the real place (of which Hardy's fictional Marygreen was not exactly a copy) which (sur-) names Jude himself, and possibly his 'folly' (as well as pin-pointing a place of destitution and despair for Hardy's Berkshire ancestors). But Marygreen (Fawley), though undeniably a place of 'humble and rustic life' has been stripped of its traditional associations, and the 'ache of modernism' hurts much more in *Jude* than in *Tess*, the novel in which the phrase originally appeared. A protagonist like Jude, mingling acquisitiveness with his child-like romanticism, might indeed fall foul of the criticism already implied by Clym Yeobright's noble scheme of assisting the local folk he 'transcended' in *The Return of the Native*. By contrast, Jude, as something of a slightly solipsistic 'scholar gypsy' or 'ineffectual angel',[9] is glimpsed as a member of the Artisans' Improvement Society only at the moment of his expulsion, for example (p.257). He may seem 'formed' to need rather than to give help, wants help to help himself. Yet he describes himself as lacking the vice of being 'selfish as a pig' to press on effectively with self-help (pt. 6 ch.1, p.278), hogging the road to self-betterment in a way that pigs—again, ironically—can't be accused of.

Ruskin College, Oxford, founded to help poor scholars, has, itself ironically enough, been styled 'the College of Jude the Obscure', but Jude, it's quite clear, would never have attended such a 'reach-me-down' institution. He is, from the outset, highly intent on, as it were, getting above himself, or, more precisely, the 'interpellated' identity which the College of Jude the Obscure would have confirmed rather than cancelled. And if anyone is to have a 'nominal' college here, it should surely be *Sue*, whose intellect 'scintillated like a star' beside that of a Jude rather endearingly confining himself to the role of 'benzoline lamp' (pt.6, ch.10, p.340) by comparison, obviously lucky to be included, you might say, in the College of Sue and Jude. This would remind us that if the novel is merely a history of Jude's aspirations it also cuts out Sue, whose pert intellectual bricolage will conspicuously fail to underwrite the

Jude-mode of 'phenomenal' reverence.[10] Sue, it seems, substitutes what Gramsci would call 'organic' (progressive) intellectualism for Jude's 'traditional' (or reactionary) intellectualism. Sue's alienation-effects here remind us uncomfortably that Sue's struggle couldn't even encompass 'not going to Oxford' in the first place. So she does not, like Jude, have to waste vast amounts of intellectual and emotional energy aspiring to it. In fact, it is as a result of Jude and Sue's *own* intellectual 'war embraces' that the novel does become an interesting intellectual set-to, recognising that its initial apostrophising of lovely Oxford obscures the intellectual view a little. A hobbledehoy encountered by Jude agrees that Christminster might perform a metamorphosis on one, but with the disconcerting results of previous mythological stories of those—the product's 'own mother wouldn't know him sometimes' (pt.1, ch.3, p.16). And this does seem a high price at which to gain recognition by an 'Alma Mater'.

But Jude seems to have forfeited his first mother's knowledge of him in any case, and is highly interested in being 'recognised' by his new Alma Mater. Jude is set on 'getting above himself' in the sense of declaring with Joyce's Stephen Dedalus that 'I am other I now', avoiding the law of interpellation, familiar in its way to the Victorians in the form of the belief that one's 'estate' had been, so to speak, 'ordered'. Initially masked by the callowness of Jude's fantasies and (quite Oedipal) longings for some kind of 'Alma Mater', in fact when he arrives at Oxford 'Hardy with a Baedeker' will present a cultivatedly brochure-ish image for Jude to toy with—the famous string of quotations from 'Oxford men' (pp.63-66). Jude knows his Alma Mater even if she doesn't as yet know him—but even here an 'oedipal' policeman will appear to shoo him away as he indulges his gentle scholarly fantasies. This small moment of coercion offers a serious anticipation of how he will be 'ha(i)led' into his (ordained) position in a much more comprehensive way.

Jude's initial affiliation is precisely to that Oxford defined by Arnold, and praised by him in terms, which might soon become censure, of being 'unravaged' ('unravished'?) by the intellectual controversies of the age.[11] We may well ask just what sort of compliment to a university that is. Blake said that he would not cease from mental strife, which sounds right for intellectuals, but Oxford, it seems, will not 'abide our question[s]', as Arnold himself might put it.[12] The compliment is one troublingly 'compounded' by issuing from the pen of a liberal historical thinker. Perhaps Arnold was so impressed by the idea of 'the return of [conservative] Burke's thought upon itself' (a kind of admission that he might be wrong), as to have engineered something of a return of Burke.[13] Jude himself is a natural Burkian, an abused orphan who hopes that familiarity with the abstruser musings of traditional Dons will eradicate contempt, and compensate for the heartlessly erased traditions of his (no-) village. What Marygreen conspicuously lacked (and Hardy spends a good deal of time establishing this [pp.5-7]) is evocative charm or a sense of timeless stability. As a result, Jude will experience himself as 'differences without positive terms': not quite the rustic swain ambiguously commended by the Gray of Gray's 'Elegy' dubious about the effects of ambition, Jude will occupy a new (no-) place, that of 'varsity man manqué'. This is obscurity, it seems, in a new, if only ironically 'improved', sense.

Another way of putting this might be to say that *Jude* is also full of Hardy's typically 'torque-like' effects as he embarrasses what seems to be his case, reversing significances and problematizing its own 'hermeneutic' clues. 'Signatures of all things I am here to read', thinks Stephen Dedalus as he faces the world in *Ulysses*, as, in his way, does Jude, but something, ideology perhaps, gets in his eyes and makes things as obscure as he is, both as himself and to himself. The reader needs to get used to the idea that it's part of the strength of *Jude* that it reveals so much about the 'obscurantism' Jude invokes as a cure for obscurity. As if in response to this, the novel's four-square, realistic, 'Hardy-in-history' effect is crossed with a disconcerting volatility: a touch of *Alice in Wonderland* (1865) attends a Jude and Arabella 'trotting along together' (pt.1, ch.8, p.39) after an escaped pig in a 'North Wessex' said to be full of them—almost developing trotters themselves, perhaps. (John Maynard suggestively describes Arabella as a 'pigwoman'.)[14]

Jude initially aspired to a bishopric—a kind of godhead in earthly form (p.27). But with Arabella he seems to descend into a porcine state, an identity in fact *lower* than that originally occupied. At this stage, Jude is not clearly capable of being able to say with 'Rabbi Ben Ezra' (a poem Hardy knew well), that 'a brute I might have been, but would not sink i' the scale'.[15] 'Better Socrates dissatisfied than a pig satisfied', wrote J.S. Mill, as if to explicate Jude and Arabella's marital tensions, and indeed this famous *mot* of his may have suggested them. Mill, a voice and presence in the novel, is mainly relayed by a Sue herself playing J.S. Mill to Arabella's porker, and husband Phillotson will soon grow as tired of the J.S. Mill thrown at his head by Sue as Jude had with the pig-part thrown further down by Arabella, demanding a 'quiet life'—as, one might say, something of a 'pig dissatisfied' with J.S. Mill (p.187). Pigs cannot speak, however, and merely grunt and squeal. A way of overcoming difficulties in representation here is to make a character use bad English, as a 'pig' might be imagined as doing. Consider, for example, the climactic events of Section One 'At Marygreen', in which Arabella's passion in the sense of her feeling desire for Jude gives way to passion in the sense of feeling very angry with Jude. This culminates in 'counter-cultural' clarity: 'I won't have *them* books here in the way' (pt.1, ch.11). But, interestingly, Arabella is of inconsistent linguistic register, and seems to be capable of expressing herself with pith and even propriety when the occasion demands. So we can conclude that here she uses a deliberate illiteracy to counteract what she considers Jude's 'ill-literacy' (she has earlier been characterised as assuming that he will 'get frightened a bit' [p.45] and relinquish his scholarly ambitions). This provides another way of showing how 'interpellation' works: the onset of 'financial realism' will bring him to his senses. Its *terminus ad quem*, as Jude is turned into a 'proper' husband, will, *inter alia*, supply her with lots of clothes.

Insensitive about Jude's sensitivity, Arabella does seem, at least momentarily, a wife from hell here, a 'poisonous remedy' indeed for a man who, we were given to understand, never had been 'in want of a wife', in Austen's phrasing, in the first place. Obviously, in terms of Jude's transcendent ambitions, life with Arabella seems decidedly *lowering* on several counts. But Hardy's ironic 'perspectivism' springs continual surprises, and no one character is collecting all the points here—in Thom Gunn's phrasing, there are 'no gods or vermin' in the case. It is perhaps finally in this sense that *Jude* may be said to be undoing 'the work of ideology' rather than in the idea that a working-class young man should go to Oxford. (This idea might itself be attacked for being 'conducive' to that carapace of 'customized concepts he had already shown to be damagingly exclusive in the form of Angel's priggish brothers in *Tess*.) Jude seems to be trying to 'liberate' himself in the wrong way, finds himself caught between the priggish and the piggish. He finds in Arabella, the 'pigwoman' he is linked to, a 'complete female animal' who will slaughter one with something too like enthusiasm. Both Jude and Arabella might be described as 'close to animals' in completely different senses, and what Hardy called 'animalism' both united and divided them. What Jude has been guilty of in particular, as the young couple address themselves to hog-slaughtering, is Hamlet-like 'awareness', 'thinking too precisely on the event' (4.4.41) (and citations of the Shakespeare play itself are well to the fore here), as they kill their (virtually) 'pet' pig. For example, Jude and Arabella have just been seen 'honeying and making love over the nasty sty' (*Hamlet* 3.4.93-4*)* (the 1996 film, *Jude*, ['starring' Christopher Eccleston and Kate Winslet] perhaps went a little too far with its honeying and making love *in* the nasty sty). Incidentally, 'event' for Hamlet meant the *result*, here the 'mere obtaining of meat' (bk.1, ch.10) which Arabella is able to concentrate on, but for Jude, it is definitely, and horribly, the sordid *process* by which it is obtained. The narrator, naturally complicit with a Jude who himself links easily to what we may as well call 'Hardy', makes an unforgettable event of the pig-killing for the reader, Jude and himself, and the keen eyes of reproach of the pig for its killers must strike chill indeed for one described earlier as being sensitively aware of his ill-treated fellow-creatures (bk.1, ch.2). Indeed, Sue herself will later exclaim, 'oh why must nature's law be mutual butchery?', Jude's sentiments exactly, and Arabella, after all, is a butcher's daughter. More extremely, Sue even wishes that 'some harmless form of vegetation might have peopled heaven', eliding all forms of carnal knowledge in a way that might prove less popular, or less than popular.

Yet, in a typically sly moment here it is shown that Jude and Sue are not themselves vegetarians—surely the logical upshot of their attitudes to the slaughter of creatures. They tuck into bacon and greens in the kindly peasant's cottage on their ill-starred jaunt from Melchester—a jaunt which harmed Sue's reputation and hastened her still more ill-starred marriage to Richard Phillotson (p.115). Besides, 'hog butcher' though she is, and unlike Sue, Arabella at least gives requital to desire (and, one suspects, is then condemned for doing so). 'Damned rough on us women', as she comments with a certain grin-and-bear-it likeableness the narrator's partisan attitude can't wholly disguise (p.269). (But we should be careful here: when David Trotter makes the prima facie good point that the pig-killing scene is 'curiously respectful to Arabella's pragmatism, and disrespectful to Jude's feeble protests',[16] unfortunately he does so with a disconfirming example. This is the point at which Arabella observes, odiously, of the dying pig which has just produced 'a tablespoonful of black clot', that they are 'artful creatures' who 'always keep back a drop like that as long as they can'.

And, by contrast, tender-hearted Sue is tough on her lovers, something of a belle-dame sans merci even, much inclined to hold them at arm's length until they die, like the leader-writer friend of whom she cruelly hopes that he 'died of consumption and not of me entirely' (p.123) (consumed, as it were by her refusal to consummate, not just consumption). It is Sue here who momentarily seems rather loathsome, not

Arabella, eager to hang the young leader-writer among her 'cloudy trophies'. The creature whom Jude was prepared to see as 'almost a divinity' after her scapegrace escape from 'the species of nunnery' (p.116) which was Melchester Training College is falling short of it now—or perhaps composing an interesting comment on the limitations of divinities themselves. As a 'Bridehead' Sue's name seems not merely a double but an at once self-cancelling and self-preserving sign: Sue wanted to have a 'special relationship' with the hymeneal, specialising in purely 'intellectual intercourse' ('Venus Urania', as she puts it [p.140]). Even her 'relations' with Jude were only initiated by pique at the thought of the possibility of his renewing 'intercourse' with Arabella (a pique fully justified in a context which shows 'sensitive' Jude at *his* worst as he completely loses the interest in Arabella's welfare he had professed after he had found 'satisfaction' with a jealously agitated Sue) (pt.5, ch.2): 'You haven't the least idea of how Arabella is able to shift for herself' (p.226).

Earlier, 'sensitive' Sue had excruciatingly *rehearsed* her marriage with Phillotson, already 'killing' to Jude (p.144), with Jude himself. As a confessed 'sensation-hunter' she is all too close, perhaps, on this occasion, to Walter Pater's injunction in *The Renaissance* (1893) to 'burn with a *hard*, gem-like flame' in seeking and savouring them. Later, admittedly as a kind of 'inverse' self (intellectually [or 'ideologically'] she and Jude have 'contrapuntally' changed places) she will leave him to die, even if only as something of a victim of her own self-punishing scrupulousness. So, despite the narrator's propaganda for them, it isn't entirely clear that 'coarse' Arabella is actually crueller than 'exquisitely fine' Sue and Jude. And, to return to hateful pig-sticking for a moment, it is also equally 'Hardy' who inserts the qualifying clause about this also being a mere 'obtaining of meat', bringing a touch of the 'dialogism' which corresponds to Arabella's powerful, if unwelcome, point that 'poor folks must live' (ch.10, p. 51), as indeed must 'rich folks' who are able to 'delegate'.

Scrupulous Hamlet types like Jude, thinking too precisely, consider pigs in relation to ourselves and find them altogether too close for comfort, part of 'the one life within us and abroad'[17] which Romanticism rediscovered (and Hardy 'rediscovered' in Romanticism). J.S. Mill also reminds us that his famous point 'better Socrates dissatisfied than a pig satisfied' also sustains the possibility that 'pigs' here might in any case be anthropomorphic: (wo-) men behaving badly rather than mere porkers. Arabella's 'piggery' bespeaks her father's vocation as well as her 'female animal' status as one fully acquainted with pig-parts in this part of North Wessex specifically said to be full of them. Yet the reader is alerted to the fact that the narrator has some special pleading on Jude and Sue's behalf which necessarily makes for unfairness to Arabella, a 'hog butcher' herself strangely akin to them. In the clash of values here, neither 'upper' nor 'lower' cases formally triumph. Indeed, if Jude is to be thought of as following Ecclesiastes' injunction to 'get wisdom, get understanding', he seems to get a knowledge of sorts from Arabella which he fails to get elsewhere.

Hardy leaves a (slim) space for Sue to fill in his description of Arabella as a female animal ('and nothing more'). But we are also shown that this 'nothing more' is not possible. For example, Arabella speaks, often to excellent effect, eloquently rallying Phillotson on the subject of runaway wives, a female devil quoting scripture on the subject of how females must be quashed (p.269), something she never is for long herself.

But the narrator repeatedly returns to the attack here. We have scarcely got used to seeing Arabella as *au naturel* in an unfortunate way when she is *equally* saddled with a repellant *artificiality*, caught dimple-making in the mirror (by a young husband himself repeatedly referred to as 'caught' [pp.46-7]) and wearing a hairpiece to eke out her own as a flirtatious young barmaid in Aldbrickham. Indeed the narrator, with yet more *parti pris*, has already made far too much fuss over Arabella's low knowledge of the 'adulteration' of beer (insinuating, perhaps, that she might herself have been 'taken in adulteration' at one time) (e.g., pt.1, ch.7), seemingly intent on investing her whole history as a barmaid with a slightly comic sense of horror which might well alienate the reader: it underlines the thorough imbrication of young Jude's educational aspirations with social ones once more. Yet, having prissily tilted things against the proletarian 'pubwoman', Hardy will later make amends with a pub-scene, of some prurience but also of a kind of proto-Joycian exuberance, as Jude watches his long-lost wife treat a (no doubt *soi-disant*)'Mr. Cockman' with 'ministering archness while he whiffed''(p.150).

Indeed, in general, although Hardy sets out to be nothing if not didactic, he is often at least as mischievous as sententious here—making of Sue a kind of inadvertent (D.H.) Lawrentian avant la lettre in her description of how 'cocksure' she was en route to describing her disastrous marital experiment (p.181), for example, and somewhat embarrassingly comparing her sexual incompatibility with Phillotson to someone's getting used to a 'wooden leg' (p.168), and we might almost describe this as Hardy's 'poking fun'. There is a definite instability of emotional 'register' here, although his facetiousness perhaps creates more empathy with Sue and her marital miseries. It isn't clear that the 'thumb in the scales' narrator has quite the same effect, though, in showing how Arabella's 'naturalness' naturally inclines her to artificiality, while her 'all-too-much' in the 'female department' is from the point of view of Jude and the narrator, itself a kind of 'lack' which slim Sue will subsequently eke out.

With more mischief-making, the male gaze itself is scrutinised in the process of establishing this, with Jude mentally comparing 'Arabella's amplitudes' with the 'apple-like' convexities of Sue's bodice (p.157). Despite the usual disclaimers by Hardy, it seems that *Jude* always was designed to be *risqué*. Indeed, we may be watching Hardy arrange his own 'exit velocity' from the novel genre itself here in making outrage—and consequent critical tirades—inevitable. Jude's weighing-up of respective female physicalities is indeed startling in its late-Victorian context, with Jude 'comparing and contrasting' like a potential examinee. Jude's mastery of the subject area is obviously felt, if in a slightly gamey way, to be a kind of 'education in itself', with Jude becoming a 'graduate' of sorts here, if only of 'Cupid's college'.[18] Apart from its subject, which is about 'desiring education', *Jude* is also about 'the education of desire'. If the subject (and object) of desire is, in a way, the subject of *Jude the Obscure*, what we seem to have learned is that desire feasts on what is, so to speak, lacking,[19] and Arabella, who enthusiastically requites passion, seems to fail to do so for that very reason—'rather rough on us women', as Arabella might put it herself. Hog-tied by marriage to 'Circe-like' Arabella, Jude's obvious fastidiousness primes him for 'spiritually-refrigerating' Sue. Yet, unsatisfied by ethereal Sue, Jude is obviously 'going after' Arabella at one point (pt.5, ch.2). As Hamlet might have said, that is the question: which woman is 'supplemental'? Was Arabella always intended to have 'missing portions', which would turn up in the form of Sue? Was Sue merely made out of what Arabella, a substantial figure, nevertheless, or rather *precisely because of this*, lacked? Arabella's 'too much' is less than Jude needs, while slender Sue, considered as a lack-supplier, is all that he hoped for (and will indeed finally prove all too much for him). In a parallel way, Arabella is an ironically 'natural' mother who fails in the role Sue will adopt, as the foster-mother of young Jude.

Indeed, *Jude* itself might be defined as a series of attempts to *matric*ulate, and Jude's attempt to be accepted by Oxford as an 'Alma Mater' runs in tandem with those other serial 'failed substitutes' for a 'natural' mother, the acerbic elderly females of Marygreen (Aunt Drusilla and the Widow Edlin), Arabella, and, most hurtfully, Sue. Lawrence, whose way with Hardy can be high-handed, gets real, and large-minded, purchase on this novel, predictably championing Arabella—but also, in a kind of 'return of his own thought upon itself', making much of Sue the Sensitive, the 'tremulous bundle of nerves' as Special Case.[20] So the novel makes us consider, not so much Sue as a character with destructive effects as the destructive effects on Sue of intrusive social and institutional matrices and the attitudes they foment. The novel promulgates the sense of the desirability of a kind of freebooting existentialism in life-choices, harmless unorthodoxy, innocuous eccentricity. In particular, Sue and Jude were 'never so happy' (pt. 5, ch.7) as when they embraced a nomadic, un-ambitious course, deserting the notion of life as a science of climbing.

So it needn't have been baleful in itself that Jude finally became a kind of pilgrim of *no progress*. According to Blake, 'without contraries is no *progression*'.[21] Hardy said his book was 'all contrasts'. But his 'quadrille',[22] as he called it (a kind of '*square dance*' made of 'queer unions' to take a phrase from 'companion-novel' *Tess*) leads formally to retrogression, not the expected advance. This 'quadrille' (finally something of a dance of death) ends, in formal terms fairly, and squarely, with Sue's shuddering return to Phillotson and Jude's fuddled return to Arabella, But, in John Donne's idiom, Hardy's 'firmness' also 'makes his *circle* just'. As if to emphasize an unhappy cycle rather than linear movement, Sue returns from Christminster to Marygreen to contritely face the music with Phillotson; and Jude, whose 'first movement' saw him journey from Marygreen to a sojourn in the 'heavenly city' of Christminster, returns to Christminster, at the end of part five. Finally he will travel in 'killing weather' (pt.6, ch.8) to his starting-point of Marygreen in part six, simultaneously to kiss Sue and initiate the process of killing himself in a kind of nomadic *Liebestod*. The novel's formal 'felicity' in J.L. Austin's sense[23] as a series of (extra-) marital 'performatives', culminates in the 'felicity' as one critic enthusiastically notes,[24] of Sue's full-blown marital re-encounter with Phillotson, as a church wedding is later followed by Sue's teeth-clenching sexual submissiveness. (Cf. the injunction from a well-known Victorian 'pundit': 'the modest woman seldom desires any gratification for herself'.)[25]

But what the (good) American critic fails to note is that the situation he indicates—the formal felicity of Sue's return to hubby—is sardonically counterpointed with Sue's deep *infelicity* in the prosaic sense of extraordinary unhappiness. Hardy, as if already following the implications of the words themselves, braids *formal* felicity with *experiential* infelicity as a final novelistic comment on society's not-so-little ironies. As if in confirmation of T.S. Eliot's reversal of Hardy's own epigraph, 'the letter killeth', to wit 'the *spirit* killeth, but the *letter* giveth life', Goetz is pointing out that Hardy is as an *artist* the beneficiary of the severe dictates Eliot was to deploy, but *failing* to point out that *as a human being* he is utterly opposed to them. Hardy is interested throughout in defamiliarizing the ways things are conventionally seen, represented or interpreted, by society, or the ways in which people are 'ha(i)led' into position by it: thus, Jude and Sue's 'legitimate' marriages were not those, merely represented as being so, while their 'sordid' and 'unsanctified' 'liaison' was indeed a 'true one'. Analogously, Jude's intellectual formation 'was not one' to college officials—they were 'programmed' to 'interpellate' as 'students' the 'millionaires' sons' (p.125), apparently. Perhaps it is such students who fail to understand even a word (according to the narrator's alarming announcement) of what we might call Jude's 'Latin creed karaoke' in the Christminster pub (later much regretted by Jude himself).

Sue's (repetition of) marriage was indeed one to those of ecclesiastical bent, like the officiating vicar here who paradoxically congratulates Sue and Phillotson on their 'second *attempt*', although the marriage service is itself a 'performative' which has ironically succeeded twice in their cases. But as a relationship it involved the sordid self-sacrifice of one of the parties and the 'defilement' of sexual relations in submission without personal affection. As if at once in requital for and fulfilment of Jude's intertextual leap into the cadences of the despairing Job, Widow Edlin will hasten over to Christminster to provide 'Job's comforter updates' on the progress of Sue's sexual submissiveness with a suspiciously keen narrative relish for the young woman's marriage bed disrelishings (p.315). This forms a kind of 'anti-ideologue's tale', becoming a potent allegory of how people, especially women, perhaps, may 'identify against themselves' and come to 'invest in their own unhappiness'[26]: 'creed-drunk' pt.6, ch.8, p.332) after the death of her babes at the hands of Jude, the 'quite Voltairean' Sue sacrifices herself on the altar of duty (and patriarchy), suffering sexual defilement at the hands of a man she still cannot stomach. 'Drunk' in a much commoner way, Jude is induced to remarry Arabella in befuddled despair helped by some discreet pressure from Arabella's butcher father and an assortment of ('Jehovah's'?) 'witnesses' (pt.6 ch.7 p.327).

Jude 'makes representations' which challenge Victorian formation narratives ('*Bildungsromane*') as much as they do 'marital states'. Those critics are clearly wrong to take at face value a reading which implies that Jude is merely an inveterate romantic whose 'desire is too difficult to tell from despair'. This plays into the hands of those privileged by society who, in Blake's idiom, 'think they have done us no injury'.[27] There is no 'exchange rate mechanism' for Jude's 'cultural capital', but the point is that this is not his fault. And, yet again, the development of the idea shows Hardy 'resisting the intelligence/almost successfully', as Wallace Stevens puts it. There is no doubt at all that the private, unpretentious, 'nomadic' existence he ascribes to Jude and Sue, a kind of 'licensed anomie', supposedly as a result of their social failure, is profoundly *attractive* to Hardy. The constrictions of Victorian conformity at Max Gate, and the domestic hell of 'two unequal wills',[28] like those of the Hardy domicile, with the silent rage of 'jealous foe' Emma to contend with (not least over the writing of *Jude* itself), all conspire to make the 'supra-marital' existence of Jude and Sue enviable.

Jude and Sue temporarily achieved a kind of notional 'solution' to several problems, and one which only a kind of 'Ibsenite' malevolence in their community combined with the work of ideology to 'utterly abolish and destroy'—against the optimistic inflection of Wordsworth's phrasing in the 'Immortality' Ode here. Hardy does step forward here as quite a serious 'ideology critic', and Jude and Sue are his deserving cases, or causes. But not everything is 'against them' here. Even the divorces of Jude and Sue were painless because the couples were not persons of consequence. To be written out of history, or in at the margins only, is, if a complex fate, hardly a wholly disagreeable one. (Hardy might just have been imagining here the hypocritical outcry that would have greeted his leaving Emma for the [in the end, insufficiently 'Shelleyan'] Mrs Henniker, one of whose names ['Florence'] is assigned to Sue herself.)

Jude will die as Arabella steals off with Vilbert (p.345), himself a highly nomadic purveyor of quack medicines (*pharmaka*) which will not bear scrutiny (an interesting role, as the book is in a sense all about them on the social and spiritual level). Vilbert, teller of tall tales to innocents, finally stole off with Arabella, and his trickster role was suggestive from the outset. In particular, when Vilbert failed to bring the grammars which would unlock Christminster's word-hoard for the schoolboy Jude (p.19), this seems a kind of anticipatory symbolism for his being traduced and excluded elsewhere, just as Jude's verbal abuse by his terrible Aunt Drusilla and physical abuse by Farmer Troutham themselves anticipated the rejecting college official Tetuphenay (p.96), whose letter was tellingly addressed to 'Mr J. Fawley, *Stone-Cutter*', with thoughts, from a dark and stony place of institutional power, (un-) helpfully suggesting a career set in stone. But even Tetuphenay would hardly have mattered tuppence-ha'penny if 'crookedness, custom and fear'[29] had not brought Sue and Jude low. Hardy succeeds here by presenting us with a *Bildungsroman* which fails. He enjoys his own 'genre trouble', impugning the social structures which enable *Bildungsromane* in the first place. Certainly it did come to seem as if Jude's 'estate' *had* been mysteriously 'ordered', after all: he was 'ha(i)led' into his '(no-) position', couldn't quite make it to a *déformation professionelle*. But it is quite typical of Hardy that the reader may well feel, for quite long stretches, that the results of this were not such a bad thing as the novel appears to commit itself to saying they were. Jude in particular is often ha(i)led into position(s) we or he might call degrading, so that the positive advantages to being a nobody in terms of social stationing—theoretically unha(i)led, if you will—assume a certain paradoxical visibility as part of the novel's formal and thematic achievement, as 'just the opposite' of 'what it came to say'.

Chapter 12

'Genetically Unmodified': *The Well-Beloved*

'Corpsing'—the actor's term for coming out of one's 'role'—might furnish an alternative title for *The Well-Beloved*[1] as it dramatises the death of desire in its 'hero', the sculptor Jocelyn Pierston. And we learn that Pierston in the last phase of his career is often (with unconscious felicity) referred to as 'posthumous' by his critics. ('His life seemed no longer a professional man's experience, but a ghost story' [p.140].) In this sense he achieves a paradoxical state aspired to by Hardy himself, which he referred to as 'dying before one is out of the flesh'.[2] 'Corpsing' might also refer here to the process which attends the failure of his 'Well-Beloved' *herself* to remain long in any earthly form which Pierston's 'desiring-machine' should select. Stage 'corpsing' might also entail a fit of the giggles, and this too would have its equivalent in the lightly sardonic humour of the novel as it moves towards narrative, but not carnal, fulfilment. But finally its true *terminus ad quem* is the ending of life of the artist *as* artist, pin-pointing the novella's sub-genre as *Kunstlerroman* or 'artist-novel'.

Patricia Ingham offers an intelligent and sophisticated feminist reading of the work in which it becomes largely about Pierston's arrogant patronage and self-absorption,[3] but this seems a little unkind: Pierston's rather gentle pursuit of his perennially unfulfilled, if 'gigantic' (p.109) fantasies ends in pathos, and he shows himself capable of magnanimity in the face of his failures—particularly towards Avice Caro III and her young Henri Leverre on their elopement (on the night preceding his own proposed wedding with Avice [!] [pp.133-39]).

Pierston's failure to keep his initial tryst with Avice Caro I in chapter one, partly because she had (innocently) taken the erotic initiative and partly because of his temporary involvement with Marcia Bencomb when he and she sought refuge from a storm under the hull of a fishing-lerret (p.15), was 'avenged', many times over, in his subsequent contacts with the Caros—and, in a more incidental fashion, by Marcia herself; and this 'relay of feminine requital' was completed by Pierston's slightly bruising encounter with the society lady, Nichola (sic) Pine-Avon. That the contingencies of 'desire' may bring in a kind of 'revenge' for social affronts is also shown in the sudden detachment of Pierston from Nichola herself, 'well-connected' and 'accomplished' as she is, in favour of the 'little laundress' Avice II (p.61). Avice I had been, if not rich, culturally aspiring, but Avice Caro II had sunk to washerwoman level. However, Pierston was, if anything, even happier to act the part of Munby, man of two worlds,[4] until he found she was already married (to one 'Ike' [pt.3, ch.1]). (Strictly, Avice II was 'Ann Avice Caro', but it seems this merely confirms for

Pierston, that she was 'An Avice Caro': in its quiet way, this is, throughout, a humorously melancholy text.)

With solicitude for Pierston combining with a prudent attempt to set the Caros up once more, Avice II encouraged the successful Jocelyn to pay court to her daughter Avice III, but Avice III herself couldn't help remarking that he was, so to speak, the Picture of Dorian Gray—so not quite Dorian. (Published in 1891, Wilde's tale of an ambitious attempt to cheat the years is an obvious influence on *The Well-Beloved*.) Jocelyn himself seems youthful for most of the novella, but, Dorian *renversé* after a final illness, might, ironically 'have passed for seventy-five', but is in fact a mere sixty-two [pt.3, ch.8].) Avice II, *herself* unflustered by his attentions when young (partly thanks of course to that—in fact, bad—marriage of hers), might amusingly declare that it would 'break her heart' if he failed to marry young Avice III (p.123)— but unfortunately no such declaration could be made by Avice III herself. In one significant moment, as Jane Thomas charmingly puts it, 'although he symbolically frees her foot from the Slingers limestone and returns her boot, she refuses to act the part of Cinderella to his creaky Prince Charming'.[5]

Avice III was a painful case, precisely because for Pierston she was 'quite the ideal'[6] as a kind of (Hegelian) *'Aufhebung'* of previous incar(o)nations of femininity. ('She was somewhat like her mother, whom he had loved in the flesh, but she had the soul of her grandmother, whom he had loved in the spirit' [p.124]). However, although Avice III seems to be a handy 'resumé' of former 'loves', Pierston is merely the more deceived in the thought that 'time' has 'reserved' her for him (p.144). Similarly, with final irony, Avice II muses on what will prove to be her deathbed that the union of Pierston and Avice III will make a fittingly *'artistic finish'* (p.131), but Hardy's 'artistic finish' results precisely from *not* having this happen. (It also becomes clear in any case that he loves the new incarnation specifically as 'reminiscence': he is in love with *the genealogical itself* as a 'trace', a flickering 'absent-presence'. His 'genealogical' quest entails 'a series of slippages', in a constant play of 'betweenities'—to cite a memorable Austen family coinage.[7] In a sense, then, Pierston finds himself perennially caught 'between repetitions'.

Hardy seems to be playing with a Lacanian idea avant la lettre here: the narrative premise is that *'desire remains unfulfilled'*, which will resolve into different versions. Narrative climaxes, especially Hardy's, deal with, perhaps even 'traffic in' 'the fulfilment(s) of desire', so there is a particular piquancy to this final narrative outing of Hardy's in which nothing of the kind occurs for a protagonist himself obsessed with the theme. The knowledge it thus withholds from its hapless protagonist is: if (his) desire *were* ever to encompass its physical 'end(s)', it would merely find an 'other place' to begin, dissatisfied in its mere 'satisfaction' through its immediate deprivation of 'fantasy fulfilments'. Ironically, then, the Caros help Pierston fulfil himself artistically through their perennial capacity to frustrate him.

In terms of 'normal' fulfilments he fares no better with Marcia Bencomb, the female offspring of the *other* successful stone-cutter of Portland. Marcia proved to be a proud, hot-tempered spendthrift—used to illustrate the idea that *Romeo and Juliet* would have ended, not merely in tears (as it did), but in tears made out of the rediscovery of the inveterate rivalry of the respective families (p.32). Parted for decades after their initial entanglement, with its inevitable contretemps, as the second wife of young Henri Leverre's father Marcia was 'nominally' hunting up 'Pierston' when she mistakenly encountered Avice II—also a Pierston, by marriage—fatefully acquainting her stepson Henri with Avices II and III as a result (p.133).

Subsequently, however, in her pursuit of the eloping pair (Henri Leverre and Avice III), Marcia re-encountered Pierston himself, not 'just married', as anticipated, but 'just jilted' in favour of Marcia's stepson Henri himself, and hence ironically 'free' once more. But in finally agreeing to 'marry' Marcia—a possibility here as young Leverre's father has predeceased her—in a sense Pierston did *not* do so as *his desire has failed*, as Ecclesiastes the Old Testament preacher, in a way, predicted. And Marcia herself is now a crone who comes to church in a wheelchair (p.172). In this respect, like the protagonist of a minor Ezra Pound poem, Pierston might be said to have intended a 'grand passion', but ended with a 'willingness-to-oblige'.[8] Interestingly, Pound, the supreme *aesthete*, is scornful about his 'character'—but isn't the ironic insinuation here, which Kierkegaard would have relished, that Pierston's true talent, despite the artistic form stamped on his life, lay in the realm of the *ethical*, or, less formally, in his kindly disposition? For example in the last chapter, as the solitary mourner at the funeral of little Avice II (a being of no social cachet) in 'the bleakest churchyard in Wessex', with 'raw rain' flying 'level as missiles' (on this 'Isle of Slingers'), we learn that he had been a 'fickle lover in the brief, faithful friend in the long run' (bk. 3, ch.8).

This late-flowering little novella is a still underestimated sample of Hardy's feline 'dance of the intellect among narratives', as Ezra Pound himself might have called it. Although the theme is of serious import, Hardy does not cease to play games with it, generating conceits as he shuttles between 'abstraction' and 'empathy' here. For example, the Caros were, in a sense, the ultimate *natives*, 'the Portland peninsula made flesh'. Sustained by (base) stone-cutting, they are ironically 'turned to stone again' in Pierston's ('superstructural') statuary.

Pierston's father, though never 'on-stage' here, had himself been a rather 'flinty' old stone-cutter well able to cut out lesser rivals like the Caros—and, as a result, afford for Pierston the expensive training which will enable Jocelyn himself to 'cut stone' to more permanent effect. His sculpting is a (dubiously) 'evolved' form of 'stone cutting' itself 'victorious in the struggle for existence' at the expense of 'the native(s)'. Hardy's conceit here is that the adage 'like father like son' applies, apparently against the odds, at this more abstract level. Only Jocelyn's emotional 'defeats' at the hands of the Caro girls ironically 'compensate' the Caros for the Pierston family's having won the economic battle hands down. (A further irony for us, not available to Hardy, is that one Anthony *Caro* was later to become a sculptor of some eminence.)

Jocelyn's career illustrates the idea that culture does not merely bespeak the 'history of the victors'; it partakes of (or results from) it: and 'superstructural' Kensington, where Pierston too easily flourished (p.33), gets satirical treatment. On the other hand, the peninsula itself, suggestively described at one point as looking like 'a vast *animal*', is made of 'oolite' (p.7), or 'egg-stone'. This suggests that this particular 'rock of ages', a neglected 'wonder', already 'offers itself' in the form of a genetic building-block which may be described as 'permeable'—porous, and pierceable, and so 'hymeneal'. As Jocelyn's normally prosaic friend Somers points out, the 'island' *itself* is such a 'romantic place' that 'a man might love a scarecrow or a turnip-lantern here' (p.89). Kensington is more obviously an 'enviable' address than Portland, if only it's implied, on the basis of the false values the novel quietly impugns. For example, for Pierston Portland contained the Caros, and, as their name also suggests, the Caros were 'inexpressibly dear' (p.61), in addition to being racially interesting as, genealogically speaking, the immemorial 'Latin' relics of Roman occupation. They were also inbred, and this too was a bonus, avoiding that 'alloy-ing' effect in genetic modification of a lover's children Hardy deals with in a poem, and in *Jude* (1895)[9] (in this respect a kind of 'companion' to *The Well-Beloved* [1897]). Another irony Hardy has tucked in here is the attitude of the natives, themselves genetically fashioned from the genes of alien imperial conquerors, to outsiders.

The Caros were ideal 'material' for Pierston in this respect, given the customary 'peninsularity' of the natives who treated the mainlanders as foreigners[10]—what they themselves describe as 'kimberlins' (p.123, p.143). This, although I'm guessing, is surely a version of 'chamberlains'—those cowed, compliant shufflers. So their aversion to 'others' suggests proud independence, resistance to 'hegemonisation', creating a kind of parallel between *social* and *genetic* self-sufficiency. This is underscored as we move to the third phase of Pierston's infatuation: there is a revealing passage which recapitulates Philip Larkin's sense of 'littoral' existence ('still going on, all of it, still going on') in his late poem 'To the Sea':

> The canine gnawing audible on the pebble-bank had been repeated ever since at each tide, but the pebbles remained undevoured. Men drank, smoked and spat in the inns with only a little more adulteration in their refreshments and a trifle less dialect in their speech than of yore (p.101).

With its 'grace dissolved in place', as T.S. Eliot puts it (in his own sea-girt 'Marina'), Portland itself sustains fantasy by retaining 'indigeneity'. It offers proudly parochial, anti-metropolitan self-containedness, parallel with the idea of a kind of 'genetically unmodified' and unfenced existence. It is possible to argue, then, that *The Well-Beloved* is a clever recapitulation of Hardy's career-long thematic concerns. Underestimated by many, though not Proust, as a suitable artistic closure, *The Well-Beloved*'s sportive ironies are much to be preferred to the plodding discursivity of the *Life* to come.

For its perennially returning native the salty actuality of Portland is contrasted with the effetely prosperous drawing rooms in which one might encounter 'a representative of Family, who talked positively and hollowly, as if shouting down a vista of five hundred years from the Feudal past' (p.50)—which sounds deliciously disrespectful. Yet much writing about him has sustained the idea of Hardy as a deferential writer, prone to snobbism(s). The tone of barbed wit here was underscored in the serial version of the novel. That version ended with a sardonic 'Ho! Ho! Ho!' from Jocelyn[11] (p.191) in the face of life's final little irony in the form of the death of desire, the 'etiolation of Portland as an artistic stimulus',[12] and the filling in of those fountains in the 'Street of Wells' (p.151) which have a transparently allegorical significance here.

They represent the *sources* of Jocelyn's inspiration and the *origin* of desire: the end to his quest for satisfaction brings, for the reader, a complex and satisfying sense of an ending. Noting how Pierston '*sat darkling*' with the dead Avice II beside him (and his last love Avice III irrevocably lost through elopement), Hardy is evoking as 'intertext' the stanza of Keats' 'Ode to a Nightingale' here, in which its speaker is said to be 'half in love with easeful death'.

The Well-Beloved is consistently Hardy-esque in being inspired by place, but rather in a *meta*-sense of being *about* 'being inspired by place', offering a kind of *précis* of previous efforts in the area, so to speak. Desire itself is evoked by a kind of *genius loci*. Even femininity itself is seen as a particular expression of this fundamental 'topophilia'.[13] (For example, Jocelyn's less than wholly passionate response to Avice I partly owes its attenuation to the fact that, although 'local to the bone', she could not 'escape the tendency of the age' in her susceptibility to the insipid cultural influences of the mainland [pt.1, ch.2].) So this curiously 'marginal' (sc. 'marginalized') example of his work is, ironically, a kind of 'essence of Hardy' which might equally constitute its 'centre'.

Yet even Hardy's admirers seem to need to be reassured that *The Well-Beloved* is a textual place to harbour in, despite its incorporation of Hardy's characteristic obsessions. D.H. Lawrence's dismissal of it was perhaps a symptom of his own persistent resistance to seeing 'desire' as other than a 'natural' phenomenon, evoked by 'culture' as well as 'nature' (while for John Fowles, who also has a significant 'creative' response to Hardy, 'taken straight, the book cannot be judged as anything but a disastrous failure by Hardy's standards elsewhere').[14] By contrast, desire in Hardy is a Lacanian 'property', always 'exceeding' its object, and, almost by definition, eluded by it. Lawrence is also intent on 'the right true end of love', with a more controversial and perhaps finally constricting attitude to 'women'. Despite Hardy's apparently 'sex-ist' generalizations, there's finally a much greater empathy with the feminine in his work. Ironically, as Rosemary Sumner intuits, Hardy is almost attaining the island of modernism here, and so closer kin than ever to the D.H. Lawrence who, in this incarnation, seems to repudiate him.[15] But there's also a hint of James Joyce in this portrait of the artist as a 'youngish older man', resulting from the work's 'makeover' of Jocelyn as a 'Dorian Gray' figure (who was, finally, 'not one', as Jocelyn's final infatuation, Avice III, made clear enough [p.123]). There also seem to be some distinctly 'Joycian' proto-'modernist' sentences in which sense or signified drops away in ironic contemplation of their signifying function: 'a warm-hearted, emotional girl was Lady Mabella, who laughed at the humorousness of being alive' (p.43); and in the claim that Mrs Pine-Avon 'was the first intellectual woman he had seen . . . that night, except one or two as aforesaid' (p.44). But such phrasings also serve to indicate Jocelyn's artistic (but also 'native-ist') alienation, indicating that the *beau monde* is not as 'beau' as it considers itself to be, and so 'mundane'. Jocelyn's *own* distaste for it provides basis for his desire for a woman who is not just a Platonic transcendence flitting from carcass to carcass (as Hardy, following Shelley, seems initially to be saying), but, more specifically a female emanation of the spirit of place—as a feminised *genius loci* which will provide an anthropomorphic version of his 'topophilia'. Murmurs and scents of the 'island' seem to pervade the drawing-room in which he hears of the death of the first Avis Caro, her withdrawal to ultimate distance awakening Pierston's desire with a vengeance, while his immediate, and 'superior' environment, suffering by the comparison, attracts his sardonic scorn.

But if Hardy floods the 'socialite' perspective with irony, equally he lets irony play over its apparent antithesis, the realm of 'true love', where 'naught may endure but mutability', a Shelleyan theme recalling not only the 'imaginative promiscuity'[16] of Shelley's 'Epipsychidion', but his 'Hymn' to that 'Intellectual Beauty' which 'visits with inconstant glance/ Each human heart and countenance'.[17] As often, Hardy is providing a kind of creative commentary on poems which mean intensely to him here. Yet in a sense the story is also one of the resistance to its own, unShelleyan counter-intuition, that of Wallace Stevens' 'Peter Quince at the Clavier'—that 'beauty is momentary in the mind/ The fitful tracing of a portal. / But in the flesh it is immortal'.

Although, pursuing an implication of the Marxian metaphor of base and superstructure, the 'base' marble hacked from the isle becomes the glorious sculpture —the 'privileged' 'superstructure'—in other respects the art becomes a metaphor for the superstructural existence itself as something suspect. And in this sense too we can say that Hardy's 'firmness makes his circle just', permitting him 'to end where he began'. The author of *Under the Greenwood Tree* (1872) made much of being 'rooted in one dear perpetual place', and 'desire(s) of upward mobility' were dubious. We see that the novelist, though in social terms well-travelled, has not 'changed his mind', as, taking stock of the evening party of the ambitious, Pierston finds that 'no principles of wise government had place in any mind, a blunt and jolly personalism as to the Ins and Outs animating all' (p. 41). Hence, s/he who finds the John Bright dictum (1858), cited here, that *'the nation of every country dwells in the cottage'* (p.45) congenial can expect short shift from these worldlings. The reader should intuit that the quest for the well-beloved is not finally separable from a political 'animus'. For example, it is Jocelyn's prosaic friend Somers who finally marries the refined Nichola Pine-Avon, and his solid 'society' marriage seems to set the seal on his artistic mediocrity as Somers sets himself to the task of 'executing many pleasing aspects of nature addressed to the furnishing householder through the middling critic' (p.118), as Hardy wickedly puts it.

So *The Well-Beloved* broaches old Hardy subjects in a new Hardy 'register' which needs a little getting used to. In its new way it is successful, particularly with respect to the ways it finds to station itself between the butterfly attachments recommended by the Shelley of 'Epipsychidion' and the pusillanimous prudentiality of the lovers of Browning's 'The Statue and the Bust'.[18] These are poems Hardy cites almost obsessively. In the Browning poem, both lovers were immortalised as works of art, 'sculpted' as if in ironic compensation for their failure to consummate their passion. But the narrator of the Browning poem did not approve of their emotional continence, their conviction that 'the world and its ways have a certain worth'.

Hence Lawrence's judgement on *The Well-Beloved* as 'sheer rubbish, fatuity'[19] is itself close to being that, particularly as *The Well-Beloved* 'distils' some lessons from earlier work of Hardy which he himself admired. (But Hardy does make a mistake in having Pierston begin the story of his infatuation(s) to Somers with some pre-Avice incarnations of the Well-Beloved—'Laura' and 'Elsie' for example [pt. 1, ch.7]. As Tess O'Toole perceptively notes, 'it is only when [Pierston's] fetish takes a genealogical bent that the narrative takes shape'.)[20] Lawrence would not have liked the ambiguously 'Platonic' transports of the Shelley poem any more than he would the prudent continence of the lovers in the Browning one. Hardy, however, cunningly notes how Pierston's ultra-romantic, Shelleyan attitude issues in more scrupulous treatment of women than that of his moralizing friend Somers, who seems, pre-maritally, to be having furtively casual sex with his artist-models, but still enjoys laying down the law to the naïve Pierston anyway (pt.1, ch.6). At the same time, Hardy treats Pierston's asexual settling-down with Marcia, an apparent concession to Browning's 'world and its ways', with sympathetic irony. In the novella the question of desire itself is involved with 'thematic repetitions' of Jocelyn's 'internal distancing' from what seems to be his allotted role, and the difficulty he has in 'knowing his place' in a double sense, marked as he is by social 'differences without positive terms', apparently. There is a persistent insinuation of Jocelyn's anomalous social 'stationing' as an unwitting victim of his own artistic 'superstructuralism', alienated from High Society but, equally, no longer quite 'indigenous' enough to 'settle down' *as* a 'cottager', if he imagines himself prepared to do so *with* one.

So the theme of 'desire' is socially mediated, more so than the novella immediately intimates. Jocelyn's sardonic observation that affairs of state are ruled by 'a blunt and jolly personalism' (p.41), relating to the ins and outs of individual careers, without any real sense of political responsibility, is related to 'the place of Jocelyn's desire', and 'desire of place'. For Pierston the word itself has a social as well as a natural register, and the novella itself is thus an affair of 'place-men' in sharply divergent, favourable and unfavourable senses. Hardy's reanimation of romanticism mingles a Shelleyan repudiation of the fashionable world and the stultifying actualities of the political process with the novella's more obviously Shelleyan allusion to the glancing, 'uncontainable' quality of desire. Depicting the consequences of a failure to 'know one's place', the text shows Jocelyn's alienation from the High Life which has 'forgotten its origins'. Yet to the indigenous of Portland he is readily identified ('hailed') as a fine gentleman and foreigner. He thus becomes, in Julia Kristeva's phrasing, something of a 'stranger to himself' in the form of what Hardy described as *his* 'simple self that *was*' in the poem 'Wessex Heights', dated 1896 (and so contemporaneous with *The Well-Beloved* itself).

The novella suggests the baseless nature of the life Pierston has made for himself, as neither 'native' nor 'of' the metropolitan world, doomed to an unhappy 'hybridity'. This is partly why he can never know quite 'what he wants' (some of F.R. Leavis's comments on Hardy himself to the effect that he 'knows what he is, what he wants, and what he values' are particularly 'unhappy'). The final point the novel seems to be making, then is that, as Adorno puts it, 'in a false life there is no right way to live'.[21] His desire is negotiating social contradiction(s). It is not just an embodiment of nature wandering at its own sweet will (and failing to find 'what will suffice').

The novella is 'handling' desire and 'its object', foretells the famous 'little object *a*', of Lacanian invention. Elisabeth Roudinesco, almost as if explicating *The Well-Beloved* itself, defines the 'little object *a*' as 'it came to stand for something left over, between the real and the nonsymbolisable: the object as lack of and the object as cause of desire'.[22] (But if Lacan will do something towards understanding *The Well-*

Beloved, the reader might easily feel that *The Well-Beloved* will do more towards an understanding of Lacan.) For us, Hardy almost seems to be toying with the possibility that 'little object "a"' is indeed 'a vice' ('Avice'). As 'The Statue and the Bust' puts it, 'the end in sight was a vice' (that's to say, 'Avice' with a little 'a' and a suggestive spacing). So Hardy's name 'Avice' is a particularly good *trouvaille* here, pursued as it is also by the familiar theme of the *rara avis*. Lacanian *avant la lettre* (particularly with respect to this particular letter), Hardy explores ideas of 'the object of desire' *qui pourtant n'existe pas*, as he keeps demonstrating—slightly against his own will. Even 'Avice' here is divided into the different beings whom she names, 'one name of many shapes' rather than the 'one shape of many names',[23] as the Shelley phrase from 'Epipsychidion' which suggested the book (and furnished its epigraph) has it. Announcing a Shelleyan programme[24] confirmed as such by Harold Bloom as well as by J. Hillis Miller, Hardy qualifies his sense of the infinity which his emphasis on 'desire' and (its) 'utopia' suggests with grimmer interventions from 'the Lords of Limit'.

Hardy used a phrase relevant to his own case in referring to 'The Mayor of Casterbridge' as 'the self-alienated man', and Jocelyn's 'structure of feeling' makes the description even more appropriate in his case. The self-alienated Pierston is finally playing a kind of *'fort-da'* game with the peninsula itself (as Freud's grandchild did with the reel) in an attempt to master a sense of absence and isolation. Hardy also describes how, on the stormy night which brought Pierston and Marcia Bencomb together, thanks to the shifting, indeterminate nature of Chesil Bank (pt.l, ch.5), the 'peninsula' *is* a 'virtual island', or rather, itself a 'betweenity', *ni l'un ni l'autre*, and as such an 'objective correlative' for a game played out in terms of the shifting nature of personal and class relations. (The ambiguity is also confirmed by the ancient name for Portland, that of 'Isle Vindilia' [pt.2, ch.3].) This game, as Hardy implicitly shows, might easily become a metaphor for social 'liminality', for someone doomed to find an assured sense of (social) 'being'—and hence of self—eluding him. As a related source of insecurity, desire, never truly possessed except by that which eludes its possession, lives in casual impulses as much as in deep-sworn vows. Its startling ephemeralities, 'too like the lightning which does cease to be ere one can say it lightens', as Shakespeare's Juliet, in lines cited here (p.31, p.38) puts it, combines with its equally disconcerting persistencies. Jonathan Dollimore has interesting points in an article about how with 'a flick of feeling', in Wallace Stevens' phrase, disgust may succeed desire, or vice versa,[25] although with respect to *The Well-Beloved* 'disgust' would have the weak, Johnsonian sense of '(slight) distaste'.

Hardy creates a final extra irony in the face of Pierston's inability to find 'the measureless consummation that he dreams', as the mores of Portland seem positively to facilitate rather than discourage 'fulfilment'. Especially exciting for outsiders would be the fact that 'island custom' (p.17) here permits or even enjoins your possession of the betrothed before the mere formalities of nuptial rites. We might put this—a little heartily—by saying that 'bedding before wedding' seems to be the 'island' slogan, but 'heartiness' in 'the place of desire' is obviously the last thing Jocelyn himself would wish for. According to Joyce a *pier* is 'a disappointed bridge',[26] and in a parallel way this 'island which is not one', this peninsula, seems finely to fit a *Pier*ston who specializes in what Joyce's Stephen Dedalus would call *'almosting* it'. Pierston is doomed, as it were, to pierce *stone* only, in a study in punctured idealism: as Hardy insists, despite his being 'subject to gigantic fantasies still' (p.109), no woman 'had been *wrecked* by him' (p.140). Oddly, as this last phrase suggests, Pierston is depicted as 'pursuing desire', in a way that the reader might easily find alienating. But, despite this '*assumed* Don Giovanni-ism' (in Joyce's idiom), he becomes endearing through compunction and scrupulousness—his genuine concern for the women who momentarily focus his sense of the everlasting 'Aphrodite' (p.22).

Pierston perhaps lacked 'animalism', a Hardy coinage used of Angel in *Tess*: art and the desire which informs it are doomed to go on 'putting divinity about'[27] objects known 'as a phenomenon of *distance*'. In this way the D.H. Lawrence idea of 'fatuity' might return in a different form to suggest that the novella is 'about' the fatuities which pursuing desire entails, and the desire of death it might finally also entail—although, as we have seen, theme and treatment here are not themselves fatuous in the way that Lawrence suggests. In fact the theme of *The Well-Beloved* is rehearsed in Hardy's startling poem, 'He Abjures Love', in which accepting the death of desire seems to entail accepting death—although the poem finally rounds on itself and its own 'logic'. For the speaker of the poem, it looks as if the reflections occasioned by 'the abjuring of love' will finally lead to his not doing so. For Pierston, however, this seems, equally finally, not to be an option.

Chapter 13

Screening Hardy: Some Recent Adaptations [*Jude, Tess, The Woodlanders*)

Jude

Like Jane Austen, Hardy is 'open' to a wider process of what we have learned to call a process of 'cultural semiosis', involving a kind of 'canonisation from below, through film, television and stage adapatation. As Roger Sales has remarked, it would be 'arrogant' not to give some consideration to a process by which canonic authors reach a considerably 'wider' audience. But even if we are not merely hopelessly canonic, in Frank Lentricchia's encouraging phrasing, but hopelessly textual (or linguistic) as well, much can be learned about the given novel itself from the attempt at adaptation. The moral of this chapter, however, is indeed that the process, however differently or divergently undertaken, is infernally difficult to carry out, or off.

This film of *Jude* got a good deal more critical attention than the other two adaptations. A slightly surprising feature of it (as directed by Michael Winterbottom and 'starring' Christopher Eccleston and Kate Winslet) is that there also seems to be a good deal of fully recorded unclothed sexual activity going on in it, despite the fact that the original Hardy emphasis was laid on the relative ethereality of the Jude and Sue connection.[1] This we might assume is on Mark Twain's 'if that don't fetch them I don't know Arkansaw' principle, avoiding the disastrous drop in curiosity which might accompany a 'U' certificate for a film which might then be held signally to have failed to take advantage of Hardy's 'quadrille' (his word) of 'queer unions' (in fact it attracts the slightly amusing 'PG' label). According to the *Guardian* this was 'a film Truffaut might have made', according to the *Independent* it was 'a triumph', while for the *Daily Mail* it was a 'rare, startling and devastating film', and the *Evening Standard* gave it 'high marks for literary fidelity'. [2]

This was a most surprising verdict. Jude doesn't die at the end of the film, nor does he re-unite with Arabella, and nor does the climax refer to the philistine festivities of Christminster as a frame for Jude's Job-like mutterings as he lies dying. Nor does Arabella elope with Vilbert, and no wonder—he isn't in fact 'in the frame' here, though a significant presence (and absence) in the novel. Nor is there a Widow Edlin to hurry over to Christminster to administer her Job's comfortings to a Jude much inclined to see himself as Job, with an essential tittle-tattling update on Sue's joyless cavortings with her 'ecclesiastically correct' husband. (Widow Edlin was herself something of a posthumous stand-in for Jude's terrible Aunt Drusilla, but she, though 'there', is sentimentally softened into aunty normalcy by June Whitfield.)

Again, instead of begging a dying Jude to leave her alone in her 'defilement', in fact, in an interview with Sue which looks to be part of an 'ongoing situation' very unlike what the Hardy novel envisions, Sue begs Jude 'not to give up on her', which picks up on an earlier invention of hers. So, in general, if this is an example of relative literary fidelity, one wonders just what 'unfaithful' screenplays might be like.

On the other hand, perhaps the film shouldn't be saddled with a tabloid newspaper's account of its virtues. And this one does seem to be aiming less for that kind of 'fidelity' than aspiring to be something of a combination of 'commentary', 'transposition' and 'analogy' (to take the three forms of adaptation specified by Geoffrey Wagner).[3] This was supposedly a holistic designation of 'adaptation' modes, but if these categories were originally supposed to apply wholesale to individual films, *Jude* definitely mingles the three. Neil Sinyard points out that adaptations have to change their original, to enter into the new combination which allows for a temporal lapse from the original cultural context, with a new directing personality and a consequent sense of new thresholds, new anatomies.[4] But of course these have to carry their own forms of artistic justification in performing something of a transposition, as opposed to their merely performing a kind of artistic 'typeover' operation on an obliterated original.

The screenwriter (Hossein Amini) was dismayed by the decision of the director here over how to 'end' the film, a compromise formula perhaps consequently with something of that slightly depressing 'designed by a committee' feeling. *Jude* finally can't really handle the tentative 'optimism' implied, surely? Is Sue really going to run away from Phillotson *again*? Or rather, where is she, exactly, at this point? In any case, Jude has *not* re-married Arabella, so Hardy's hugely sardonic artistic investment in this criss-cross path to propriety and seemliness, to a final ecclesiastical correctness which crucifies, has been by-passed. And Jude's death, no less than his earlier fuddled perception 'that there is something wrong with our social formulas' is surely an absolutely necessary terminus ad quem here, even if precise details of the plot are expendable (itself a hard saying for a Hardy novel). Instead, the emphasis was placed on the idea of its 'taking three generations to do what I tried to do in one' [Jude on his return to Christminster], which seems to underline a simple *mistake*, a (culpable) naivety over how society 'functions' rather than anything of 'radical' implication.

This moment of revelation, together with Sue's 'imploding' compliance with all she previously despised, combined with Jude's fuddled surrender to Arabella, makes a complete statement of a kind of wholesale cultural despair. In Hardy this is amplified and overdetermined as part of a 'narrative' of 'what happened to romanticism' in the senses both of the romanticism of folk art, and the romanticism of the revolutionary decade of the 1790s.[5] The film had intimations of this interest the novel had in 'whatever happened to radicalism', as it were, but dissipated them. (Perhaps one might just about see the film's 'sense of an ending' functioning as an exquisite reference to the *origins* of *Jude*, in the pathetic excitements of Hardy over Mrs Henniker and his plaintive requests for her to be a little more 'Shelleyan'. Quite. (['Do[n't] give up on me, Tom'?!])

Indeed, with newspapers ecstatic, we might be allowed to spend a little time on inappropriate 'substitutions' without being intemperately unfair. For example, Jude and Sue didn't sleep together here only because at first Sue said she 'wasn't ready' (not invoking the 'Venus Urania' principle with which the original Sue daunted her suitors)—presumably to make this Sue a more 'generic' example of those who bolt from partners in the 1990s; but the 'original' Sue was 'special', as even D.H. Lawrence conceded: to be fair, they do indeed sleep together here because of the apparent imminence of Jude and Arabella 'getting together', as in the novel, but they show no solicitude about her over her anxiously announced problems.

It was the amusing 'relay' of their concern about Arabella which complicates the purely sexual tensions of the episode in such a way as to keep Sue, if not Jude, reasonably likeable in situations in which the reader musn't be alienated from them, even if s/he is from nearly everything else. It was also intimated that Arabella was simply cold and hard here (pure negative), rather than coarse and buxom (ambiguous), necessarily so by comparison with Sue. And in the film she was also unintellectual (pure negation) rather than so spiritedly anti-intellectual (ambiguous) as to turn into a philosopher of sorts herself—so the label 'Arabella' now indicates a character functioning in a quite different way. The film, that's to say, casts a colder eye, and in doing so it seems to do something to desensitise Jude and Sue themselves, almost '*nineteen*-ninety-ists' avant la lettre and the worse for it. For example, Phillotson confessed to *Jude* here, not to his friend Gillingham, that Sue and he made a sort of Platonic couple as moieties of the same paradoxical personality, Shelleyan twins.

But this was mainly conveyed by Jude and Sue's happy sense of 'tertiary education' prattling—important in the novel—but very little of it survives here (when it does surface, as in Sue's appreciation of Jude's copy of Catullus poems, the film becomes much 'stronger', against the ethos of its apparent commitment to 'modernist' transposition, suggesting that even films partake in a kind of 'chronotopic imperative'). Films are made of images, we know, but unfortunately the 'Jude and Sue connection' is 'made out of words' in a rather special sense. Their 'wordy' relationship should release a glorious sense, especially for Jude, of a male-female relationship based on intellectual affinity as well as 'basic instinct', a marriage of true minds to which several impediments would subsequently be admitted.

As we saw, Phillotson also admits openly to *Jude* here that Sue finds him physically repulsive, in an unusual abrogation of male vanity. As in the novel, but now much more so, Phillotson is dangerously noble at this point, and indeed he came close to looking like the 'hero' of the novel itself when he relinquished Sue. Here it seems distinctly mean of Jude not to say something encouraging or consolatory here. Kingsley Amis has a culminating phrase in a poem about 'our own nasty defeats, nastier victories', and it seems clear that the film lets Jude, whom we 'relate to' as 'agreeable loser', win a rather nasty one hands down here. The trouble is partly that the novel *itself* is on the verge of making Sue and Jude a little troublesome at points, and has to work hard not to 'lose' the reader's sympathies in this respect.

This also shaded Sue's running away from Phillotson in a way Hardy might not have liked. She tormented Phillotson by alleging a theoretical right to 'be with' Jude, but jibbed when it came to simply jumping into bed with him. In the novel, Jude entrained them for impersonal Aldbrickham, not (suspicious) Melchester, but Sue declined the offer of a single room and there was no question of that kind of 'stand-off' here. It's true that 'fleshy' Arabella did turn up like the proverbial bad penny and a kind of 'one-night stand' with one's wife seemed yet again to be on offer. But, by occluding the strange relay of concern for Arabella's welfare (marital difficulties—with pub-bound Australian husband—once more rather awkwardly 'cut') amid the sexual tensions of the scene, Sue became more 'ordinary', seemed less sensitive, or less than sensitive even.

Also (incidentally?) Hardy was not so unkind as to suggest that even Sue would herself be unkind enough to demand that they should (as it were) 'sleep together' without 'sleeping together' as they do here. When Sue does finally agree to 'go to bed' (although they are already in it), thanks to Arabella's threatening erotic proximity, she immediately takes all her clothes off, precisely not what one would imagine Sue doing (and not what Jude would want, surely?). While Kate Winslet, good actress though she be, is perhaps a little buxom to play Sue, and, in the film persona she presents, is definitely a coper; as such she is not completely suited to playing the 'bundle of [not-quite-emancipated] nerves' Hardy said Sue was. In general the film seems as much a 'hoard of de- (con) - structions' as *hommage*.

There are points here which show the possibility of intelligent 'transposition', refracting rather than merely attempting to 'reproduce': for example, in the case of the heavily-accented Scottish agitator who points out that 'their sort' (the Christminster 'mob of gentlemen who speak with ease', presumably) have all the words to win their points—that physical contiguity seems to occlude scrutiny of huge social divisions and their effects. These are words which Sue and Jude 'attend to', in a happy example of 'interpolation' here. But the advantage of this was erased by a Scottish *student* voice in the pub later derisively demanding that Jude recite a creed in Latin. Surely the courage to use a 'millionaire's son'-style 'plummy voice' to criticizable effect was absolutely essential here? Attractive too, however, and something of a critique of the original was that the Jude's fellows among the working men of the stoneyard are much more likeable and rejoice in both the company and the relationship of Sue and Jude in an unthreatening way here. Hardy's working men, by contrast, tend to be unlikeably proletarianised, lumpen, and composed less of good- than ill-will (partly in order to legitimise Jude's quest for something 'finer'). Also, showing the film helpfully 'in dialogue' once more, one implication was that Jude, if less scrupulous, might have prevented the marriage, by actually 'having' Sue (as they were destined to 'live in sin' anyway, it might be suggested that they needn't have complicated things with Sue's crushingly unhappy marriage to someone else in the first place). In the novel, there seemed to be two 'opportunities', missed on account of the innocence of the couple: a kindly peasant innocently offers them a bed together on their jaunt from Melchester [novel only], and the intense affection for Sue engendered in Jude by her 'Ganymede appearance' when she turned up dripping wet as a result of absconding from the punitive conditions of Melchester Training College at Jude's lodgings—and this was 'handled' by the film.

In this case, when Sue explains that men don't approach unless you encourage them ('sensual savages' not included) with a particular look, 'Kate-as-Sue' definitely 'gives it' to a Jude, too 'stupidly good', in Milton's idiom, or simply in awe of Sue, or burdened with the knowledge of his formally married state, to respond. That seemed to be a perfectly legitimate response to 'the original', taking Sue's theoretical provocations *à outrance*. This shows that, in adaptations, because the original will have its *non-dits*, there are cultural spaces left for the film transposition to fill. This is not to say that the 'original' is merely a kind of cultural 'landfill site'.

Tess of the D'Urbervilles[1]

It's difficult to supply a satisfactorily 'taxonomic' account of possible relationships between the film adaptation and its 'original' (partly because of the extremely various critical practices involved here, as well as the different assumptions which govern the process of adaptation itself). Different forms of adaptation may also be telling us something about historical developments in media transpositions. But not only are critics gradually supplying descriptive models of greater sophistication, but the adaptors themselves develop a subtler approach, although a simple evolutionary metaphor would not be apposite. Perennial pressures brought to bear may include (incompatible?) efforts to 'reproduce' the novel, to 'interpret' it—even unto this last desire, frankly to replace it with something else, possibly even 'something completely different'. And, one might say, why not? After all, the novel is still *there*, as, in Wallace Stevens' idiom, 'the plum survives its poems'. 'Go read it, gentle reader', is the injunction which provides a simple resolution to difficulties here, perhaps?

But of course the vast majority of viewers will not in fact have read the 'original'. Why should poor Jane Austen be saddled with the latest film version of *Mansfield Park,* for example (1998), even if its impetus seemed partly to be to 'replace' its heroine, little Fanny Price, with a resumé of 'Jane' herself in the sense of propria persona provided by what remains of her letters (as a feisty young miss whose mores were greatly at odds with those of the quiet and timid Fanny), as if to offer a conceit of 'Jane Austen destroyed by Jane Austen'? The emphasis then shifts to the 'state' of the viewer herself as 'naïve' or 'sophisticated' consumer in this respect. For example, from responses of secondary school children inferred from their internet questions, it seems that she who watches the film does indeed, slightly depressingly, take the novel as 'read by other means' (the *terminus ad quem* in this instance, 'reading off' (or 'reeling off') the film as the book, would entail the perpetuation of nothing less than uproarious absurdities).

The triad elaborated above by Wagner, of 'transposition, commentary or analogy', though a highly interesting 'pot-shot', still seems to him, though inconsistently with his schema, to offer the possibility of 'the novel given on screen',[2] a surprisingly naïve idea, and perhaps particularly in relation to a novel like *Tess*, in which the means of re-presentation are highly 'intertextual' and thus volatile in a way a film can't capture (see the chapter on *Tess* for a sense of the 'metamorphic' 're-presentations' of the heroine in the novel). It must be conceded that discussion of adaptations tends to have a strong and rather automatically applied sense of 'medium priority', with film as the slightly despised Johnny-come-lately.[3] The idea of an 'intrinsic quality' pre-emptively earmarked for the 'text' is particularly unfair as the idea of 'performance' makes the natural point of comparison here *other adaptations*, with 'orchestral scores' for a music which lives only when played provides only a partial analogy, if still a suggestive one here. However, this might be the amusingly reversed fate of the individual cultural production: for example, the *novel* of the *film*

The Piano by Jane Campion (1993) was pronounced (and denounced as) insufficiently nuanced compared with its richly-textured original.[4] This set up an instructive contest ('priority of medium' versus 'priority of production'), which brought a healthy destabilisation and relativity to the scene of cultural bullying. This is a battle of 'cultural capital' which also involves canonicity with other forms of cultural appropriation—cultural 'use-value' might be transposed to a fan-like investment in 'sustaining' fictions, with films offering a repository of embodied attitudes affecting 'life-choices' in a society without traditional signposts.

'Ideology critique' has flourished in relation to Austen and Shakespeare adaptations, as they seem to be more readily recuperable as 'Heritage sites', the source of much critical interest. (Hardy, for example, figures hardly at all in the recent wide-ranging look at the adaptations industry edited by Cartmell and Whelehan [1999] despite his prominence in the adaptations field.) Hardy is a much more ambiguous figure than Austen or Shakespeare in this respect, and more nuanced critical descriptions are perhaps made necessary to accommodate his complex intertwining of social 'inquisition' and nostalgia. As we saw, Wagner also uses the helpful word 'commentary' in suggesting what a film adaptation might do: as here, there are further possibilities of cultural allusion, including that of this (attractive) film version of *Tess*. In a particular sense it might be said to have what Norman Holland would call an 'identity theme'. This seemed to me to be based fundamentally on *an idea (or myth) of Hardy himself*, who has already attained an 'independent existence' as a kind of purveyor of 'rural imaginaries'. Hardy here is less an embodiment of 'the sociological imagination' than an intelligent folk-teller with a burr on his coat and in his voice.

In this sense the film might even be styled a kind of 'hidden polemic' for 'a pure Thomas Hardy', as a sort of psychological parallel to his own campaign to uphold Tess's 'purity'. Handled partly by means of 'educated countryman' voice-overs, Hardy himself immediately became a kind of character in the film. This character might even be thought of as originating in a strain in his critical reproduction: for example, Davidson's once-famous essay on Hardy as a survivor of an archaic, ballad-like tale-telling[5]—gentle, restrained, intelligent but nurtured by a rural idiom and culture (rather than the 'high' or 'metropolitan' versions of this). Again, the parallel with Tess herself is obvious, and underlines the point made by some critics that Hardy's emotional investment in his women characters can make them the figure of the artistic psyche and hence of the artist (him?) self, as something of a 'shesoul', in Joyce's idiom. Hence we may think of Hardy himself as naturally estranged from those sophisticated places we were specifically told Tess herself tried to avoid— indeed, as if this vital 'unsophistication' in Tess really were tied in with the 'hiding places of his [own] power' (*The Prelude* 12.279-80). However, the film confirmed this in rather strange way, one hand tied behind its adapting back, as the whole story of Tess's journey from Flintcomb-Ash to Emminster was sacrificed—as was the Reverend Clare and his wife, and hence the Pauline but charitable churchman's consequential intervention in Alec's (and Tess' and Angel's) existences: 'Mr Clare' (the Father) converts 'Alec' and 'Mr Clare' (the Son), through Tess, will 'deconvert' him, but also 'reconvert' him to Tess, (i.e., 'Mr Clare's wife') herself, with the added irony that Alec was approached by the Reverend Clare specifically on account of *his sexual impropriety*. It was also significant that the parents embodied warm-heartedness as well as ecclesiastical rigidity, so that Hardy made it clear they would have been Tess' allies if she had only had the strength to approach them, but was repelled by an unlucky piece of eavesdropping on the priggish and prudish brothers of Angel, and Mercy, his alleged 'intended'.

Brian MacFarlane has re-animated Barthes' distinction between 'cardinal functions' (or 'nuclei') and 'catalysers' as elements of narrative in order to make some judgements as to what is relatively essential or extraneous across media.[6] Yet film adaptations may trouble theoretical analysis rather than merely illustrate it by transposing one function into another in the adapting process. Finally it wasn't clear that the film *did* 'destroy' its version of *Tess* by abolishing her complex imbrication with and timidity over the Clare family as a whole. The logic of this 'Thomas Hardy' led to a dramatic departure from the generally 'realist' feel of film adaptations. In a startling development of the idea, the film introduced what purported to be *Hardy himself* as a character, hat-doffing and sad-eyed, 'in propria persona'—very much the Older Hardy—on the occasion of the terrible night at Wellbridge when Angel wanders abroad, quietly distraught, followed by 'the soft and silent Tess'. As sad lovers in the novel itself they were reportedly seen by a farmer, but here are briefly greeted by 'folk-teller' Hardy. This was 'artistically justified' in that Hardy was here paraphrasing the poem ('Beyond the Last Lamp') in which he catches the pathos of desolate lovers himself (although the key point in the poem is the *repetition* of their appearance). Hardy's cameo role here beguilingly 'takes back' from John Fowles what Fowles added to Hardy in introducing an 'authorial' presence in the Hardy-inspired *French Lieutenant's Woman*, itself set in 'Hardy country' and with a critical examination of Victorian *mentalité*—postmodernistically 'breaking frame', as it were. Yeats once wrote that *A Shropshire Lad* deserved its fame but that 'a mile further and all had been marsh'. A similar verdict might be reached about the greater work, *Tess*, and what the film does is to 'go the extra mile' to that emotional marsh—if sometimes to excellent effect.

Angel, for example, is less a return of fierce Clym Yeobright of *The Return of the Native* than an educated yet naïve boy, warm- (and open-) hearted: Angel-Clym of the novel is shocked and scornful of Tess' thoughts of suicide out of solicitude for him at Wellbridge, but appears to be about to practise it here (on) himself as the Tess who has just murdered Alec in 'The Herons' boarding-house at Sandbourne catches up with him. By contrast, partly because of the homogenising realism of character presentation which remains a problem for film adaptations in particular, Alec becomes a 'stronger' (and a 'rounder') character, and it becomes harder to resist Lawrence's (irritating) idea that, 'in a way', Alec 'was her mate' here. D'Urberville's 'savage indignation' as the Durbeyfields were evicted, for example, was impressive and almost winning (if ineffective). This is also partly because the 'Liza-Lu' theme in which Tess 'wills' her younger sister to Angel is omitted. This, unfortunately, makes *Alec* the final benefactor of the Durbeyfield family – it isn't clear Angel will have any further contact with them at all: so that 'house with walled garden' in the never-quite-identified village in which the Durbeyfield family 'subsidised' by Alec found a refuge of sorts looks distinctly imperilled: the idea that it may be better if Angel 'does *not* make it' back from those fever-inducing slopes of Curitiba in Brazil becomes a much more plausible one.

Dolled-up in what seems almost *Mikado* style as she descends from her quarters with Alec at 'The Herons' (is *Tess'* well-attested popularity in Japan alluded to here? [!]), she resists Angel quite firmly at first, but succumbs to a tearful, melting sensibility at the sight of him which seemed almost more pathological than endearing. Once again, it seemed clear that Angel should *not* have reached her at Sandbourne: her family, solicitude about whom is Tess' constant point of reference, will be unprotected, and finally, that 'murder is murder' seems much more clear-cut here— even if we, Angel, and Hardy can see that Tess didn't deserve her fate, exactly. (Perhaps amusingly, the viewer couldn't *really* [or at least readily] agree with Oliver Milburn's likeable young Angel in his vehement insistence to Tess that she 'had *done nothing wrong*'.)

The earlier, slightly alarming claim by Jane Marcus that abused and 'have-not' women will enter the cinema to watch 'Tess kill Alec D'Urberville'[7] seems to find an enthusiastic response here in the 'full frontal' confrontation of a Tess, slightly 'out of herself', killing Alec with the bread knife, whereas in the novel this was distanced and refracted through the initially uncomprehending reactions of the imaginatively *bornée* landlady of 'The Herons', which is much more in artistic 'keeping', unless one wishes to foreground other problems—a legitimate aim, although one likely in turn to create more of them.

For example, the murder itself here was memorably cued by Alec's gleefully *schadenfroh* revelation of his prosaic *name* (slightly altered to 'Stokes'), picking up on information given much earlier in the *novel* by the narrator, and well dramatised, as Hardy's interest in what might be called 'the naming of parts' forms a significant part of his artistic effect. 'Naming' and 'name-calling' are indeed fairly decisive in *Tess*, and the substitution of the idea of something intrinsically evil in the purely 'nominal' deception presented as the immediate stimulus to her killing of D'Urberville, is in fact quite 'in keeping' artistically. Reversing the novel's emphasis, however, the killing of Alec is done, as it were, under our very noses, while the killing of Tess is entirely elided. And this does mute the *political* impact of the work. The killing of Alec before our very eyes also eschews the particularly memorable moment when the reader is distanced from the scene and the perception of the fact of murder is refracted through the prosaic landlady Mrs Brooks' horrified realisation that the growing, blood-red diamond shape on her ceiling is indeed formed by, and of, blood.

Angel earlier addressed Tess as 'the most perfect woman ever seen' (if this merely underlines something in the original, why protest?): of course she both is and isn't. 'Perfect' brings hymeneal thoughts in both the sense of Tess' eligibility and of her hymen, the (no) thing which is 'not there', in Wallace Stevens' idiom from his 'Snow Man', which is what Angel will prove to be here. In a sense Angel is composing his own empty conundrum, seeing 'nothing that is not there but not the (no-) thing that isn't' which will temporarily but decisively destroy his love for Tess, the marriage, and, effectively, Tess herself. The film turns up the sheer pathos here, making their relationship more mawkish: in the case of the ancestral mural portraits of ladies D'Urberville at Wellbridge, Tess' alleged similarity to the ferocious figures became a mere joke (just as Angel himself was a gentler creature), and this was partly the result of modes of presentation in the film—Hardy's boldly various 'perspectivising' is intellectually reduced: Tess can hardly be 'a Fellowship' one minute and a 'friendly leopard at pause' the next. We *see* Tess unequivocally, so Hardy's ricochet of re-presentations, constantly re-adjusting the reader's perspectives, has no parallel here.

Originally so 'hymeneal' that even ethereal Angel could hardly be imagined as keeping his hands off her for long, Tess, proved not to be intact, becomes a kind of untouchable, and this the film underlined, almost in its caste sense, as Tess declines in the social scale to the roughest forms of agricultural labour to swede-hacking and feeding the threshing machine (and getting more than a little 'threshed' herself in the process). However, it also omits some of the patriarchal 'overdeterminations' of Tess' plight—Groby, for example, punched by Angel in the novel on his denying that Tess was a 'maid' on their Christmas eve visit to the (unidentified) town near Talbothays has not been included. Significantly, though, in the novel he turned up as the bullying employer at Flintcomb-Ash who 'would have cuffed her if he had dared' *yet was still preferable to Alec.* The tension between the 'lover' who is more feared than the brutal persecuting employer is a suggestive one, while the letter sent by Marian and Izz to Angel emphasized more than anything else the real danger Tess was in. Here, though, the audience might well conclude that her surrender to the forceful and by no means wholly unlikeable Alec was both inevitable and not quite such a bad thing after all, especially after the feckless Durbeyfield family had eaten their 'seed potatoes'.

This in itself raises questions of modes of representation of character: Hardy tries to keep Alec stereotypical but doesn't quite succeed, and the characters themselves are framed by comparisons in that Hardy is much less a taxonomic 'open and shut case' of nineteenth century realism than is generally supposed. But here Alec's mode of existence as a character is not significantly differentiated from the others, and Hardy did do *something* to restrain empathy with persistent attempts to keep Alec 'stereotypical', combined with 'diabolic' associations and points of reference which function to keep Alec functional, ancillary, and faintly odious as the 'respectable' gentleman 'who is not one'. And then Hardy almost always supplies some thickly implicated plotting which any film would have to scamper to keep up with. A television film in several episodes would have a better chance of succeeding here, as the respective fates of recent Austen adapatations seem to indicate (with the highly indulged 'Colin Firth' *Pride and Prejudice* running out a clear winner). For example, the almost 'Marxian' theme of the uprooting of the immemorial villagers *in general* is not here, nor is the intensely dramatic scene in the family vaults at Kingsbere when Alec starts up from the sarcophagus, and, likewise, the strange scene in the allotment as Spring approaches, when Alec (as himself a kind of version of the Miltonic Satan he cites) turns up the pressure on Tess and alienates the reader more (and necessarily?) is also missing. Again, such omissions and media-special 'effects' make the undesirability of Tess' being 'won back to' Alec more ambiguous and troubling.

Earlier, we might have had Tess' 'tender' and eerily foreshadowing killing of the wounded pheasants, and, approaching the dénouement, the highly cinematographic incident in which the landlady at 'The Herons' watches horrifiedly as the red spot on the ceiling expands has been cut. (David Lodge pointed out that Hardy is a kind of 'man of the cinema' *avant la lettre* and never more so than here, surely?)[8] The 'Winchester hanging' is omitted (necessary not only to a sense of the sheer horror of Tess' fate, but as a thematically apposite 'climax'?)—and highly significant in the novel as leading into the famous conclusion concerning 'The President of the Immortals'.

But change and omission is emphatically *not* necessarily for the worse. Here, as an indication of his 'liberation' from his priggish environment, Angel plays an unpretentious concertina, not a harp, part of his resistance to bourgeois constraints, its plaintive quality also surrounding him with some of the 'pathos of the victim' and its melody becomes a kind of emotional *aide-mémoire* for Tess herself. He does not have Hardy's Angel's Clym-like decisiveness, underscoring his psychological distance from his strait-laced brothers, but has a 'friendly puppy' quality, which accompanies his serious-minded boyishness. His tentative 'concertina-ing' supplies the leitmotif of lost love.

Home from his unfortunate Brazilian adventure, Angel, again somewhat boyish and quite without the 'Clym Yeobright' formidableness of Hardy's Angel, gets a good verbal drubbing from a Mrs D'Urberville herself a 'stronger' and more intelligent character than in the novel, as well as from a quite censorious Marian when he reaches her at Flintcomb. In general, too, the Durbeyfield family's helplessness isn't quite as absolute as in the novel. For example, even silly Jack Durbeyfield is able to ironize his 'antiquity' here (Jack's idea of the collection hat to be passed around antiquarians is something he, as opposed to the reader, treats as a joke in this film), and the country scenes are pretty, rural-nostalgic (though the hardships of Flintcomb Ash are well presented and unsentimentalised). Text-sensitive, the film cites many of the essential lines. It was particularly well carried off that Tess begins her foiled pre-marital narrative with the statement that her 'Durbeyfield' is in fact 'D'Urberville', and Angel scoops up the offer—'and is that all your trouble?' The answer is, of course, 'Yes'.

Her story, then, is at once told and not told, and this is the sort of thing Hardy is extremely good at 'engineering'. It forestalls her confession, since, as her name is her trouble she has, in a sense, made it: 'What's in a name?' might even be an alternative title, we realise, with the implication 'quite a bit', not the 'nothing' which Shakespeare's Juliet implied. Many will surely find this film 'engaging' in both senses. Perhaps its greatest lack is the specific nineteenth century intellectual context for Angel's partially completed 'revolution from within', a real sense of what Bakhtin would call the novel's 'chronotope',[9] a persistent problem in the screen version of *Jude* also.

The Woodlanders

For Ezra Pound, cutting and condensing was an (or quite possibly *the*) artistic merit, but this film,[1] which goes in for a great deal of it, distinctly fails to make it a virtue, and many of what Barthes would call 'nuclear' incidents and Seymour Chatman 'kernels'[2] ('narrative moments that give rise to cruxes in the direction taken by events') are (not-so-'tree-surgically') removed: for example, the obsession of Marty's father, sick John South, with the tree outside which threatened, yet, in the event, apparently sustained him (he died when the tree was felled on Fitzpiers' instructions, and his reactions to this focalised his crassness, based partly on his snobbery); and the incident provides the psychological core of the novel, which furnishes a sardonic notation of the high romantic sense of 'the one life within us and abroad'. It was also the incident which precipitated Giles's eviction and the disaster which followed. It combined disastrously with the displeasure he incurred over the refusal to give way to Mrs Charmond's coach with his oak-laden wagons. The dropping of South from the cast list is on the same level of crassness as Fitzpiers' 'tree-felling as cure'.

What we may surely call South's manic-depressive state as projected in his tree-fixation is associated with the theme of 'organic' existence and 'the one Life within us and abroad'. But to the extent that South's depression is cued by *social* anxieties, the episode becomes a revelation, slightly after the manner of the left-wing playwright Edward Bond, of the 'origin of superstition' which Hardy as sociologist is himself well up to enunciating. The incident also warns you of Fitzpiers' callousness, twinned in this case with his insecurely snobbish contempt for his *locale*. This film proceeds by eliding such things in such a way as to gradually attenuate a sense of Hardy's mordantly sociological approach, stripping it down to a theme of 'organic' existences versus those of no 'natural piety'. In a sense the film excavates a form of the Wordsworth who influenced Hardy, but whom Hardy himself was also critiquing not merely 're-producing'. This is an interesting idea, however, and needn't be aprioristically condemned as a 'cultural initiative'.

But the film does demonstrate that 'less' is not necessarily 'more' (to cite Van der Rohe's 'modernist' cliché). Quite startling at times, if hardly in a happy way, this *Woodlanders* is interesting in individual character performances–but this does subtend what we are asked to imagine 'about' them, hard to accommodate to a sense of the original *Woodlanders*. For example, Marty South, the would-be 'lover' of Giles (though hardly even 'in shot' enough to earn the privilege of being spurned), looks as pretty as a motion picture and somehow even more intellectually sprightly than this film's clearly overanxious, unspontaneous, costively bourgeoisified version of Grace.

Unfortunately, too, Marty's despair over the way Giles channels his niggardly-received affections for the benefit of finishing-schooled Grace is lightly pencilled in. She even seems fairly unfazed when Giles teases her over her shorn locks. And Hardy gave her a highly 'catalytic' role, bringing the already tottering relationship of Fitzpiers and Charmond crashing to the ground with her shocking tonsorial disclosures, then, in a brilliantly pathetic pay-off, made Marty highly 'nuclear' again in giving her the exit-line the opening of the novel initially seemed to promise with its prolonged picture of Marty as 'Elegy in a Country Churchyard' material pursued by Percombe as an unusual kind of 'lock-smith'. But here the hair motif ceases to be what Seymour Chatman calls a 'kernel', or perhaps, in Barthesian terminology, we are watching a *nucleus* becoming a mere *catalyser*—what Chatman describes as a *satellite* (roughly, a small, ancillary action). Marty of course succumbs to Percombe's demand for her hair as a dramatisation of the appropriative power of the idle rich, almost as if they might 'control' the 'workings' of desire itself, but the ultimate point of this was to give weak Marty a weapon in the war against powerful Charmond which would prise her and Fitzpiers apart with Edred's 'finely satirical' observations on the origins of some of the Charmond charm(s). But nothing is heard of all this subsequently and no letter is sent.

Things do seem rather complicated by the film's being in some respects 'in denial' rather than in dialogue with its original as it actually ends with Grace coldly *rejecting* cold fish Fitzpiers, in a complete reversal of what actually occurred (and thus boldly throwing down a gauntlet of sorts), apparently declaring its independence and claiming its own creative logic. Grace, who is socially more, is humanly less than the rejected Marty, faithful unto death and beyond. Fidelity was a theme of the novel, and might be transposed here into an artistic sense of fidelity of sorts (even in adaptations) as being desirable. As it happens, the film might be said to be 'as "unfaithful" to *The Woodlanders* as Fitzpiers was to Grace'. This may remind us of Giddings' point that the adaptor is in a kind of aporia: 'if we modernise, it is in a sense a way of admitting they are no longer appropriate or relevant in their original form [but] . . . we slavishly endeavour to recreate them . . . we produce a fake antique'. [3] This film modernizes in a sense, but paradoxically only in order to reach *back* to Wordsworth, the 'origin' of the novel which is not uncritical towards its 'source'. And indeed in the novel the re-uniting of Grace and Fitzpiers was of serious *ideological* import—the survivors, however unworthily, are 'life-rafted' by bourgeois structures. However resourceful and characterful Giles is, still he is vulnerable. However dissipated and even devilish Fitzpiers is, still his social cachet and acquired skills shall see him unworthily through. Thus we 'lose the plot' not only in the obvious sense, but in the novel's logical inferences about the results of Grace's educated velleities, and its sense of the sordid but sustaining 'survivorships' for those of bourgeois provenance and training, especially when contrasted and counterpoised with the wordless Wordsworthian fidelities and vulnerabilities of woodcraft folk.

As it stands, this film might in fact have the function of gratifying those annoyed or frustrated by the novel, with its passivities and unhappily 'determined' feel. It might be argued that Melbury becomes the unlikeable character here he always had the potential to become, deprived of the pathos which attended his social mortifications (the idea advanced here to Grace that 'I broke my back to better you' is nasty: his investing *himself* with old man's pathos seems to preclude genuine love for his daughter and his exclusive focus on her has issued in a kind of *ressentiment*). So, Grace's rejection of Fitzpiers here might make a potentially interesting statement of her repudiation of her father's attempt to ru(i)n her life (although in the novel it was *he* who did not approve of Grace's return to Fitzpiers). At the same time in the film he sounds vaguely censorious about her 'obstinate condolment' over Giles, which we can't now see her abandoning, so that the contrast with Marty's excruciating dirge for a Giles posthumously deserted by Grace also falls out of the frame – the ultimate (or 'extreme') point Hardy at least was working towards—Grace's 'posthumous' infidelity versus Marty's "Wordsworthian woodlander" absoluteness of ('useless'?) affection. So the film actually seems to be hacking away at these fine Hardyan juxtapositions and 'special effects'.

This would mean, then, that Grace *did* know her own mind all along (where the novel stakes everything on her *not* quite knowing it), and that it was merely *Melbury's* frantic social aspiration which was at fault. Grace's reply to Melbury's peevishness here—'you have bettered me. You have torn me up by the roots'—seems unhappily paradoxical. Again, on the dramatic evidence here, Giles should indeed betake himself to Marty at once and avoid the tortuous self-lacerations which will prove to subtend Melbury's all-too-finely-calibrated sense of social registers, which ensures that

Fitzpiers will feel fully justified in his patronising attitude to Grace, Melbury and Little Hintock generally.

Again, it was of fundamental importance that Fitzpiers was a local scion of the aristocracy down on his luck—hence the rural conservative Melbury's extreme awe of the man. Oddly, though, Fitzpiers here is a kind of 'man in black with a "Celtic" look', and hence something like an 'undead' version of a Scottish (TV) doctor—a sort of 'Dr Finlay from hell'. His wider intellectual interests in Kant, Spinoza and Shelley, for example, have been deftly cut, and they survive only as he becomes a transcendent exponent of the idea that neither people nor things have souls (an anti-'organic' point which is, admittedly, highly a propos). Indeed his own seems to have been deftly removed by aliens, or possibly he may even be one himself. Fitzpiers was, however haughtily, a local man, but this Edred is quite definitely a 'Mephistophelian visitant' here.

Melbury here seems more unpleasantly set on anything that looks 'upwardly mobile' as a kind of diffuse revenge for early slightings over his educational 'underprivilege' (the sympathy which accrues to him in the brief important scene in which, after being disrespectfully addressed by a monocled huntsman type, he pleads that Grace will 'look away' if she encounters him after her grand marriage, is also missing). On the other hand, it can hardly be claimed that Grace is unaffected by ideas of social advancement and simply wishes to marry Giles here. Her education is 'a forgetting of apples', and she is as pleased as Melbury is that Mrs Charmond seems to offer to take her up. We are not shown the scene in which she does, however, and Charmond's declining to do so is awkwardly unexplained – in the novel Charmond 'thought herself impaired' by Grace's younger charms as she glimpses them both juxtaposed in a mirror as Grace leaves after everything seems to be 'set up'—a scene, incidentally, which might have been filmed to excellent effect. In such ways the film seems to offer commentary only inadvertently and hence is productive of what might be called 'differences without positive terms'.

It also forgets the artistic shape of the relationship of Charmond and Fitzpiers— Edred did, after all, 'commit' to a Mrs Charmond, and although disillusioned with her had got her pregnant, apparently, and only the 'deranged Carolinian (ex-) lover' of Mrs Charmond got him off the hook by killing her. Only then did he return to Grace, contrite after his fashion (and all of this seems eminently suitable for film treatment). None of it survives, but what was also of significance was the early rejection of impoverished young student Fitzpiers' suit to Mrs Charmond in Heidelberg, as an (in effect) ironically 'transposed' version of Giles' experience with Grace as a kind of apple just out of his social reach. Hence Mrs Charmond became a mere function or 'actant' in the film, whereas in the novel we saw the trajectory or teleology of her existence as something on all fours with that of the other major characters. It has often been said that Hardy's novels anticipate cinematic modes of presentation, but the film itself seems paradoxically embarrassed by the most stunning instances of this. Grace's inadvertent sympathy with the other women 'had' by Fitzpiers, that noble reflex of solidarity unexpectedly attending on her shock at finding what Edred is like, is missing, so that the touchingly 'quasi-lesbian' moment in the woods with Mrs Charmond as well as the striking line—'"Great God—he's had you! Can it be? Can it be?'" in which the injury to Grace herself is 'folded' under her spontaneous sympathy for the suffering Charmond—is also cut.

Adaptations are tricky things, invitingly suggesting possibilities of light and easy pastiche in the mode of allusion, and a kind of light-fingered cultural appropriation from places in which cultural capital is already helpfully invested by educational processes and institutions. But although they may initially seem like the cultural equivalent of 'hitching a lift' in an 'easy commerce of the old and new' which is nothing if not commercial, it seems that the very completeness and self-sustaining virtuosity of the 'prefabricated' structures the original provides become a bit of a problem as things drop out of the frame and significance dissipates. This particular version seems vulnerable in being pushed for time (and resources?). Curiously, the (empty) spaciousness that results from excessive eradication itself puts pressure on the actors, who are left with very little to 'play with'. Grace's frustration as she is deprived of 'organic' Giles and cohabiting with a cold fish Fitzpiers who clearly 'murders to dissect' with relish, is imaged briefly by her fondling a rather rough-barked tree until Marty sensibly warns her of possible danger to her fine skin. Indeed, it looks as if the poor actors may have been asked to improvise a little when not actually left with much to say, so Rufus-Sewell-as-Giles is quite startling when he seems about to enter the dense verbal thickets of Gerard Manley Hopkins with the idea that, as he puts it, 'Heart hopes out of where all's hopeless'.

The film does not enact a wholesale repudiation of its original: on the one hand, the respect for the idea of the 'organic' world of woodlands and its denizens implies a respect for Hardy, but the new satisfaction of seeing Grace reject Fitzpiers *implies* disrespect by arranging a 'feistier' conclusion for the reader who finds the Hardyan pathos intolerable. This adaptation finally seems to subsist less in dialogue than in denial, almost a costume drama version of a soap opera without the narrative space necessary to transpose a Hardy sometimes at his concatenating best here. Although the skills brought to bear by directors, actors and screenwriters aren't being denied, what is most instructive is predicated on 'perceived' absences which are 'educational' in the unhappy sense of showing that what Hardy does is irreplaceable—rather than in happily transposed versions which don't traduce the original. So, also *necessarily* missing is the distraught scouring of the countryside by Melbury with his (tired) rustics, finally establishing only that Grace is snugly enclosed in the 'Earl of Wessex' Hotel once again. Hardy's novel, itself a trap of sorts, converged on the trap set by Tim Tangs, which inadvertently caught Grace's pretty dress, not Fitzpiers' 'pretty shins', as Tim terribly predicted, and the rest followed. But all of this too is missing. Perhaps the film has, despite its talents, and its moments, its own way of being a trap which catches relatively little in its jaws.

Chapter 14

Spectres of Hardy's Poetry: Back to the Future

How do we ascribe 'literary value'? For example, to approach Hardy's poetry with 'theory' might seem almost 'sacrilegious' to some readers. 'Theory' might suggest the intellectual bent of someone with a blueprint for (new) social arrangements, highly anti-'Burkian'. Edmund Burke's *Reflections on the French Revolution* (1791) implied a philosophy of 'organic' conservatism which 'proved the state a tree'. And Hardy himself, the Older Hardy of the poems in particular, has always had the image of 'organic' intellectual in the sense of having a 'conservative' imagination with unradical roots, in the soil. On the other hand, addressing himself to the business of poetry he announces a 'Shelleyan' programme, which is dedicated to overturning received ideas and social formulas. Colin MacCabe, however, warned against a Theory, not so much as a threatener of the status quo as stuck in formalist repetitions,[1] and the point will bear repetition. He suggests the need for theoretical enquiry to mesh with problems associated with class, gender, subjectivity, and the effects of power. This agenda might lead us to establish what is 'questionable' 'in theory' itself, and raise the question of the fate of 'literary value', often ascribed as a result of simple 'culture war' bullying.

The High Noon of Leavisism, for example, was underpinned by fiats: 'I am Sir Oracle, / And when I ope my mouth let no dog bark'. Evidence suggests that the Leavisian project had itself a surprisingly 'neo-Burkian' *terminus ad quem*, even if it set out as something quite different. This could be a starting point for a re-consideration of Hardy, who, as poet, barely survives Leavis's 'Booby-trap commendations', based on a kind of 'varsity man' patronage of the naïve countryman Hardy turns out not to have been. Hardy, ironically, wouldn't sustain the cultural conservatism Leavis himself came to exhibit. Hardy's was a complex fate, as one in various ways an 'insider' and 'outsider': alternating currents of social exclusion and inclusion made his social existence volatile and uncertain. He was a paradoxically triumphal underling of sorts, a 'peasant' turned 'patron', although this did not, equally ironically, prevent his being patronized. Consequently, his poetry rehearses this persistent sense of instability and 'liminality', emerging from a negotiation of the intimate and the historically 'momentous', unforgettably marrying a larger music of alienated nostalgia to the intimately elegiac 'work of mourning'.[2] As 'the unconsoled', his 'black sun of melancholy' seems to 'back into' one of the oddest forms of social critique.

Ironically, critics of Hardy may summon an 'ideology of poetry' itself to contest this kind of intellectual 'linkage'. William E. Buckler, for example, enters upon a full-blown, Arnoldian rhetoric of poetry as a religion substitute and a 'guarantee' that 'man [sic] will never be wholly historical'.[3] Taking Hardy 'out of history' has been the reflex response of many a Hardy critic. Yet, although 'making assays' of Hardy's poetry is a tricky business,[4] we can show that Hardy is a quirky version of an 'organic intellectual' in a semantically 'riven' version—at once 'organic' in the sense of his post-Darwinian 'ecological' awareness of 'the world's body', but with a line in intellectual inquisition which probes received ideas and orthodoxies.

Hardy only 'emerged' as a poet in the 1890s, so that he is more consistently identifiable as a writer of alienated 'nostalgia' here than in his role as novelist. Pressing some 'reveal codes' key might show that a common drama underlying the poems would be the change from *Gemeinschaft* to *Gesellschaft*, terms used to characterise the change from close-knit communities to a competitive 'noncommunity'.[5] Hence for Hardy the 'progressive' is often the antithesis of anything he could regard as 'progress'. In the attitudes most associated with Hardy's poetry, what Yeats called 'some vague Utopia' could not compete with the plenitude of the past. This might be grasped as a social version of Freudian *Nachtraglichkeit*,[6] a 're-visionary' awareness which found words to stand for a past, which, unmediated, no one could now stand. So if Weber helps to 'explain' Hardy, Hardy also helps to 'explain' Weber, elucidating Weber's sense of the shift from communal modes of being to 'instrumental reason' ordering the work place: poems about the lapse of time are also about the lapsing of a particular sense of community. These are a kind of an after-image, an idealizing, wistful glimpse of what he came to imagine was 'left behind'.

Hardy, then, seems to have seen *Gemeinschaft* become *Gesellschaft* (though, to put it informally, the half-brutalized, hard-drinking [and wife-beating] reality of Puddletown we glimpse in biographies seems to give the lie to the only slightly off-key, lightly-penumbra'd idyll of *Under the Greenwood Tree* [1872]). However, most radical writers, as Gillian Rose puts it, have 'defined the divisiveness . . . of society (*Gesellschaft*) in terms of each other and recommended some sort of struggle in order to obtain communality (*Gemeinschaft*)'.[7] If so, surely Hardy really is a dissenting 'pessimist' here, a word he resisted (but in this context it's a meritorious condition: how on earth could one 'get back' or 'go forward' to 'obtaining' *Gemeinschaft* ['again']?).

His socio-historical themes take flight from the 'unhappy consciousness' which reflects it, enabling him to establish that 'I think where I am not therefore I am where I do not think,' (Lacan's famous modification of Descartes' 'Cogito'). This is the 'message' of the somehow quintessential lyric, 'The Self-Unseeing', and seems also to be the burden of 'Night in the Old Home' where unreflective ancestors upbraid the 'thinker of crooked thoughts upon Life in the sere'.

At 'Life in the sere' certainly seems to be where to find him: in the famous poem 'During Wind and Rain' Hardy almost seems to be writing the 'missing portion' of Shelley's life, that of the 'still young' poet drowned in the Bay of Lerici at twenty-nine who found his textual complement in a Hardy who emerged as a poet only in his late fifties—just as Shelley's bright Italy, 'paradise of exiles', contrasts with drizzling England and Romantic-as-Revolutionary bohemianism with jaded, nostalgic Victorian respectability, youth with old age, utopian hope with wan retrospection: the refrain of

'Ah no, the years, the years!' is a post-Shelleyan disconfirmation, the poem an example of all time has disproved. The happiness of the poem, the Shelleyan moment in which 'music and moonlight and feeling/Are one' (in 'To Jane') is given to others, 'altogether elsewhere'. Those 'others' seem to be the relations of the wife whose maledictions Hardy had just been reading—Emma's posthumously discovered notebook with its singularly ominous title, 'What I Think of My Husband'. Identifying against a Shelleyan poetic self, he also identifies with the relations of the wife who identified against him in propria persona.

The Hardy poem offers a union of what Yeats called the primary and the antithetical imagination which Hardy would more humbly define as the contrast between the idea of 'life as an emotion and [that of] life as a science of climbing'.[8] A line like 'They move to a new high house' suggests a slight turn on the word 'high'— seeming at once to 'fulfil' ambition and to 'transcend' it—as if 'wobbling' between the two conditions. The poem shows imagination projecting a version of 'the ceremony of innocence,' preserving 'life as an emotion' while, or even by, 'climbing', a combination which, in his habitual *mentalité* he had in fact 'impossibilised'. The implication would be that Hardy's imaginative reach may be greatest when he deserts rather than fulfils the Shelleyan programme he announces. In his relations with Shelley there is an odd 'oedipality' which makes Hardy a kind of 'morning after' to Shelley's Utopian 'night before': Hardy is a 'son-as-father' here, with 'winter words' of retrospection cancelling 'social hope'.[9]

As a standard-bearer of Shelley, he is alert to the fact that poetry is scrutinised with unavowed reference to its imputed ethics or politics, yet in his own poetic practice he takes flight by reversing Shelley's own emphases. But if Shelley was launched on a poetic career which would not rehearse the 'history of the victors', then in this sense Hardy's modestly muttering marginalia seem also, in their own way, to have got the point. (Frederic Jameson seems to have thought that nostalgia might provide the impetus for 'radicalism'.) Hardy is scarcely programmatic, however: the poems, in progressing, establish a norm of discordance rather than dialogue. Some of them simply occlude the radical programme he announces (see the deferential poem to Victoria, for example ['V.R. 1819-1901']. As a politic practitioner of 'good little Thomas Hardy-ism' he seeks protective coloration. But Tom Paulin has noted how use of dialect seems to 'incriminate' someone 'by association': denying the use of it is correlated with the deepest betrayal in 'In the Servants' Quarters'.[10] Yet Hardy's own defence of Barnes's cult of dialectal purity may be contrasted with his defensive over-insistence that it was 'never used at home'(!)[11]

So the pleasures of (re-) reading Hardy must include a sense of the ways in which he 'interferes' with his Shelleyan intentions as a 'bold enquirer into morals and religion' after the manner of Shelley's Milton.[12] One notes how his 'metaphysical iconoclasm' is contradicted by physical solicitude, in his membership of the Society for the Preservation of Ancient Buildings (mainly ecclesiastical). Here, it seems, are attitudes of 'mutually assured destruction'. Hillis Miller speaks of Hardy's poems as 'the juxtaposition of unrelated, even discordant, effusions.'[13] Hardy himself claimed to offer 'unadjusted impressions' or 'a series of fugitive impressions' which were produced by '*humbly* recording diverse readings of life's phenomena as they [were] forced upon [him] by chance and change',[14] in tension with High Romantic theories of imperious imaginings. 'Humbly' seems here to echo the 'humble' creatures of 'An August Midnight' who bumble their way into Hardy's study at night: 'earth's humblest they,' he muses, but concludes that 'they know earth-secrets that know not I', it being somehow characteristic of Hardy to be humbled by the humblest. Curiously, this tender, innocuous ['decentring'] of (sc.) 'man' is already potentially 'subversive': the feeling that nature offers a gentle reproach of sorts suggests the transposition of common Romantic tropes into critique. This is a poetry of (in fact, textual [after-]effects of) perception which 'keeps warm/ Men's wits to the things that are' (Hopkins), resistant to (say) T.S. Eliot's 'clerical' inquisitions, his characteristic forms of response. Hardy wants to 'hold the line' for a kind of intellectual integrity against the mystifications of a religiosity which may express itself in stunting social effects. This is clearly shown in his sardonic 'death-bed epitaph' on a G.K. Chesterton 'who'd prove and never turn a hair/ That Darwin's theories were a snare'. (Hardy seems to have seen *The Origin of Species* as enabling an *ethical* advance, in the very awareness of our oneness with the other creatures with which we share the earth.)[15]

Hence Hardy is attracted to sages like Darwin or David Hume, who might have been felt to be 'cutting poetry's throat'. And when Bachelard claims that 'the world of possibility . . . is the source of *both* scientific and poetic creation,'[16] he is saying something Hardy would have found deeply congenial, as a poem like 'Proud Songsters,' with its birds emerging mysteriously from 'earth, and air, and rain' would confirm. Similar conclusions might be inferred from 'The Year's Awakening', or the Darwinian 'In a Wood', which surely glances at Wordsworth's 'one impulse from a vernal wood' (in 'The Tables Turned'). In the Hardy poem nature is (sardonically) confirmed as a great 'teacher': fleeing to his Wordsworthian retreat, the speaker of Hardy's poem finds the trees, like human protagonists, are 'combatants all!' The speaker who has thought himself fleeing from the 'Darwinian nature' of society which offers no easy survival to the finest, finds Nature herself is engaged in an equally desperate struggle. So 'poetry' entails intellectual integrity, underwritten by an emphasis on 'perceptions', which cannot, as it were, lie. Hence Hardy's becomes 'the poetry of perception'. Yet there may be the lie of the notion of 'perception' itself. Bachelard, for example, claims that 'what man *imagines* dictates what he *perceives*'.[17] This sounds like the message of Freud's notes on the 'mystic writing pad' [in which] 'the establishment of permanent traces in the psychic apparatus preclude the possibility of immediate perception'.[18]

In a poem like 'Nature's Questioning', for example, close kin to the nature of Baudelaire's '*Correspondances*' which '*laissent parfois sortir de confuses paroles*,'[19] Hardy's message of cosmic entropy offers the excuse for the plaintive sentiments expressed ('We wonder, ever wonder, why we find us here!' [implicitly, abandoned]). 'Thus things around', concludes the supposedly bemused poet actually constructing himself as his own 'Doomster'.[20] In 'While Drawing in a Churchyard', the message 'soughed' by the yew ['"Now set among the wise"/ They say, "Enlarged in scope, / That no God trumpet us to rise/ We truly hope".'] is the speech of the (imagined) dead imputed *by* the yew as imputed *to* the yew by the *speaker*—an artistic 'ricochet' which involves him. It foregrounds the absurdity of the yew's actually speaking. The apparent naivety, and 'folkloric' primitivism here is sophisticated. Impression also slides into demonstration in 'Neutral Tones': the sun which is 'white, as though chidden of God,' becomes, at the end, less speculatively, the 'God-cursed sun' in this continuum of cosmic, natural, and emotional 'wrong'—of which the conspicuously missing term is the 'social', a deafening silence.

It was Raymond Williams who 'made strange' the gestures of critical patronage which have characterised the 'varsity man' responses to Hardy the good little autodidact.[21] Peter Widdowson infers that 'Hardy' is 'a product of the processes of his reproduction', which would permit us to cast a cold eye on both process and product. Michael Alexander, for example, is anxious to allay fears that Hardy might be identified as a 'Tolpuddle curmudgeon,'[22] [referring to transported trades unionists], but art may with perfect propriety enact a 'politics of refusal' and Hardy is well placed, particularly in his poetry, to sustain Marcuse's claim that 'all authentic art is *negative*.'[23] Cultural documents may be monuments to past barbarism which record the 'history of the victors', in Walter Benjamin's pessimistic phrasing, but there may be an art of resistance to 'affirmative culture'.

Hardy re-enacts Shelleyan recognitions that writing poetry has unavoidable 'political' bearings, cites with approval as a verdict on the world the line from *Hellas*: 'Victorious Wrong, with vulture scream, salutes the risen sun!' He announces, that is, a Shelleyan programme of expressing 'in verse ideas and emotions which run counter to crystallized opinion[s] which the vast body of men have vested interests in supporting . . . if Galileo had said in verse that the world moved, the Inquisition would have let him alone'.[24] This seems close to the Lacanian 'if they'd known what I was saying they'd never have let me say it'. Leavis' perhaps surprisingly negative response to his poetry is the suspicion conveyed by Kierkegaard's diagnosis of an opponent to the effect that 'his energy . . . was consumed in asserting *negativity*'.[25]

However, if this were merely negativity on behalf of 'the powerless and dispossessed', to use Paul Ricoeur's phrase,[26] of what Hardy himself calls 'the frail ones' who 'gyrate like animalculae / in tepid pools,'[27] may be seen in a more positive light. But Hardy notes that often the situation of the 'victim' *forbids patronage*. See, e.g.—'Four in the Morning' ('Though pleasure spurred, I rose with irk:/ Here is one at compulsion's whip/ Taking his life's stern stewardship/ With blithe uncare, and hard at work/ At four o'clock'). Given its class 'distance' (with himself on the 'wrong' side), this also makes a fascinating contrast with the image of Baudelaire's '*Recueillement*' (*Oeuvres Complètes I* [pp.140-1]): '*Pendant que des mortels la multitude vile, / Sous le fouet du Plaisir, ce bourreau sans merci . . .*'. In 'A Wet Night', the poet finds that 'hardship to be calendared' leads him to his 'history of the vanquished'

> Yet sires of mine now perished and forgot,
> When worse beset, ere roads were shapen here,
> And night and storm were foes indeed to fear,
> Times numberless have trudged across this spot
> In sturdy muteness on their strenuous lot,
> And taking all such toils as trifles mere.

Curiously, the poem itself has the sturdy, stoical quality of the forebears and as such is not 'radical' as this is usually construed, its tone being unlike that of the hysterical (if appealing) idea of Baudrillard's in relation to the vanquished dead 'crying out for justice' which Hardy certainly also mediates. It is the lack of self-pity, of any utopian aspiration on the part of the speaker, which the poet finds moving. In similar style is the 'sodden tramp' seeming to rebuke the 'despondent' poet of 'Christmastide', as he 'breaking/ Into thin song, [bears] straight/ Ahead, direction taking/ Toward the Casuals' gate'. Also suggestive is the poem about the giant led by a dwarf ('At a Country Fair'), which the speaker regards as the 'sorriest' of sights, presumably for allegorical reasons possibly derived from the Shelley of 'The Mask of Anarchy'). A more direct 'intervention' is 'A Sunday Morning Tragedy', which deals with an attempted abortion which leads to the death of the young mother whose plight is one 'so scorned in Christendie', chronicling the cruelties of the social effects of established religiosity.

Nicely 'chiasmic' ('criss-crossed'), if perfunctory, is 'The Seasons of her Year' ('she' was happy in winter and 'ruined' by summer)—her lover 'leaves [her] to pay/ Alone! Alone!' This poem of female pathos makes a provocative contrast with 'The Dark-Eyed Gentleman' and 'One Ralph Blossom Soliloquizes,' in which women 'admit' to enjoying illicit sex or to finding the results of giving illicit birth less than tragic. All this, taken together with 'The Coquette, and After' ('Of sinners two/ At last one pays the penalty--/ The woman—women always do!') may serve to pacify feminists who might protest about poems taken singly (Blossom's 'assumed Don Giovanni-ism', in Joycian idiom, being a little hard to take in conjunction with the irony at the expense of his female victims).

'The Bedridden Peasant' cloaks its socialist theme in its purely metaphysical iconoclasm, and, likewise, the poem addressed 'To an Unborn Pauper Child' may 'affect the metaphysics', but the theme is ultimately social, and the suspicion of a 'socialist' penumbra rather than the croak of the fatalist provided the real foundations for expressions of critical distaste. In 'The Farm-Woman's Winter' an economic process lies behind the farmer's physical decline. Hardy's poetry, though flexible as to 'affinities', certainly offers 'art *among* the ideologies'. Master-narratives of liberation, including Marxism, arise partly from Romanticism itself: Shelley influenced Marx, in his way, as well as a rum lot of poets to 'take the strains' of the young revolutionary— Hardy, Browning, Yeats and Wallace Stevens, for example. Unlike the others, Hardy seems implicitly in touch with Shelley's 'Marxian' side, yet, as we saw, gets poetic impetus from filling up places and postures the antithesis of that enunciated by Shelley. Despite Anthony Easthope's claim that Romantic poetry has 'always already surpassed' the social,[28] it would surely be wrong to assume that it could only act 'recuperatively'. Later in the same book, Easthope speaks more congenially of 'the specificity and subversive vitality of poetic Darwinism' (p.148). However, as an unexpected result of Darwinising, usually considered as unsentimental to a fault, Hardy is able to read a new kind of pathos into Nature, a modification of the 'red in tooth and claw' image of Tennyson's perception. The 'perception' is perhaps 'always already' transposed from social conditions, about the power 'which subtly interpenetrates an entire societal network'. It is as if Hardy were trying to come to terms with the idea that Shelley's (benign) 'Unseen Power' (in 'Hymn to Intellectual Beauty') had turned out to be a Foucauldian double agent. His cosmos becomes a kind of hastily abandoned Panopticon; while Foucault's parting thought, that 'intellectuals are themselves agents of this power' is one that has already struck Hardy.

It is interesting to recall here that Larkin is thought to have done something for Hardy by appropriating him in the name of the eternal banalities about the fading of love and the passing of time,[29] but, as a version of Hardy the poet, it is highly edited. And, even where these poets share a subject, differences of tone and attitude are considerable—cf., for instance, Hardy's tender but unsentimental 'Wives in the Sere' ('Never a careworn wife but shows/ If a joy suffuse her, / Something beautiful to those/ Patient to peruse her . . .') and the Amis-like note of Larkin's reference to the women 'moustached in flowered frocks' of 'Faith Healing'.

And Larkin fails to note the 'side' of Hardy which makes him something of a Dorset Burns. Hardy is not 'like' Burns in the sense that Burns isn't too bothered about the discreet charms of respectability, although Hardy, while sharing the feeling, has nevertheless quite definitively entered what we might call the timid new world of net curtains and prurience. But Burns is suggested by the astringent jocularity of 'The Levelled Churchyard', and it is interesting that Hardy's debut as a published poet (1875) was with the heavily dialectal 'The Bride-Night Fire'. Yet his private, unpublished 'start' would appear to have been with 'Domicilium', a Wordsworthian poem with some of the beauty of Wordsworth's deliberately 'fading' closures ('So wild it was when first we settled there'). Here we can almost watch him choosing 'what kind of poet to be', beginning with the sophistications of High Romanticism and choosing second the unsophisticated rusticity 'look'. His forms show Hardy as 'political' in an unLarkinian way: Dennis Taylor claims that Hardy found himself on a 'fault line' of conflicting linguistic traditions in the study of 'dialects of the tribe,' one of which sees that 'the standard language' is 'a momentary construct, one dialect among many' (*Hardy and Victorian Philology*, p.62). The choice of poetic form(s) is also relevant, since, as Panofsky observes, 'there would be nothing wrong in seeing the history of art as an articulation of the history of social conflicts and violence: as a *history of conflicts in the sphere of aesthetic forms*. . . . in its deepest foundations form is always an ideology, . . . [and] the world view is the postulate of every form'.[30] Hardy is highly inclined to 'folkish' forms, his social 'liminality', between patron and peasant, is always to consider, the fact that the people he necessarily wrote for were not, on the whole, the people he wrote about.

Indeed, in social and political terms Hardy's poetry is so variously 'vectored' as to make the once-influential Leavis' treatment of it particularly unhappy. In his *New Bearings in English Poetry* almost every sentence on Hardy is written so as to form a contrast with the sophisticated modernity of Eliot's *Waste Land*, a 'Hardy' is fashioned as 'a naive poet of simple attitudes and outlook' (p.57), hugging the traditional pieties as one who knows, in his *sancta simplicitas* way, 'what he wants, what he values, and what he is' (p.57). Yet Hardy's poems, collectively considered, know none of these things. 'Hardy' here is, as the title of one poem suggests, 'So Various' as to initiate a comparison between himself and Dryden's Zimri— 'everything by fits and nothing long'. 'Afternoon Service at Mellstock' is a famous instance of how he was 'not aware/ That I have gained by subtle thought on things/ since we stood psalming there', but still claiming the subtle thought anyway. We might describe this as a painful form of enlightenment in terms of a paradoxical failure to achieve that.

Hardy is also a sophisticate in showing how desire and its signifiers exceed a signified, and that imaginary attachments alone are real, as one desires to possess what cannot be possessed, or 'possession' itself obliterates desire, as a seasoned explorer of the velleities of desire, where strength of desire is an inverse function of 'availability' and variations on ideas of absence may include the ultimate absence, death. Hardy constantly moves towards a zenith of aphrodisiac regret. Desire contaminates or suffuses 'perception,' and this desire is, in turn, socially 'vectored'. His poems suggest the turn on the word 'eroticist' in Kierkegaard's 'the observer should be an eroticist— no feature, no moment should be indifferent to him'.[31] A poem like 'In a Eweleaze near Weatherbury' looks like rustic naiveté but seems to be poised between the sublimated promiscuity of Shelley's 'Epipsychidion' and the 'reconsidered passion' of T.S. Eliot's 'Gerontion':

> The years have gathered grayly
>   Since I danced upon this leaze
> With one who kindled gaily
>   Love's fitful ecstasies!
> But despite the term as teacher,
>   I remain what I was then
> In each essential feature
>   Of the fantasies of men.
>
> Yet I note the little chisel
>   Of never-napping Time
> Defacing wan and grizzel
>   The blazon of my prime . . .
> Still, I'd go the world with Beauty,
>   I would laugh with her and sing,
> I would shun divinest duty
>   To resume her worshipping.
>
> But she'd scorn my brave endeavour,
>   She would not balm the breeze
> By murmuring "Thine for ever!"
>   As she did upon this leaze.

Hardy's poem seems typically unpretentious: yet if, as Derrida says, 'to deconstruct a text is to disclose how it functions as desire, as a search for presence and fulfilment which is interminably deferred,'[32] then here 'Hardy's reality' is a kind of text which at once initiates and thwarts the search for presence and fulfilment. Hardy makes uneasy appeasements with absence rather than presence (absence is 'more reassuring'), giving a sense of 'anchored transcendence', of boundless feeling at once excited and annulled in a stasis of 'hopeless hope'.

This is emphatically a poem by the married novelist for whom the métier of poetry is itself part of a tentative but persistent 'escapology', unlatching the posterns of Max Gate. Like much of Hardy's work it brings to mind Kierkegaard's thoughts about the nuances of the German phrase *'er hatte sich verandert'* ['he had changed/altered himself/ = *married*'],[33] which runs smartly to meet Hardy's forebodings—as in the (minor) poem 'Mismet', with its popular-song-like honesty about an ill-chosen 'partner'—and with his sense of marriage/ career as an emotional straitjacket. See also 'The Conformers'; 'The Christening' and the effect of these poems on Lawrence's 'Gypsy' ('Thou shall shut doors on me'). Marriage 'goes with' a sad process of confining bourgeoisification. In accordance with this, the 'Eweleaze' poem is at once confessional and reticent, with the boundless desire excited by his retrospection but bounded by the 'Lords of Limit'--memory and the body. The immediate context for the word 'dance' here perhaps discourages literal-mindedness about this, suggesting a general and appropriately dignified romantic excitement, evoking sexuality in an appropriately 'refined' way, as an affair of feelings but not squeamish about physicality, succumbing neither to 'moralism' nor 'immoralism'. (Compare comments by R.P. Blackmur on Hardy's poetic subjects which recall the influence of T.S. Eliot, with an interesting note of hysteria: 'surely no serious writer ever heaped together so much *sordid* adultery . . . as Hardy did in these poems' [p.55]).[34] In fact Hardy's 'In a Eweleaze' is 'mixing memory and desire' in a more personally engaged and engaging way than Eliot can hope to with his bookish sublimity, despite his dazzling mixture of textual collage and expressionist extremity. We can appreciate both poets, as Ezra Pound certainly did. In its curious way the rustic poem is no less 'sophisticated' than Eliot's own.

Although critics like Peter Widdowson have shaped to us a 'radical' Hardy, the cultural nostalgia, the peer-crowded *Life*, the sheer instability of perspective on class and language entails the conclusion that his 'radicalism' is ambiguously related to his 'meliorism' in his poetic texts: but 'melior for whom?' is a legitimate question where civilisation may mean only 'mechanic furtherance' (see 'The Jubilee of a Magazine'). This would be a civilisation which, in Leopardi's words, 'trumpets its retrogression as gain'. Hardy and Leopardi also share a suspicion of a wholly 'romanticised' nature ('Why do you cheat your children so?').[35] Hardy is a kind of poetic detective here, with the universe not so much the scene of a crime as a crime in itself. But is his culprit, finally, Nature or Culture? Stan Smith gets some interesting mileage out of contemplating an unusually 'radical' version of Hardy, while Gilles Deleuze emphasizes Hardy's view of people being given only one life and thus only *one chance* in untoward social conditions (*Dialogues*, p.51). In fact to attack Nature as doing what Wordsworth denied in 'Tintern Abbey' ('betray/ The heart that loves her'), is to attack less 'Nature' than the Victorian 'recuperation' of Wordsworth, Browning's 'lost leader' born again as 'the wrong kind of guru'. Yet Hardy and Wordsworth are, poetically speaking, close kin, responsive to 'humble and rustic life'. Indeed, thanks partly to Wordsworthian mystifications, although Hardy's polemic tone in 'The Dorsetshire Labourer' (1883) is genuine, his approach to actual working conditions is misty-eyed and dulled to bourgeois distance. Indeed, as no one has ever clearly exhibited a folkloric 'underpinning' of Hardy's literary tradition, it might even be argued that Hardy offers 'simulacra' of the curiously elusive 'folk-tradition', and that his poetic practice is, in this respect, completely simular. It might be a future (re-) source of critical insight to note that some of his poems may be 'retro-chic-anery'.

Donald Davie used the word 'engineer' to suggest a different, if still highly Victorian Hardy, as a kind of Isambard Kingdom Brunel of poetry, to contradict or counteract the patronising rustic version of Hardy as a low-key poetic 'thatcher' in *Thomas Hardy and British Poetry* (1973). Contesting the idea of the simple (-minded) Hardy in a different way in 'Hardy's Virgilian Purples', originally published in *Agenda* [1972], he produced an extremely bookish and rather Eliot-like Hardy, adjusting nuances of Virgil and Dante. In general, though, Davie's is an eminently middle-class, meliorist Hardy seeing a moment of proletarian levity in the British Museum as presaging the death of 'art and literature' (*Thomas Hardy and British Poetry,* p.19). He fails to see the intertextuality of this graveyard of dead Romanticisms, the dialectics of social difference, the siege of ideological contraries which show that Hardy will not 'stay still' textually to be labelled as he would wish. For example, although fascinated by the fact and consequence of the French Revolution, Hardy's rural solicitudes are in tension with the French Revolution itself considered as a culmination of the forces of Enlightenment which were destructive of many of the cultural features with which Hardy is affiliated. Paul Ricoeur, in claiming that 'to give people back a memory is also to give them back a future . . . and . . . release them from the "instantaneous mind",' simultaneously attacks the Revolution as 'representing a rupture with the patrimony of . . .folklore' (cited in Kearney, *op. cit.* p.28), which might be construed as a somewhat 'folkloric patrimony'.

But Hardy mediates a confused sense of rupture and opportunity. He might easily be led to feel, by contrast, that his age is indeed one which, as Leopardi put it, 'stumbling backwards/ Trumpets its retrogression as gain'. However, against the curmudgeonliness this might encourage, in 'An Ancient to Ancients' he produces a poem of brio and assurance to match a sense of Victorian expansiveness – although, with an exquisite turn, the refrain-like 'Gentlemen' is finally addressed, not to the Old Guard, but to the 'hungry generations' which will 'tread down' those who relished 'Bulwer, Scott, Dumas and Sand', for example. In Auden's phrasing, he concludes that 'another time' has 'other lives to live'.

In his poems, in effect, are many ideological mansions. Often they seem *overdeterminedly* 'bourgeois', from 'The Musical Box' with its 'dusky house that stood apart, / And her, white-muslined, waiting there/ In the porch with high-expectant heart . . .' to the hale and hearty daintiness of 'Great Things'. Hardy ushers in, often, a thoroughly 'Victorian' world of excursions and domesticity, and poems to be 'placed' in *Palgrave's Golden Treasury*—'Any little old song' etc. Hardy forces one to confront the difficulty of knowing which poems have the tentacular roots and which are merely the plastic flowers.

Why not indeed, put that arbitrary sequence, from which there are also many poetic spillages, 'Poems of 1912-13', *sous rature* as possible 'plastic flowers' concealing the searching, sardonic preoccupation with desire?

> The passion the planets had scowled on,
> And change had let dwindle,

Her death-rumour smartly relifted
   To full apogee.

Here, in 'My Cicely', where all might be pathos, there is also a saving irony. And even at best the widower's 'Poems of 1912-13' to the dead Emma are triumphs of the *antithetical* imagination, in which Hardy is prepared to weave Emma's snobbery into a sequence in which he is on his best linguistic behaviour, perhaps as if slightly cowed by her in death as in life, in posthumously tender reminiscence of their shared 'epiphanies' and 'moments of being'. In 'At Castle Boterel', for example ('But was there ever / A time of such quality'), the set phrase 'persons of quality' overpowers the philosophical whiff of the word commemorating persons of no consequence who once wove an aristocracy of feeling. The high points of the sequence are rather against his characteristic voice and posture: (e.g.) '*I am just the same* as when / Our days were a joy, and our paths through flowers' is a most 'unHardyan' assertion.

In terms not so much of a Bloomian 'anxiety of influence' as a quest for poetic integrity, we can see Hardy's creative struggle with Wordsworth. It is possible that this could have the kind of ideological aspects Bloom seems anxious not to invoke, although his own critical quest must certainly have them, plainly inspired by a desire to swerve away from High Modernism to the humaner politics of Romantic poetry. Here Hardy seems to be noting that Wordsworth, in a carefully edited version, was proving something of a metaphysical prop – for example, the Wordsworth of 'Tintern Abbey', whose exquisite 'topophilia' merges a communion of loved one and landscape to produce intimations of immortality is in Hardy's mind in 'At Castle Boterel', where empathy

   . . filled but a minute. But was there ever
   A time of such quality, since or before,
   In that hill's story? To one mind never,
   Though it has been climbed, foot-swift, foot-sore,
       By thousands more.
   Primaeval rocks form the road's steep border,
   And much have they faced there, first and last,
   Of the transitory in Earth's long order;
   But what they record in colour and cast
       Is—that we two passed.

Here Wordsworth's 'metaphysic' is undercut by a sense of crowds (that jostling of other bodies as well as minds is a scandal to subjectivity), and the discourse qualifies its own initial assertiveness. The presentation of the scene, tagged by the new 'geological' awareness, undercuts the robust absoluteness with which Wordsworth celebrated the 'beautiful and permanent forms of nature'.

In 'The Second Visit' the speaker finds that the 'sweet especial rural scene' is deceptively altered, where for Wordsworth the sense of 'confirmation' and continuity was a secret underpinning of 'the self' and its purposes. 'The Impercipient' contradicts the 'Immortality' Ode, and 'To Sincerity' also uses him to attack worshippers who 'say [they] rejoice, though grieving, / Believe while unbelieving'. Perhaps, then, the ultimate 'literary contortionist' is Wordsworth rather than Chesterton. Certainly Hardy associated some aspects of the response to Wordsworth with a Victorian 'pietism', lacking intellectual integrity, unwilling to confront the social or natural dispensation as in itself it really was. Like Arnold of 'Growing Old' he also knew that one might become the ghost of one's self, as Wordsworth had, although his concept of ghostliness cuts deeper. 'Ghostliness' mediates his sense of the cost of 'mobility', and suggests the emotional springs of his poetry. While his quotidian self 'does not believe in' ghosts, his poetic self can speak of little else, apparently. Ghosts are an absent-presence which mediate and (im-)mobilize desire.

The extended definition of ghostliness by Stephen Dedalus in *Ulysses* might initially strain the concept for some readers, but surely illuminates Hardy:

> What is a ghost? said Stephen, with tingling earnestness:
> one who has faded into impalpability through death, through
> absence, through change of manners . . .[36]

The most lightly-pencilled-in item deserves scrutiny here: 'change of manners' is a kind of 'behavioural' concomitant of the attempt to transcend one's milieu by strenuous self-improvement, social 'climbing', which will almost certainly issue in behaviour suggesting 'remoteness'. Marx said communism was the spectre haunting Europe, Derrida recently evoked his 'hauntology', and the spectral in Hardy mediates a sense of the communal. The concept also 'infolds', however, to suggest not only the ghostliness of what is abandoned, absent or 'derelict', but the ghostliness of the consciousness which emotionally cleaves to what has formally been abandoned. 'I travel as a phantom now' is a poem whose opening marries a characteristic matter-of-factness with its surprising intimation, cognate with the feeling in 'He Revisits his First School' that 'I ought to have gone as a ghost': and cf. 'Night in the Old Home' and 'The Dead Man Walking'. And he has already revealed what he calls a 'melancholy satisfaction' in what might be called proleptic ghostliness, as in 'I went and stood outside myself', while he often becomes the ventriloquist of skeletons, as in 'Channel Firing' or 'Ah are you digging on my grave?' (a slighted lover becomes a ghost who leaves 'his grave for an hour or so' in 'I rose up as my custom is'). The props of ancient literary forms like the ballad, with its use of the natural/supernatural, mediate modern forms of consciousness and the insights of psychoanalysis. The pace of social change and the sense of having journeyed far psychologically stirs visitation, as in 'The House of Hospitalities':

> . . And the worm has bored the viol
>   That used to lead the tune,
>   Rust eaten out the dial
>   That struck night's noon.
>
> Now no Christmas brings in neighbours,
>   And the New Year comes unlit;
>   Where we sang the mole now labours,
>   And spiders knit.

> Yet at midnight if here walking,
>   When the moon sheets wall and tree,
> I see forms of old time talking,
>   Who smile on me.

This conflates the passage of time and the loss of a specific social dispensation and sense of community. Naming the opponent of this *traditionalism* as capitalism itself, Weber claims that

> A man does not "by nature" wish to earn more and more money, but simply to live as he is accustomed to live and to earn as much as is necessary for that purpose. Wherever modern capitalism has begun its work of increasing the productivity of human labour by increasing its intensity, it has encountered the immensely stubborn resistance of this leading trait of pre-capitalist labour (Cit. Kasler, p.78).

Stan Smith prefers the latter emphasis: 'communities rose and fell, not in any timeless natural rhythm, but according to the dictates of what "The Two Men" calls "the Market's sordid war".' *(Inviolable Voice* [p.26].) Yet what, in Hardy's verse, 'so thrusts on, so throngs the ear,' in Hopkins' idiom, may be a 'forgèd feature' in which the 'forging' is also a forgery, creating a configuration of the present with an '"original" which never existed', as Stan Smith says in another book.[37] The 'biographical' tradition is immensely powerful in forging a critical reception of Hardy, but the poem 'resists' biography. Hardy's 'organic community' is, one way or another, always slightly 'out of reach'. So the case of Hardy can be put more sympathetically in saying that for him the trouble is that the cause of 'radicalism' is one of 'progressivism' which ignores the ambiguities of the idea of progress in itself, an altering concept for altering things. So Hardy's imagination was perhaps unShelleyan in its retrogression, in speaking of things 'silently destroyed' by the dominant culture. Something of the complexity of his position is suggested by Jean Baudrillard in his *Échange Symbolique et la Mort*. Seeking 'an intellectual vantage point' from which to criticise the 'dominant mode of signification', Baudrillard locates the model for protest in *death* (!), as 'in capitalism the dead are excluded from the circulation of meanings in society. The ancestors no longer function, as they did in primitive society, in continuity with the living. In a fundamental sense, then, the dead provide a model for the living and a radical basis for the overthrow of capitalism'.[38] This suggests something of the 'owl service' of Hardy's voracious and caressing memory. Indeed, Baudrillard's ghostly claim is itself given life by Hardy's 'necrologic scrawls' (see 'In a Former Resort after Many Years').

Hobbes opined that 'imagination and memory are but one thing, for which divers considerations have but divers names', a quotation Hardy would have endorsed. But it is interesting to contrast Hardy's memory with a Wordsworth inclined to rehearse 'strength through joy': for Hardy, if imagination is memory, memory is melancholia. The art of memory may be a memory of art, although memory's apparent fidelity is already a form of 'treason', and here too there is a split between the 'radical' and the 'progressive.' For example, Hardy 'remembered' a 'harvest home' he attended as a child, after which 'the orally transmitted ditties of centuries' were 'slain at a stroke' by the London comic songs in the wake of the coming of the railway. Progress can 'seriously damage a sense of cultural autonomy, and 'folk-art' stands ready to be reconstituted as the bearer of 'social imaginaries'. Hardy's 'instinct to preserve' poetic forms of communication doubles back to become what Baudrillard calls 'the history of the vanquished dead crying out for justice' and tells Ricoeur's 'story of the powerless and the dispossessed'. This ambition vies with his personal awareness of having transcended an apparently 'ordained' position.

Hardy has much truck with the *ancien* while not exactly going over to the *ancien régime*. Indeed, he has quite a few 'Enlightenment' poems which slaughter misplaced pieties with post-Shelleyan gusto. These are poems of anti-metaphysical polemic, although they may turn on what seems to be the ambiguous presentation of an 'alternative metaphysic': in style and tone they suggest, rather, a 'refusal of the metaphysical', with Hume and Darwin in attendance. This 'refusal' is made explicit in 'A Sign-Seeker', and a number of others, like 'The Sleep-worker', 'Agnostoi Theoi', 'A Dream Question', 'New Year's Eve', 'God's Education', 'A Plaint to Man', and 'God's Funeral', which teach us, in words of Foucault paraphrasing Nietzsche, to 'laugh at the solemnity of the origin' [the discourse of origins?], and have a conspicuously light touch. He creates 'joke teleologies' which pretend to clear up 'uncertainties, mysteries, doubts' and reveal what Derrida calls 'the origin and end of the game', the 'revelation' being one of 'non-revelation', conveying a sense that '[The] Epiphany has been Cancelled'.

Hardy's poems naturally embody 'Victorian values', yet often refuse the flattering self-representations of Victorian culture, but do often present the drama of a Shelleyan 'desire' always already dispelled by a High Victorian 'looking before and after'. Although the phrase is Shelley's own, it was the Victorian Age in which this modern consciousness reached apogee – see Hardy's 'Before Life and After', for example, in which Darwin and geology beautifully combine with a sense of intimate personal feeling(s). Such poems are hardly the innocuous fruit of the 'rustic recorder' made (too) familiar by critical processing.

Notes

Chapter 1: *Desperate Remedies*

1 W.B. Yeats, *The Poems* (revised edition), ed. Richard J. Finneran (Basingstoke: Macmillan, 1991), p.214

2 Donald Davie, *Thomas Hardy and British Poetry* (London: Routledge, 1973), p.4 and Peter Widdowson, *Hardy in History* (London: Routledge, 1989), p.26. For Laurence Lerner and John Holmstrom: 'nothing . . . in the book . . . suggests a writer of genius', in *Thomas Hardy and His Readers* (London: Bodley Head, 1968), p.14. Catherine Neale intelligently follows-up on Derek Longhurst's claim in *Gender, Genre and Narrative Pleasure* (London: Unwin Hyman, 1989), that 'popular genres . . . evolve interactively in relation to specific historical formations' (p.5), in '*Desperate Remedies*: The Merits and Demerits of Popular Fiction', in the *Critical Survey* 5, no.2 (1993), 115-122, as 'a text to be read for its symbolism and language of the unconscious' (p.121).

3 See Hardy, *Two on a Tower* [1882] (London: Macmillan, 1975), p.76.

4 Thomas Hardy, *The Life and Work of Thomas Hardy*, ed. Michael Millgate London: Macmillan, 1984), p.63.

5 Michael Millgate, *Thomas Hardy: A Biography* (Oxford: Oxford Univ. Press, 1982), p.110. For Macmillan's caution, see Gaye Tuchman (with Nina E. Fortin), *Edging Women Out: Victorian Novelists, Publishers and Social Change* (London: Routledge, 1989), p.42.

6 Raymond Williams *The Country and the City* (London: Chatto and Windus, 1973), p.203.

7 Michael Millgate, *Thomas Hardy: A Biography*, p.110.

8 Thomas Hardy, *Desperate Remedies* (London: Macmillan, 1986), p.310. Hardy swathes this incident in the ambiguity remarked by critics in the case of Tess on the occasion of her 'violation' by Alec D'Urberville. Pamela Dalziel concludes that 'to trace the absorption of *Poor Man* material into *Desperate Remedies* is to recognize that the . . . concerns that material originally embodied were not so much dissipated as subtly misplaced', in 'The Genesis of Hardy's *Desperate Remedies*', *Journal of English and Germanic Philology* 94, no.2 (1995), 232.

9 *Punch* described the sensation 'product' as 'devoted to Harrowing the Mind, making the Flesh Creep . . . giving shocks to the Nervous System, destroying Conventional Moralities, and unfitting the Public for the Prosaic Avocations of Life'. Cited by Lyn Pykett in *The Sensation Novel: From 'The Woman in White' to 'The Moonstone'* (Plymouth: Northcote House, 1994), p.3.

10 T.S. Eliot, '*Ulysses*, Order and Myth' [1923], in: *Selected Prose*, ed. Frank Kermode (London: Faber and Faber, 1975), pp.175-78.

11 W.H. Auden, 'September 1, 1939': in *Another Time* (London: Faber and Faber, 1940).

12 Rosemarie Morgan, 'Bodily Transactions: Toni Morrison and Thomas Hardy', in *Celebrating Thomas Hardy* (Basingstoke: Macmillan, 1996), p.148.

13 Lovers in Shelley's *The Revolt of Islam* (1818); cited by Hardy in *Jude the Obscure* ed. Norman Page (London: W.W. Norton 1978), p.185.

14 Keats, 'Ode on Indolence': *Poetical Works,* ed. H.W. Garrod (Oxford: Clarendon Press, 1958), p.449.

15 Mallarmé, *Oeuvres Complètes* (Paris: Gallimard, 1945), p.75.

16 'The Bride-Night Fire': in *Selected Poems*, ed. Samuel Hynes (Oxford: Oxford Univ. Press, 1996), pp.9-12.

17 'Friends Beyond': in (e.g.) *Selected Poems*, ed. Samuel Hynes, pp.4-6.

18 Gray speaks of 'Cytherea' in writing that 'O'er her warm cheek and rising bosom move/ The bloom of young Desire, and purple light of Love': in Thomas Gray, 'The Progress of Poesy', *Complete Poems*, ed. H.W. Starr and J.R. Hendrickson (Oxford: Clarendon Press, 1966), p.14.

19 Leo Bersani, *A Future for Astyanax: Character and Desire in Literature* (London: Marion Boyars, 1978), p.6.

20 Peter Widdowson, *Hardy in History* (London: Routledge, 1989), p.93.

21 Stephen Greenblatt, *Renaissance Self-Fashioning* (Chicago: Univ. of Chicago Press, 1980), p.204.

22 Jane Austen, *Emma* (London: Oxford Univ. Press, 1971), p.438.

23 Gillian Beer, *Darwin's Plots: Evolutionary Narrative in Darwin, George Eliot, and Nineteenth Century Fiction* (London: Routledge and Kegan Paul, 1983), and Gillian Beer, 'Finding a Scale for the Human: Plot and Writing in Hardy's Novels', in *Critical Essays on Thomas Hardy*, ed. Dale Kramer (Boston: G.K. Hall, 1990).

Chapter 2: *Under the Greenwood Tree*

1 Barbara Johnson, *The Wake of Deconstruction* (Oxford: Blackwell, 1994), p.5.

2 *Under the Greenwood Tree* [1872] (London: Macmillan, 1990), p.61.

3 'Locksley Hall', *The Poems of Tennyson*, ed. Christopher Ricks (London: Longman, 1969), p.695.

4 Norman Page, 'Hardy and the English Language', in *Thomas Hardy: The Writer and His Background* (London: Bell and Hyman, 1980), pp.152-53.

5 Quoted in Dirk Kasler, *Max Weber: An Introduction to his Life and Work* (London: Polity, 1988), p.78.

6 John Milton, 'L'Allegro', 133-4 in: *Complete Shorter Poems* ed. John Carey (London: Longman, 1997), p.141.

7 Jacques Derrida, *Éperons: Les Styles de Nietzsche* (Paris: Flammarion, 1978), pp.100-102.

8 Susan Bordo, '"Material Girl": The Effacements of Postmodern Culture', in *Literary Theory*, ed. Julie Rivkin and Michael Ryan (Oxford: Blackwell, 1998), pp.1099-1115.

9 See Robert Gittings, *Young Thomas Hardy* (London: Heinemann, 1975), p.175; Frances Widdowson, *Going up into the Next Class: Women and Elementary Teacher Training* (London: Hutchinson, 1983).

10 Michael Millgate, *Thomas Hardy: A Biography* (Oxford: Oxford Univ. Press, 1982), p.16: for the 'leaves' see Marjorie Garson, *Hardy's Fables of Integrity: Woman, Body, Text* (Oxford: The Clarendon Press, 1991).

11 Jonathan Sobol, *Ghetto* (London: Nick Hern Books, 1989).

12 Raymond Williams *The Country and the City* (London: Chatto and Windus, 1973), p.202.

13 Cited in Lawrence Jones, '*Under the Greenwood Tree* and the Victorian Pastoral', in *Art and Society in the Victorian Novel: Essays on Dickens and His Contemporaries*, ed. Colin Gibson (Basingstoke: Macmillan, 1989), pp.149-167.

14 Paul Dave, 'The Bourgeois Paradigm and Heritage Cinema', *New Left Review* 224 (1997), p.119.

15 'In the Victorian era, publishers, authors and public all recognised the might of the [circulating] libraries, and the structure and content of novels conformed to their wishes': Guinevere L. Griest, *'Mudie's Circulating Library' and the Victorian Novel* (Newton Abbot: David and Charles, 1970), p.5.

16 See John Goode, *Thomas Hardy* (Oxford: Basil Blackwell, 1988), p.12.

17 See Roger Sales, *English Literature in History 1780-1830* (London: Hutchinson, 1983), pp.15-18. If, as Jan Marsh points out, Hardy gave an impetus to nostalgic pastoralism, his art entails resistance to the sentimentality he is supposed to have fostered. See Jan Marsh, *Back to the Land: The Pastoral Impulse in England, 1880-1914* (London: Quartet Books, 1982), pp.29-30.

18 Tennyson, 'Come Down O Maid' ('Shepherd's Song'), in 'The Princess', *The Poems of Tennyson*, p.836.

19 Baudelaire, *Oeuvres Complètes* (I) (Paris: Gallimard, 1975), p.11.

20 Ezra Pound, *Literary Essays* (London: Faber and Faber, 1954), p.6.

21 Wallace Stevens, *Opus Posthumous* (London: Faber and Faber 1959), p.189.

22 Teresa M. Brennan, *History after Lacan* (London: Routledge, 1993), p.113.

23 Merryn and Raymond Williams, 'Hardy and Social Class', in: *Thomas Hardy: The Writer and His Background*, Norman Page (ed.) (London: Bell and Hyman, 1980), pp.29-40.

24 Marjorie Levinson, *Keats's Life of Allegory* (Oxford: Blackwell, 1988), p.260.

25 Marjorie Garson, *Hardy's Fables of Integrity: Woman, Body, Text* (Oxford: Clarendon Press, 1991), p.31.

26 Shadia Drury, *Alexandre Kojève: The Roots of Postmodern Politics* (London: Macmillan, 1994): 'In Kojève's account of [modernity], it is the feminine principle that triumphs' (p.25).

Chapter 3: *A Pair of Blue Eyes*

1 See *Thomas Hardy: The Critical Heritage*, ed. R.G. Cox (London: Routledge and Kegan Paul, 1970), pp.xvi-xvii. For the novel's popularity, see Charles P.C. Pettit, 'Merely a Good Hand at a Serial? From *A Pair of Blue Eyes* to *Far from the Madding Crowd*', in *The Achievement of Thomas Hardy*, ed. Phillip Mallett (Basingstoke: Macmillan, 2000), pp.4-5.

2 *Collected Letters,* ed. R. L. Purdy and Michael Millgate (Oxford: Clarendon Press, 1978-88), V, p.282.

3 See *The Feminist Reader*, ed. Catherine Belsey and Jane Moore (London: Macmillan, 1997), p.255; and Hélène Cixous 'Sorties' [1975], reprinted in *Modern Literary Theory: A Reader* (3rd.ed.), ed. Philip Rice and Patricia Waugh (London: Edward Arnold, 1996), pp.137-144.

4 Thomas Hardy, *A Pair of Blue Eyes* [1873] (London: Macmillan, 1986), p.260.

5 See Morag Schiach, *Hélène Cixous: A Politics of Writing* (London: Routledge, 1991).

6 Jane Thomas, *Thomas Hardy, Femininity and Dissent: Reassessing the 'Minor' Novels* (London: Macmillan, 1999), p.71.

7 Michael Millgate, *Thomas Hardy: A Biography* (Oxford: Oxford Univ. Press, 1982), p.143.

8 See Madan Sarup, *An Introductory Guide to Postmodernism and Poststructuralism*, p.23.

9 Tennyson, 'Maud: A Monodrama', *The Poems of Tennyson*, p.1063.

10 Keats, 'Endymion', 2.758: *Poetical Works* (Oxford: Clarendon Press, 1958), p.119.

11 Keats, 'Lamia' 1.197, in *The Complete Poems*, ed. Miriam Allott (London: Longman, 1970), p.625.

12 Flaubert's *Éducation Sentimentale* (Paris: Flammarion, 1985), p.500.

13 The term is Seymour Chatman's, translating Barthes' *'noyau'*: see *Story and Discourse: Narrative Structure in Fiction and Film* (Ithaca: Cornell Univ. Press, 1978), p.53.

14 See Eve Kosovsky Sedgwick, *Between Men* (New York: Columbia Univ. Press, 1985).

15 Oscar Wilde, *The Importance of Being Earnest* [1895] ed. Richard Allen Cave (London: Penguin, 2000), p.310.

16 See, e.g. *The Feminist Reader* (London: Macmillan, 1997), p.108.

17 Freud, 'Dissolution of the Oedipus Complex' in *Complete Psychological Works,* vol. 19 (London: Hogarth Press, 1925), p.178.

18 Joan Rivière, 'Womanliness as a Masquerade', in *Formations of Fantasy*, ed. Victor Burgin, James Donald and Cora Kaplan (London: Routledge, 1986); also Marjorie Garber, 'Cross-dressing, Gender and Representation', in *The Feminist Reader*, pp.166-67.
19 See John Goode, *Thomas Hardy: the Offensive Truth* (Oxford: Blackwell, 1983), pp.5-11.
20 Shelley, *Prometheus Unbound* 1.748 (in *Poetical Works* [Oxford: Oxford Univ. Press, 1969], p.225).

Chapter 4: *The Hand of Ethelberta*

1 Thomas Hardy, *The Hand of Ethelberta: A Comedy in Chapters* [1876] (London: Penguin, 1996), p.259.
2 Eco's idea of 'intertextual frames' is illustrated in Hardy. See Umberto Eco, *The Role of the Reader* (London: Indiana Univ. Press, 1979); Shlomith Rimmon-Kenan, *Narrative Fiction: Contemporary Poetics* (London: Methuen, 1983), p.123.
3 Paul Turner, *The Life of Thomas Hardy* (Oxford: Basil Blackwell, 1998), p.6.
4 Wallace Stevens, 'The Comedian as the Letter C', *Collected Poems* (London: Faber and Faber, 1955), p.43.
5 'Garreteer': Hardy describes Christopher as living in a garret (pp.46-7), using this word in 'Dream of the City Shopwoman' (dated 1866), in *Complete Poems*, ed. James Gibson (London: Macmillan, 1979), p.609.
6 W. B. Yeats, 'The Lover Mourns for the Loss of Love', *The Poems*, ed. Richard J. Finneran (London: Macmillan, 1991), p.61; and *The Seminar of Jacques Lacan*, Jacques-Alain Miller (ed.) (London: Routledge, 1992).
7 *The Oxford Dictionary of English Christian Names*, ed. E.G. Withycombe (Oxford: Oxford Univ. Press, 1977), p.108.
8 Simone De Beauvoir: in Toril Moi, 'Feminist, Female, Feminine', in *The Feminist Reader: Essays in Gender and the Politics of Literary Criticism*, p.106.
9 Donna Haraway, 'A Cyborg Manifesto' [1991], in *Contemporary Literary Criticism: Literary and Cultural Studies*, ed. Robert Con Davis and Ronald Schleifer (Harlow: Longman, 1998), pp.696-727.
10 Julie Rivkin and Michael Ryan (eds), *Literary Theory: An Anthology* (Oxford: Blackwell, 1998), p.348.
11 A.L. Le Quesne, *Carlyle* (Oxford: Oxford Univ. Press, 1982), pp.50-51.
12 Samuel Johnson, *Lives of the English Poets* (London: Everyman, 1963), p.254.
13 Penny Boumelha, 'A Complicated Position for a Woman: *The Hand of Ethelberta*', in *The Sense of Sex: Feminist Perspectives on Hardy*, ed. Margaret Higonnet (Chicago: Univ. of Illinois Press, 1993), pp.242-259.
14 D.H. Lawrence, *Study of Thomas Hardy and Other Essays*, ed. Bruce Steele (London: Grafton, 1986), p.19.
15 Perhaps with Wordsworth's 'it is not now as it hath been *of Yore*' in mind: *The Poetical Works of Wordsworth*, ed. Thomas Hutchinson (Oxford: Oxford Univ. Press, 1907), p.587.
16 See Rosemarie Morgan, *Cancelled Words: Rediscovering Thomas Hardy* (London: Routledge, 1992).
17 See Thomas Hardy, *The Hand of Ethelberta: A Comedy in Chapters* [1876] (London: Penguin, 1996), p.208.
18 'maistrye': Geoffrey Chaucer, 'The Wife of Bath's Tale', 1221-1264, in *The Riverside Chaucer*, 3rd ed. (Boston: Houghton Mifflin, 1987), pp.121-122.
19 'Ozymandias' [1818], in P.B. Shelley, *Poetical Works*, ed. Thomas Hutchinson (Oxford: Oxford Univ. Press, 1970), p.550.

20 W.B. Yeats, 'In Memory of Major Robert Gregory', *The Poems*, ed. Richard J. Finneran (London: Macmillan, 1991), p.135.

21 W.B.Yeats, 'The Magi', *The Poems*, p.126.

22 Leo Bersani, *The Culture of Redemption* (London: Harvard Univ. Press, 1990), p.58.

23 See Juliet Mitchell's *The Stone and the Scorpion: the Female Subject of Desire in the Novels of Charlotte Bronte, George Eliot and Thomas Hardy* (London: Greenwood Press, 1994), p.155. See also Sarah Davies, 'The Hand of Ethelberta: De-Mythologising "Woman",' in *The Critical Survey* 5 no.2 (1993), 123-130.

Chapter 5: *The Return of the Native*

1 See, e.g., Tony E. Jackson, *The Subject of Modernism: Narrative Narrative Alterations in the Fiction of Eliot, Conrad, Woolf and Joyce* (Ann Arbor: Univ. of Michigan Press, 1994).

2 W.B. Yeats, 'The Indian to His Love', *The Poems*, ed. Richard J. Finneran (London: Macmillan, 1989), p.14.

3 Thomas Hardy, *The Return of the Native* (London: Macmillan, 1995), p.231.

4 W.B. Yeats, 'All Souls' Night', *The Poems*, p.230.

5 Hermann Melville, 'Bartleby the Scrivener': in *Bartleby and Benito Cereno* (New York: Dover, 1990).

6 T.S. Eliot, *Selected Essays* (London: Faber and Faber, 1934), p.288, p.296.

7 Robert Lowell, *For Lizzie and Harriet* (London: Faber and Faber, 1973), p.34.

8 W.H.Auden, *The Double Man* (New York: Random House, 1941), p.103.

9 William Wordsworth, *The Prelude*, bk.2, l.309: ed. E. De Selincourt (London: Oxford Univ. Press, 1926): p.59.

10 John Lucas, *The Literature of Change* (Brighton: The Harvester Press, 1980), p.150.

11 Rush Rhees, *Ludwig Wittgenstein: Personal Recollections* (Oxford: Blackwell, 1981), p.143.

12 See *The Return of the Native*, ed. Simon Gatrell (Oxford: Oxford Univ. Press, 1990), p.450.

13 Robert Lowell, 'Caligula', *For the Union Dead* (London: Faber and Faber, 1965), p.49.

14 James Joyce, *Ulysses* (London: Penguin, 1968), pp.455-489.

15 Wallace Stevens, 'Of Modern Poetry', *Collected Poetry and Prose* (New York: Library of America, 1997), p.218; Wallace Stevens, 'Ésthetique du Mal', *Collected Poems* (New York: Knopf, 1955), p.325.

16 Gerard Hopkins, 'Inversnaid', *The Poems*, ed. W.H.Gardner and Norman Mackenzie (London: Oxford Univ. Press, 1979), p.89.

17 Stephane Mallarmé, '*Un Coup de Dés*': *Oeuvres Complètes* (Paris: Gallimard, 1945), p.457. For Pascal and the wager, see Donald Adamson, *Pascal: Mathematician, Physicist and Thinker about God* (Basingstoke: Macmillan, 1995).

18 Browning, 'Pippa Passes' (1841), ll.227-8, in *The Poetical Works of Robert Browning*, III, ed. Ian Jack and Rowena Fowler (Oxford: Clarendon Press, 1988), p.40.

19 Thomas Paine, *Collected Writings* (New York: Library of America, 1995), pp.479-80.

20 'Hexed': Robert Lowell, 'Exorcism', in *Selected Poems*, ed. Jonathan Raban (London: Faber and Faber, 1974), p.151; 'witchery': Robert Lowell, *The Dolphin* (London: Faber and Faber, 1973), p.48. A passage in Barthes relates the image of the witch to that of the alienated intellectual. (Cited in Andy Stafford, *Roland Barthes, Phenomenon and Myth* [Edinburgh: Edinburgh Univ. Press, 1998].)

21 See P.N. Furbank, *Unholy Pleasure: or the Idea of Social Class* (Oxford, Oxford Univ. Press, 1985), p.97.

22 Wallace Stevens, 'Le Monocle de Mon Oncle': *Collected Poetry and Prose*, p.12.

23 See *The Return of the Native*, Simon Gatrell (ed.) (Oxford: Oxford Univ. Press, 1990), p.442.

24 Matthew Arnold, *Culture and Anarchy and Other Writings*, ed. Stefan Collini (Cambridge: Cambridge Univ. Press, 1993), pp.126-137.

25 Stefan Collini, 'Matthew Arnold', in *Victorian Thinkers: Carlyle, Ruskin, Arnold, Morris*, ed. A.L. Le Quesne (Oxford: Oxford Univ. Press, 1993), p.222.

26 Martin Jay, *Adorno* (Cambridge, Mass.: Harvard Univ. Press, 1984), p.36. See also Jonathan Beecher, *Charles Fourier: The Visionary and His World* (Berkeley, Cal.: Univ. of California Press, 1986).

Chapter 6: *A Laodicean*

1 Martin J. Wiener, English Culture and the Decline of the Industrial Spirit, 1850-1980 (Harmondsworth: Penguin, 1985), p.162.

2 Thomas Hardy, *A Laodicean: A Story of Today*, ed. Barbara Hardy (London: J.M. Dent and Sons, 1997), p.53.

3 Thesis 7 of 'Theses on the Philosophy of History', cited in: *Walter Benjamin and the Demands of History*, ed. Michael P.Sternberg (Ithaca, New York: Cornell Univ. Press, 1996), p.207.

4 'To the Queen': *The Poems of Tennyson*, ed. Christopher Ricks (London: Longman, 1969), p.990.

5 Ellen Meiksins Wood, *The Pristine Culture of Capitalism: A Historical Essay on Old Regimes and Modern States* (London: Verso, 1991).

6 Rosemarie Morgan, 'Bodily Transactions: Toni Morrison and Thomas Hardy in Literary Discourse', in *Celebrating Thomas Hardy*, Charles P.C. Pettit, ed. (London: Macmillan, 1996), pp.136-158.

7 'Replicant': See the discussion of the film *Blade Runner* in *Postmodern Arts: An Introductory Reader*, ed. Nigel Wheale (London: Routledge, 1996).

8 Oscar Wilde, *The Importance of Being Earnest* [1899] Act 1; in: (e.g.) *The Complete Works of Oscar Wilde*, (London: Collins, 1966), p.333.

9 An innuendo in French, most famously in Mallarmé, *Oeuvres Complètes* (Paris: Gallimard, 1945), p.75.

10 Ben Jonson, *Volpone, or The Fox*: 2.1.25; ed. John W. Creaser (London: Hodder and Stoughton, 1978), p.103.

11 James Joyce, *Ulysses* [1922] (London: Penguin, 1992), p.174.

12 *Two on a Tower* [1882] (London: Penguin, 1995), p.125.

13 The church clerk was described as 'a kind of bowdlerized rake' in *Desperate Remedies* [1871] (London: Penguin, 1998), p.126.

14 Tennyson, 'The Palace of Art', [rev.1842]: *The Poems of Tennyson*, p.400.

15 See Homi K. Bhaba, 'Interrogating Identity', in *The Real Me: Post-modernism and the Question of Identity*, ed. Lisa Appignanesi (London: ICA, 1987), p.5.

16 Michael Millgate, *Thomas Hardy: A Biography*, p.282.

17 W. L. Phelps, *Autobiography with Letters* (London: Oxford Univ. Press, 1939), p.391.

18 'Copying Architecture in an Old Minster [Wimborne]', reprinted in *Complete Poems*, ed. James Gibson (London: Macmillan, 1976), p.438.

Chapter 7: *Two on a Tower*

1 Michael Millgate, *Thomas Hardy: His Career as a Novelist* (London: Macmillan, 1994), p.183.

2 Thomas Hardy, *Two on a Tower: A Romance* [1882] (London: Penguin, 1995), p.178.

3 See John Maynard, 'Conclusion: Hardy's *Jude*: Disassembling Sexuality and Religion', in *Victorian Discourses on Sexuality and Religion* (Cambridge: Cambridge Univ. Press, 1993).

4 Wordsworth, 'To a Highland Girl' [1803], *The Poems,* vol. 1 (London: Penguin, 1977), p.599.

5 Jacques Derrida, *'Différance'*, in *Literary Theory: An Anthology* ed. Julie Rifkin and Michael Ryan (Oxford: Basil Blackwell, 1998), p.400.

6 Shakespeare, 'Sonnet 20', *Shakespeare's Sonnets*, ed. Katherine Duncan-Jones (London: Thomas Nelson and Sons, 1997), p.151.

7 John Henry Newman, 'The Pillar of the Cloud' [1833], in *Collected Poems and the Dream of Gerontius* (Sevenoaks: Fisher Press, 1992), p.65.

8 F.E. Halliday, *Thomas Hardy, His Life and Work* (London: Panther, 1978), p.102.

9 See *Letters of John Keats*, Robert Gittings (ed.) (Oxford: Oxford Univ. Press, 1970), p.250

10 See 'Ideology and the State', in *Lenin and Philosophy and Other Essays*, rep.in *Modern Literary Theory*, Philip Rice and Patricia Waugh (eds) (London: Edward Arnold, 1989), pp. 54-62.

11 For Hardy's Darwinian sense of 'the tenuousness of the "natural" self constructed out of 'arbitrary social conventions', see George Levine, *Darwin and the Novelists* (London: Harvard Univ. Press, 1988), p.239.

12 See 'Media, Simulations and the End of the Social', in *Jean Baudrillard: From Marxism to Postmodernism and Beyond* (Oxford: Polity Press, 1989), pp.60-92.

13 In 'Analysis of a Theme', Wallace Stevens states that 'We enjoy the ithy oonts and long-haired/ Plomets, as the Herr Gott/ Enjoys his comets', aware of the etymological connection between hair and comets, in *Collected Poems*, p.349.

14 See Catherine Belsey, *Critical Practice* (London: Methuen, 1980), pp.56-63.

15 See, e.g. J. Hillis Miller, *Tropes, Parables, Performatives: Essays on Twentieth Century Literature* (Brighton: Harvester Press, 1991). See Jacob Korg, 'Astronomical Imagery in Victorian Poetry', in *Victorian Science and Victorian Values: Literary Perspectives*, James Paradis and Thomas Postlwait (eds) (New Brunswick: Rutgers Univ. Press, 1985), p.139.

16 W.B. Yeats, 'The Song of the Happy Shepherd', *The Poems*, p.7.

17 Greimas's third pairing for his description of 'the actors of narrative', is 'helper vs opponent'. See Ronald Schleifer, *A.J. Greimas and the Nature of Meaning* (London: Croom Helm, 1987), p.95.

18 Gerard Manley Hopkins, 'The Leaden Echo and the Golden Echo', *The Poems*, 4th ed. (London: Oxford Univ. Press, 1970), p.91.

19 Leo Bersani, *A Future for Astyanax* (London: Marion Boyars, 1978), p.6.

20 Matthew Arnold, 'Dover Beach' [1867], *Poetical Works*, ed. C.B. Tinker and H. F. Lowry (London: Oxford Univ. Press, 1950), p.210-12.

21 See Stephen Regan, *The Eagleton Reader* (Oxford: Basil Blackwell, 1998), p.171.

Chapter 8: *The Mayor of Casterbridge*

1 Thomas Hardy, *The Mayor of Casterbridge* (London: Macmillan, 1985), p.27.

2 See Anthony Easthope, *Poetry and Phantasy* (Cambridge: Cambridge Univ. Press, 1989), p.43.

3 Proust, *À La Recherche du Temps Perdu* 3: ed. Pierre Clerac and André Ferré (Paris: Gallimard, 1954), p.376.

4 See Peter J. Casagrande and Charles Lock, 'The Name "Henchard"', *Thomas Hardy Society Review* 1 (1978), 115-18.

5 See Peter Widdowson, *Thomas Hardy* (Plymouth: Northcote House, 1996), pp.50-51.

6 See 'The Marriage of Heaven and Hell', in: *The Selected Poetry of Blake*, David Erdman (ed.) (London: New English Library, 1976), p.74.

7 See 'Preface' to *Lyrical Ballads*, R. L. Brett and A. R. Jones (eds) (London: Methuen, 1965), p.245. Michael Valdez Moses discusses 'the proto-modern character of even this provincial backwater', in *The Novel and the Globalization of Culture* (New York: Oxford Univ. Press, 1995), p.41.

8 Ronald Blythe: cited in Terry Hawkes, *That Shakespeherian Rag*: *Essays on a Critical Process*, p.15.

9 See David Underdown, *Fire from Heaven: Life in an English Town in the Seventeenth Century* (London: HarperCollins, 1992), p.264.

10 See, e.g. Marjorie Garson, *Hardy's Fables of Integrity: Woman, Body, Text* (Oxford: Clarendon Press, 1991), p.109; and Martin Seymour-Smith, *Hardy* (London: Bloomsbury, 1994), p.341.

11 Kevin Z. Moore, *The Descent of the Imagination: Postromantic Culture in the Later Novels of Thomas Hardy* (London: New York Univ. Press, 1990), p.235. As Lance St. John Butler points out, '[Farfrae's] origins in a particular part of Scotland are never made clear', in *Registering the Difference: Reading Literature through Register* (Manchester: Manchester Univ. Press, 1999), p.173.

12 For the *pharmakon*, the 'poison/remedy' as a theme from Socrates picked up by Derrida, see Jonathan Culler, *On Deconstruction* (London: Routledge and Kegan Paul, 1982), pp.142-149.

13 Shlomith Rimmon-Kenan, 'Deconstructive Reflections on Deconstruction', originally in *Poetics Today*, 2 (1980-1); reprinted in *Modern Literary Theory: A Reader* (London: Routledge, 1989), pp.185-189; see also Freud's essay 'The Uncanny', in *Psychological Writings and Letters*, Sander L. Gilman (ed.) (New York: Continuum, 1995), pp.120-153.

14 In a discussion of 'The Sandman' by Kleist initially broached by Jentsch. See Morag Schiach, *Hélène Cixous: A Politics of Writing* (London: Routledge, 1991), p.46.

15 'On Sitting Down to Read *King Lear* Once Again', in *The Poems of John Keats*, Jack Stillinger (ed.) (London: Heinemann, 1978), p.225.

16 This Kantian phrase 'passes into' a sense of (Schopenhaurian) undirected 'willing', recognizable in Hardy's 'Immanent will which stirs and urges everything'. See David Carroll, *Paraesthetics* (London: Methuen, 1987), pp.131-154.

17 William R. Rutland, *Thomas Hardy: A Study of His Writings and Their Background* (Oxford: Basil Blackwell, 1938), p.93.

18 See, e.g., Martin Heidegger, *Nietzsche*, ed. David Farrell Krell (London: Routledge and Kegan Paul, 1981), pp.37-43.

19 James Joyce, *Ulysses* (London: Penguin, 1992), p.103.

20 W.H.Auden, 'Letter to Lord Byron', in *Letters from Iceland* (London: Faber and Faber, 1937), p.53.

21 'In the Servants' Quarters', Thomas Hardy, *Selected Poetry* ed. Samuel Hynes (Oxford: Oxford Univ. Press, 1996); discussed by Tom Paulin, *Thomas Hardy: The Poetry of Perception*, 2nd ed. (London: Macmillan, 1986), pp.7-8.

22 L. Althusser, 'Ideology and the State', in *Modern Literary Theory: A Reader*, Philip Rice and Patricia Waugh (eds) (London: Edward Arnold, 1989), pp.54-62.

23 Henchard claimed that Elizabeth-Jane (as well as her mother) was dead.

24 James Joyce, *Ulysses* (London: Penguin, 1992), p.266.

25 Thomas Hardy, *The Return of the Native* [1878], p.332.

26 See Gillian Beer, 'Origins and Oblivion in Victorian Narrative', in *Sex, Politics and Science in the Nineteenth-Century Novel*, Ruth Bernard Yeazell (ed.) (Baltimore: Johns Hopkins Univ. Press, 1986), pp.63-87.

27 Hardy uses this phrase in connection with Leslie Stephen in 'The Schreckhorn' ('June 1897'), in *Satires of Circumstance* (1914), reprinted in *Complete Poems*, James Gibson (ed.)

(London: Macmillan, 1976), p.322. The mountain in the Swiss Alps is neatly associated with Stephen's character, which is also announced by his having been its first 'conqueror'.

28 A Jonathan Culler point seems à propos: 'one can continue the pursuit of signs, the attempt to grasp, master, formulate, define, even though one knows that one is caught up in a signifying process that one cannot fully control . . .' (See *The Pursuit of Signs: Semiotics, Literature, Deconstruction* [London: Routledge and Kegan Paul, 1981], p.XI.)

Chapter 9: *The Woodlanders*

1 Thomas Hardy, *The Woodlanders* [1887] (London: Penguin, 1981), p.59.

2 Carlyle, in *On Heroes and Hero-Worship* exhorts us to think of 'Igdrasil, the Ash-Tree of Existence' as an inclusive image for the cosmos, then asks us to consider 'The "*Machine* of the Universe"' as the 'image of' modernity. See Mary Jacobus' essay on 'Tree and Machine: *The Woodlanders*', in *Critical Approaches to the Fiction of Thomas Hardy*, Dale Kramer (ed.) (London: Macmillan, 1979), pp.116-134.

3 For Hardy, 'the great intellectual event of the age . . . was the publication of Darwin's *Origin of Species*'. (See Leo J. Henkin, *Darwinism in the English Novel 1860-1910* [New York: Corporate Press, 1940], p.224.) But for Darwin, as for Spencer, 'the natural sciences were far better guides to reality than the social sciences': see Cynthia Eagle Russett, *Sexual Science: The Victorian Construction of Womanhood* (Cambridge, Mass.: Harvard Univ. Press, 1989), p.133. Hardy might formally assent to the idea but his creative practice writes otherwise. See George Oppen, *Evolution and Poetic Belief: A Study in Some Victorian and Modern Writers* (Oxford: Basil Blackwell, 1956), p.298. And Robin Gilmour finds 'resistance' in his response to Darwin in *The Novel in the Victorian Age: A Modern Introduction* (London: Edward Arnold, 1986), p.188.

4 'It would be a great mistake to settle for seeing in these novels a representation of country life as an idyllic and timeless enclave': Penny Boumelha, 'The Patriarchy of Class: *Under the Greenwood Tree, Far from the Madding Crowd, The Woodlanders*', in *The Cambridge Companion to Thomas Hardy*, ed. Dale Kramer (Cambridge: Cambridge Univ. Press, 1999), p.131.

5 Thomas Gray, 'Elegy Written in a Country Churchyard', in *The Poems of Gray, Collins and Goldsmith*, ed. Roger Lonsdale (London: Longman, 1969), pp.103-141.

6 William Empson, *Some Versions of Pastoral* [1935] (London: Penguin, 1995), pp.11-12.

7 That is, he has *not* been 'cuckolded', as Marjorie Garson asserts in her excellent book on *Hardy's Fables of Integrity: Woman, Body, Text* (Oxford: Oxford Univ. Press, 1991), p.85.

8 Matthew Arnold, 'Requiescat', *Poetical Works* (London: Oxford Univ. Press, 1950), p.20.

9 See Freud, 'On the Universal Tendency to Debasement in the Sphere of Love', reprinted in *The Freud Reader*, ed. Peter Gay (London: Vintage, 1985), pp.394-400.

10 As Chris Weedon puts it, 'class is a contested term and its precise meaning depends on the discursive context in which it occurs', in *Feminism, Theory and the Politics of Difference* (Oxford: Basil Blackwell, 1999), p.134.

11 Catherine Belsey, *Critical Practice* (London: Methuen, 1980), pp.56-63.

12 See Michel Foucault, *Language, Counter-Memory, Practice* (Oxford: Basil Blackwell, 1977).

13 Steven Connor points out that the word sublime 'derives apparently from [the] Latin *sublimis*, i.e. *sub* up to and *limen* the lintel. The notion . . . that height is to be measured in terms of proximity to or distance from the lintel, the point of division between upper and lower, becomes simplified in a use of "sublime" to mean simply high or elevated', in *Theory and Cultural Value* (Oxford: Blackwell, 1992), p.47.

14 See Immanuel Kant, *The Critique of Judgement* (1790), tr. James Creed Meredith (Oxford: Clarendon Press, 1952), p.91; Jean-Francois Lyotard, 'Answering the Question: What is Postmodernism?' in *The Postmodern Condition: A Report on Knowledge*, trans. Geoff Bennington and Brian Massumi, (Manchester: Manchester Univ. Press, 1984), p.81.

15 Kevin Z. Moore brilliantly describes Hardy's transpositions of Romantic poetry in *The Descent of the Imagination: Postromantic Culture in the Later Novels of Thomas Hardy* (New York: New York Univ. Press, 1990).

16 Ezra Pound, 'Canto LXXXI', *The Cantos* (London: Faber and Faber, 1986), p.522.

17 See 'She Charged Me', in 'Satires of Circumstance' (1914), subsequently in *Complete Poems*, p.365.

18 'Afternoon Service at Mellstock', in 'Moments of Vision' [1917], *Complete Poems*, p.459.

19 W.H. Auden, 'Letter to Lord Byron', in *Letters from Iceland* (London: Faber and Faber, 1937).

20 W.B. Yeats, 'Meditations in Time of Civil War', *The Poems*, Daniel Albright (ed.) (London: Macmillan, 1990), p.247.

21 'Preface' to *A Pair of Blue Eyes*, discussed in Donald Davie's 'Hardy's Virgilian Purples', *The Poet in the Imaginary Museum: Essays of Two Decades* (Manchester: Carcanet Press, 1977), ed. Barry Alpert, p.222.

22 Florence Emily Hardy, *The Life of Thomas Hardy, 1840-1928* (1962), p.185.

Chapter 10: *Tess of the D'Urbervilles*

1 Thomas Hardy, *Tess of the D'Urbervilles* [1891], ed. Tim Dolin (London: Penguin, 1998), p.189.

2 See Norman Holland, *Five Readers Reading* (New Haven: Yale Univ. Press, 1975); and Jonathan Culler, *On Deconstruction: Theory and Criticism after Structuralism* (London: Routledge, 1983), pp.64-5, pp.69-70.

3 Michael Warner: 'femininity is learned as a way of constructing oneself as an object, a way of attributing full subjectivity only to the masculine', in 'Homo-Narcissism; or, Heterosexuality' (1990), reprinted in *Literary Criticism*, ed. Robert Con Davis and Ronald Schleifer (London: Addison Wesley, Longman, 1998), pp.624-640.

4 Cited in *Social Postmodernism: Beyond Identity Politics*, ed. Linda Nicholson and Steven Seidman (Cambridge: Cambridge Univ. Press, 1995), p.27.

5 Simone de Beauvoir, 'Introduction' to *The Second Sex*, in *New French Feminisms: An Anthology*, ed. Elaine Marks and Isabelle de Courtivron (Brighton: the Harvester Press, 1981), pp.41-56. Also Ellen Rooney, 'Tess and the Subject of Sexual Violence: Reading, Rape, Seduction', in *Tess of the D'Urbervilles: Case Studies in Contemporary Criticism*, ed. John Paul Riquelme (Basingstoke: Macmillan, 1998), pp.462-483.

6 'Freud . . . described femininity and masculinity as *constructions*, [identifying] proper femininity with passive aims . . . and, in its extreme form, pleasure in pain', in Rosalind Coward's 'Are Women Passive by Nature?' in *Our Treacherous Hearts: Why Women Let Men Get Their Way* (London: Faber and Faber, 1992), p.177.

7 Philip Larkin, 'A Study of Reading Habits', *Collected Poems* (London: Faber and Faber, 1988), p.131

8 See Norman Page, 'Hardy and the English Language', in *Thomas Hardy: The Writer and His Background* (London: Bell and Hyman, 1980), pp.150-172. Cf. Roger Bromley here: ' . . . for Lacan subject-formation takes place at the intersection of the body and the signifier; Derrida and Kristeva focus on intersections of body, self and culture'. See his 'Imagining the Puritan Body: the 1995 Cinematic Version of Nathaniel Hawthorne's *The Scarlet Letter*' in *Adaptations: from*

Text to Screen, Screen to Text, ed. Deborah Cartmell and Imelda Whelehan (London: Routledge, 1999), p.64.

9 Matthew Arnold, 'A beautiful and ineffectual Angel, beating in the void his luminous wings in vain', in 'Shelley' (1869), *The Portable Matthew Arnold*, ed. L.Trilling (Harmondsworth: Penguin, 1980), p.405.

10 Tennyson, 'In Memoriam A.H.H', *The Poems of Tennyson*, p.864.

11 Words assigned to Marian in the 1998 television version of *Tess*.

12 Robert Greer Cohn, *Towards the Poems of Mallarmé*, (Berkeley: Univ. of California Press, 1965), pp.223-224.

13 Robert Browning, 'By the Fireside' (1855), in *The Poetical Works of Robert Browning, V*, ed. Ian Jack and Robert Inglesfield (Oxford: Clarendon Press, 1995), p.62.

14 David Musselwhite, 'Tess of the D'Urbervilles: "A Becoming Woman"', in *Textual Practice* 14 (3), 508.

15 See Jane Marcus, 'A Tess for Child Molesters: Polanski's *Tess*', in *Tess of the D'Urbervilles* ('New Casebooks'), ed. Peter Widdowson (Basingstoke: Macmillan, 1993), pp.95-108. As Joseph Bristow and Angelia R. Wilson put it: 'differences about sexual identity . . . are accompanied by the uneven distribution of social, cultural and economic power', in *Activating Theory: Lesbian, Gay and Bisexual Politics* (London: Lawrence and Wishart, 1993), p.6.

16 D. H. Lawrence, *A Study of Thomas Hardy and Other Essays*, ed. Bruce Steele (London: Grafton, 1986), p.77.

17 See Nietzsche, *Beyond Good and Evil*, trans. R.J. Hollingdale (Harmondsworth: Penguin, 1973).

18 See Paul Turner, *The Life of Thomas Hardy* (Oxford: Blackwell, 1998), p.124.

19 'Lycidas' (1638), ll.68-9, in: *The Poems of John* Milton, ed. John Carey and Alastair Fowler (London: Longman, 1968), pp.244-245.

20 'Miss Campbell . . . duly danced with the strange peasant boy' [i.e., Hardy]: a typically patronizing moment in Robert Gitting's *The Young Thomas Hardy* (Boston: Little, Brown and Co., 1975), p.12. For the 'erotic' hanging, see Gittings, p.59.

21 Renée Balibar, *Les Francais Fictifs* (Paris: Hachette, 1974), p.13.

22 'Tess's Lament' [1897?], reprinted in *Selected Poems*, ed. Tim Armstrong (London: Longman, 1993), p.100.

23 D. E. Musselwhite notes the 'barbed humour in Angel's final stealing away with his deceased wife's sister' in 'Tess of the D'Urbervilles: "A Becoming Woman"; *or* Deleuze and Guattari go to Wessex', in *Textual Practice* 14 (3), 511.

Chapter 11: *Jude the Obscure*

1 See Louis Althusser, 'Ideology and Ideological State Apparatuses', *Lenin and Philosophy and Other Essays*, tr. Brewster (London: NLB, 1971), pp.121-173.

2 John Bayley, *An Essay on Hardy* (Cambridge: Cambridge Univ. Press, 1977), p.213.

3 'Afterwards', *Selected Poems* ed. Tim Armstrong (London: Longman, 1993), p.242.

4 Seamus Heaney, *The Redress of Poetry* (London: Faber and Faber, 1995), pp.xvi-xvii.

5 Thomas Hardy, *Jude the Obscure* (London: Pan Macmillan, 1995), pp.8-9.

6 Hardy's diary, April 28, 1888: 'A short study of a young man – "who could not go to Oxford" – His struggles and ultimate failure.'

7 H.G.Wells, *Saturday Review* (8 February 1896), reprinted in *Thomas Hardy: The Critical Heritage* 279-283; for the *Bildungsroman* see Deborah L. Collins, *Thomas Hardy and his God* (London: Macmillan, 1990), p.139; and Frank Giordano, Jr. '*Jude the Obscure* and the *Bildungsroman*', *Studies in the Novel* 4 (1972), 580-591.

8 Constance Rover, *Love, Morals and the Feminists* (London: Routledge and Kegan Paul, 1970), p.132.

9 Matthew Arnold, 'The Scholar Gipsy', in *Poetical Works* (Oxford: Oxford Univ. Press, 1950), pp.255-261; and Matthew Arnold, 'Shelley' (1869), in: *The Portable Matthew Arnold* ed. L. Trilling (Harmondsworth: Penguin, 1980), p.405.

10 Marjorie Garson, *Hardy's Fables of Integrity*, p.165.

11 Arnold's apostrophe in 'Thyrsis' ('Lovely at all times she lies, lovely tonight!') seems to have entered into Jude's own lover-like feelings about the place: *The Poetical Works* (London: Oxford University Press, 1950), p.263.

12 Matthew Arnold, 'Shakespeare', *Poetical Works*, pp.2-3.

13 Matthew Arnold, 'The Function of Criticism at the Present Time', in *Culture and Anarchy and Other Essays*, ed. Stefan Collini (Cambridge: Cambridge University Press, 1993), pp.34-5.

14 John Maynard, *Victorian Discourses on Sex and Religion* (Cambridge: Cambridge University Press, 1993), p.284.

15 Browning, 'Dramatis Personae', in *Poetical Works 1833-1864* (London: Oxford University Press, 1970), p.813.

16 See David Trotter, *The English Novel in History, 1895-1920* (London: Routledge, 1993), p.12; John R. Doheny, 'Characterisation in Hardy's *Jude the Obscure*: The Function of Arabella', in *Reading Thomas Hardy*, Charles P.C. Pettit (ed.) (Basingstoke: Macmillan Press, 1998), pp.57-82.

17 Coleridge, 'The Aeolian Harp', *Selected Poetry*, Richard Holmes (ed.) (London: Penguin, 1996), pp.36-7.

18 John Keats, 'Lamia', in *Poetical Works*, ed. H.W. Garrod (Oxford: Clarendon Press, 1958), p.196.

19 See Catherine Belsey, *Desire: Love Stories in Western Culture* (Oxford: Blackwell, 1994), p.60.

20 D.H. Lawrence, 'Study of Thomas Hardy', in *Phoenix: The Posthumous Papers of D.H. Lawrence*, ed. E.D. MacDonald (New York: Viking, 1936).

21 William Blake, 'The Marriage of Heaven and Hell' [1790-93], *Poetical Works* (London: Oxford University Press, 1976), pp.148-158.

22 'All contrasts': Letter to Sir Edmund Gosse, [November 20 1895], p.347; 'quadrille': Letter to Sir Edmund Gosse [January 4, 1896].

23 See: J. L. Austin, *How to Do Things with Words* (Oxford: Clarendon Presss, 1975).

24 W.Goetz, 'The Felicity and Infelicity of Marriage in *Jude the Obscure*', *Nineteenth Century Fiction* 38 (1983), 189-213.

25 Lord Acton (1862); cited in Penny Boumelha, *Thomas Hardy and Women: Sexual Ideology and Narrative Form* (Brighton: Harvester Press, 19782), p.14.

26 Terry Eagleton, *Ideology* (London: Verso, 1991), p.9.

27 William Blake, 'The Chimney-Sweeper' [*Songs of Experience*], *Complete Writings*, p.212

28 Coleridge, 'A Letter to _____, April 4 1802', *The Complete Poems* (London: Penguin, 1997), p.304.

29 Thomas Hardy, '*In Tenebris II*' ['1895-96'], in *Selected Poems*, ed. Tim Armstrong (Harlow Longman, 1993), p.98.

Chapter 12: *The Well-Beloved*

1 See *The Well-Beloved: A Sketch of a Temperament* [1898] (London: J.M. Dent, 1997), p.86.

2 In a diary entry of 1888: reproduced in Thomas Hardy, *Selected Poems,* ed. Tim Armstrong, p.4.

3 Patricia Ingham, *Thomas Hardy: A Feminist Reading* (Brighton: Harvester, 1989); and 'Provisional Narratives: Hardy's Final Trilogy,' in Lance St. John Butler (ed.), *Alternative Hardy* (London: Macmillan, 1989). See also Lyn Pykett, 'Ruinous Bodies: Women and Sexuality in Hardy's Fiction', in the *Critical Survey* 5, no.2 (1993), 157-166.

4 See Derek Hudson, *Munby: Man of Two Worlds* (London: Abacus, 1974), for this middle-class connoisseur of 'working women.'

5 Jane Thomas, *Thomas Hardy, Femininity and Dissent* (London: Macmillan, 1999), p.145. See also John Kucich, 'Moral Authority in Hardy's Late Novels: The Gendering of Art', in *The Power of Lies: Transgression in Victorian Fiction* (Ithaca, New York: Cornell University Press, 1994), p.216.

6 See 'I Rose up as My Custom Is' (1914): in *Complete Poems* [Variorum Edition, ed. James Gibson], p.379.

7 See Clara Tuite, *Romantic Austen: Sexual Politics and the Literary Canon* (Cambridge: Cambridge University Press, 2002), p.23.

8 Ezra Pound, 'Epitaph', *Selected Poems*, ed. T.S. Eliot (London: Faber and Faber, 1959), p.104.

9 *Jude the Obscure*, ed. Norman Page (ed.) (New York: W.W.Norton, 1978), p.141; and 'To a Motherless Child', in *Complete Poems*, ed. James Gibson, p.65.

10 A visitor cited in Sophie Gilmartin's interesting *Ancestry and Narrative in Nineteenth-Century British Literature* (Cambridge: Cambridge University Press, 1998), treats the Portlanders as 'racial others', interesting 'primitives'.

11 See Thomas Hardy, *The Well-Beloved: A Sketch of a Temperament*, ed. Norman Page (London: J.M. Dent, 1997), p.xxxvi. This is the conclusion to Chapter 33 of the serial version.

12 Donald Davie's phrase, 'the etiolation of Hellenism as an artistic stimulus' in the discussion of a Pound poem.

13 W. H. Auden, 'Hardy's Poetry', in *Hardy: A Collection of Critical Essays* (Englewood Cliffs, N. J.: Prentice-Hall, 1963).

14 John Fowles, 'Hardy and the Hag', in *Thomas Hardy After Fifty Years*, Lance St. John Butler (ed.) (London: Macmillan, 1977), p.30.

15 Rosemary Sumner, *A Route to Modernism: Hardy, Lawrence, Woolf* (Basingstoke: Macmillan, 1999).

16 Tom Paulin, *Thomas Hardy: The Poetry of Perception*, 2nd ed. (London: Macmillan, 1986), p.67.

17 Shelley, *Selected Poems*, Timothy Webb (ed.) (London: J. M. Dent, 1975), pp.1-2 and Shelley, *Poetical Works*, Thomas Hutchinson (ed.) (Oxford: Oxford University Press, 1971), p.523.

18 Robert Browning, 'The Statue and the Bust', *Poetical Works 1833-1864* (London: Oxford Univ. Press, 1970), p.628.

19 D. H. Lawrence, 'Study of Thomas Hardy' (1914): reprinted in *Study of Thomas Hardy and Other Essays*, ed. Bruce Steele (London: Grafton Books, 1986), p.235.

20 Tess O'Toole, *Genealogy and Fiction in Hardy* (Basingstoke: Macmillan, 1997), p.133.

21 T. W. Adorno, quot. Susan Buck-Morss, *The Origins of Negative Dialectics* (Brighton: Harvester Press, 1977), p.168.

22 Elisabeth Roudinesco, *Jacques Lacan*, trans. Barbara Bray (Cambridge: Polity Press, 1997), p.283.

23 Shelley, *Revolt of Islam*, 1.27: used as epigraph to *The Well-Beloved*.

24 *The Later Years of Thomas Hardy 1892-1928* (London: Studio Editions, 1994), p.57.

25 See *Oxford Literary Review* 20 (1998), pp.47-77.

26 James Joyce, *Ulysses* (London: Penguin, 1968), p.29.

27 W. H. Auden, 'Letter to Lord Byron', in *Letters from Iceland* (London: Faber and Faber, 1937).

Chapter 13: Screening Hardy

Jude

1 *Jude* (1996): Director, Michael Winterbottom; screenplay by Hossein Amini, Christopher Eccleston as Jude, Kate Winslet as Sue Bridehead, Rachel Griffiths as Arabella. Polygram, ('in association with BBC films').
2 Cited in: Hossein Amini, *The Shooting Script of Jude* (London: Nick Hern, 1996).
3 G. Wagner, *The Novel and the Cinema* (Cranbury: Associated Univ. Presses, 1975), pp.222-3.
4 Cited in *Adaptations: from Text to Screen, Screen to Text*, ed. Deborah Cartmell and Imelda Whelehan (London: Routledge, 1999).
5 Neil Sinyard, '"Lids tend to Come off": David Lean's film of E.M. Forster's *A Passage to India*', in *The Classic Novel: From Page to Screen*, ed. Robert Giddings and Erica Sheen (Manchester: Manchester University Press, 2000), p.147.

Tess of the D'Urbervilles

1 *Tess of the D'Urbervilles* ('London Weekend Television' [1998]). Director Ian Sharp; Adapted by Ted Whitehead. Justine Waddell as Tess; Jason Flemyng as Alec [second in billing]; Oliver Milburn as Angel; John McEnery as Jack Durbeyfield; Lesley Dunlop as Joan Durbeyfield.
2 G. Wagner, *The Novel and the Cinema* (Cranbury: Associated Univ. Presses, 1975), pp.222-3.
3 Imelda Whelehan, 'Adaptations: The Contemporary Dilemmas', in *Adaptations*, ed. Deborah Cartmell and Imelda Whelehan, p.3; G. Bluestone, *Novel into Film* (Berkeley: Univ. of California Press, 1973), p.xiii.
4 Ken Gelder, 'Jane Campion and the Limits of Literary Cinema': in *Adaptations*, Deborah Cartmell and Imelda Whelehan (eds), pp.157-171.
5 See 'The Traditional Basis of Thomas Hardy's Fiction', in *Thomas Hardy: A Collection of Critical Essays*, ed. Albert J. Guerard (Englewood Cliffs, N.J.: Prentice-Hall, 1963), pp.10-23.
6 B. McFarlane, *Novel to Film: An Introduction to the Theory of Adaptation* (Oxford: Clarendon Press, 1996), p.18.
7 Reprinted as 'A Tess for Child Molesters', in Peter Widdowson, ed., *Tess of the d'Urbervilles* (Basingstoke: Macmillan, 1993), pp.90-94.
8 See Dale Kramer, ed. *Critical Approaches to Thomas Hardy* (London: Macmillan, 1979).
9 See Robert Stam, *Subversive Pleasures: Bakhtin, Cultural Criticism and Film* (Baltimore: Johns Hopkins Univ. Press, 1989).

The Woodlanders

1 *The Woodlanders* (Channel Four Television [1997]): starring Rufus Sewell as Giles Winterborne, Emily Woof as Grace Melbury, Cal Macaninch as Edred Fitzpiers, Tony Haygarth as George Melbury, and Jodie May as Marty South.
2 Roland Barthes, 'Introduction to the Structural Analysis of Narratives', in *Image-Music-Text* (Glasgow: Collins, 1977), p.94); Seymour Chatman, *Story and Discourse: Narrative Structure in Fiction and Film* (Ithaca, N.Y.: Cornell Univ. Press, 1978), p.53; also Brian McFarlane, *Novel to Film*, pp.13-15.
3 See Robert Giddings and Erica Sheen, *The Classic Novel: From Page to Screen* (Manchester: Manchester Univ. Press, 2000).

Chapter 14: Spectres of Hardy's Poetry

1 Colin MacCabe, *Theoretical Essays* (Manchester: Manchester Univ. Press, 1985), pp.132-3.

2 Peter Sacks, *The English Elegy* (Baltimore: Johns Hopkins Univ. Press, 1985), 227-259, Jahan Ramazani, 'Hardy's Elegies for an Era: "By the Century's Deathbed"', *Victorian Poetry*, 29 (1979), 131-43; and Linda M. Austin, 'Reading Depression in Hardy's "Poems of 1912-13"', *Victorian Poetry* 36 (1998), 1-15.

3 William E. Buckler, *The Poetry of Thomas Hardy* (New York: New York Univ. Press, 1983), p.1.

4 See Edward Neill, 'How They Brought the Bad News from Essex to Wessex: or, What We Talk about When We Talk about Hardy's Poetry', *Victorian Literature and Culture* (1998), 489-505.

5 Dirk Kasler, *Max Weber: An Introduction to His Life and Work* (London: Polity Press, 1988), p.78.

6 J. Laplanche and J.B. Pontalis, *The Language of Psychoanalysis* (London: The Hogarth Press, 1973), p.111-13.

7 Gillian Rose, *The Melancholy Man: An Introduction to the Thought of Theodor W. Adorno* (London: Macmillan, 1978), p.29.

8 Florence Hardy, *The Early Life of Thomas Hardy, 1840-1891* (1928; rpt. London: Studio Editions, 1994), p.70.

9 Harold Bloom, *A Map of Misreading* (New York: Oxford University Press, 1975), p.23.

10 Tom Paulin, *Thomas Hardy: The Poetry of Perception* (London: Macmillan, 1986), p.63.

11 Norman Page, 'Hardy and the English Language', in *Thomas Hardy: The Writer and His Background*, ed. Norman Page (London: Bell and Hyman, 1980), pp.152-53.

12 Shelley, *Selected Poems,* ed. Timothy Webb, p.31.

13 J. Hillis Miller, *The Linguistic Moment* (Princeton: Princeton Univ. Press, 1985), p.279.

14 Thomas Hardy, 'Preface' to 'Poems of the Past and the Present' in *The Variorum Edition of the Complete Poems of Thomas Hardy*, p.84.

15 *The Later Years of Thomas Hardy, 1892-1928* (1930; London: Studio Editions, 1994), p.141.

16 G. Bachelard, *On Poetic Imagination and Reverie,* tr. Colette Gandin (New York: Bobbs-Merrill, 1971), p.23.

17 R. Kearney, *Poetics of Imagining: From Husserl to Lyotard* (London: HarperCollins Academic, 1991), p.92.

18 Madan Sarup, *An Introductory Guide to Modernism and Post-Modernism* (London: Harvester Wheatsheaf, 1993), p.42.

19 Charles Baudelaire, *Oeuvres Complètes (I)* (Paris: Gallimard, 1975), p.11.

20 Cf. 'To an Unborn Pauper Child': 'The Doomsters heap/ Travails and teens around us here'.

21 Raymond Williams, *The English Novel from Dickens to Lawrence* (London: Hogarth Press, 1984), p.95.

22 Michael Alexander, 'Hardy Among the Poets', in *Thomas Hardy After Fifty Years*, ed. Lance St. John Butler (London: Macmillan, 1977), p.51.

23 Richard Kearney, *Dialogues with Contemporary Continental Thinkers* (Manchester: Manchester Univ. Press, 1984), p.74.

24 *The Later Years of Thomas Hardy*, pp.57-58.

25 S. Kierkegaard, *The Concept of Irony* (London: Collins, 1996), p.335.

26 Richard Kearney, *Dialogues with Contemporary Continental Thinkers*, p.17.

27 Cited by Harold Orel, 'What *The Dynasts* meant to Hardy', *Victorian Poetry*, 17 (1979), 109-123.

28 Anthony Easthope, *Poetry and Phantasy* (Cambridge: Cambridge Univ. Press, 1989), p.138.

29 Philip Larkin, 'Wanted: Good Hardy Critic' in *Required Writing* (London: Faber, 1983), p.75.

30 Franco Moretti, *Signs Taken for Wonders* (London: Verso, 1983), p.8.

31 Kierkegaard, *The Concept of Irony*, p.35.

32 Derrida, in Kearney, *Dialogues*, p.74.

33 S. Kierkegaard, *Fear and Trembling: Repetition*, ed. H. and E. Hong (Princeton, N.J.: Princeton University Press, 1983), p.52.

34 'The Shorter Poems of Thomas Hardy', in *Language as Gesture* (New York: Harcourt, Brace and Co., 1935), p.55.

35 From 'Broom' and 'To Sylvia', in *A Leopardi Reader*, ed. and tr. Ottavio M. Casale (London: Univ. of Illinois Press, 1981).

36 See section on 'Ghosts' in *Introduction to Literature, Criticism and Theory* (2ⁿᵈ Ed.), by Andrew Bennet and Nicholas Royle (London: Prentice Hall Europe, 1999), pp.132-140.

37 Stan Smith, *The Origins of Modernism: Eliot, Pound and the Rhetorics of Renewal* (London: Harvester Wheatsheaf, 1994), p.7.

38 See Mark Poster, 'Semiology and Critical Theory: From Marx to Baudrillard', in *The Question of Textuality* (Bloomington: Indiana Univ. Press, 1982), p.284; also 'The Politics of the Dead', in Tim Armstrong's *Haunted Hardy: Poetry, History, Memory* (Basingstoke: Palgrave, 2000), pp.89-110.

Concise Bibliography of Secondary Reading

Amini, Hossein. *The Shooting Script of Jude*. London: Nick Hern, 1996.

Armstrong, Tim. *Haunted Hardy: Poetry, History, Memory*. Basingstoke: Palgrave, 2000.

Austin, Linda M. 'Reading Depression in Hardy's "Poems of 1912-13"'. *Victorian Poetry* **36** (1998): 1-15.

Bayley, John. *An Essay on Hardy*. Cambridge: Cambridge Univ. Press, 1977.

Beer, Gillian. *Darwin's Plots: Evolutionary Narrative in Darwin, George Eliot and Nineteenth Century Fiction*. London: Routledge and Kegan Paul, 1983.

Beer, Gillian. 'Finding a Scale for the Human: Plot and Writing in Hardy's Novels'. In: *Critical Essays on Thomas Hardy*. Ed. Dale Kramer. Boston: G.K. Hall, 1990.

Belsey, Catherine. *Desire: Love Stories in Western Culture*. Oxford: Blackwell, 1994.

Bennet, Andrew and Nicholas Royle, Eds. *Introduction to Literature, Criticism and Theory*. 2nd Ed. London: Prentice Hall Europe, 1999.

Bersani, Leo. *The Culture of Redemption*. London: Harvard Univ. Press, 1990.

Bhaba, Homi K. 'Interrogating Identity'. In *The Real Me: Post-modernism and the Question of Identity*. Ed. Lisa Appignanesi. London: ICA, 1987.

Boumelha, Penny. '"A Complicated Position for a Woman": *The Hand of Ethelberta*'. In: *The Sense of Sex: Feminist Perspectives on Hardy*. Ed. Margaret Higonnet. Chicago: University of Illinois Press, 1993.

Boumelha, Penny. 'The Patriarchy of Class: *Under the Greenwood Tree, Far from the Madding Crowd, The Woodlanders*'. In: *The Cambridge Companion to Thomas Hardy*. Ed. Dale Kramer. Cambridge: Cambridge Univ. Press, 1999.

Bristow, Joseph and Angelia R. Wilson. *Activating Theory: Lesbian, Gay and Bisexual Politics*. London: Lawrence and Wishart, 1993.

Bromley, Roger. 'Imagining the Puritan Body: the 1995 Cinematic Version of Nathaniel Hawthorne's *The Scarlet Letter*'. In: *Adaptations: from Text to Screen, Screen to Text*. Ed. Deborah Cartmell and Imelda Whelehan. London: Routledge, 1999.

Butler, Judith. *Gender Trouble: Feminism and the Subversion of Identity*. London: Routledge, 1990.

Butler, Lance St. John. *Registering the Difference: Reading Literature through Register*. Manchester: Manchester Univ. Press, 1999.

Casagrande, Peter J. and Charles Lock. 'The Name "Henchard"'. *Thomas Hardy Society Review*, **1** (1978): 115-18.

Cixous, Hélène. 'Sorties' [1975]. Reprinted in *Modern Literary Theory: A Reader*. Ed. Philip Rice and Patricia Waugh. London: Edward Arnold, 1996.

Collini, Stefan. 'Matthew Arnold'. In: *Victorian Thinkers: Carlyle, Ruskin, Arnold, Morris*. Oxford: Oxford Univ. Press, 1993. Ed. A.L. Le Quesne. Oxford: Oxford University Press, 1993.

Connor, Steven. *Theory and Cultural Value*. Oxford: Blackwell, 1992.

Dainotto, Roberto M. *Place in Literature: Regions, Cultures, Communities*. Ithaca, New York: Cornell Univ. Press, 2000.

Dalziel, Pamela. 'The Genesis of Hardy's *Desperate Remedies*'. *Journal of English and Germanic Philology* **94**, no.2 (1995).

Davie, Donald. 'Hardy's Virgilian Purples'. *The Poet in the Imaginary Museum: Essays of Two Decades*. Ed. Barry Alpert. Manchester: Carcanet Press, 1977.

Davies, Sarah. '*The Hand of Ethelberta*: De-Mythologising "Woman"'. *The Critical Survey* **5** no.2 (1993), 123-130.

Derrida, Jacques. *Éperons*. (1978). Translated as *Spurs: Nietzsche's Styles*. By Barbara Harlow. Chicago: University of Chicago Press, 1979.

Derrida, Jacques. *Acts of Literature*. Ed. Derek Attridge. London: Routledge, 1992.

Doheny, John R. 'Characterisation in Hardy's *Jude the Obscure*: The Function of Arabella'. In: *Reading Thomas Hardy*. Ed. Charles P.C. Pettit. Basingstoke: Macmillan Press, 1998, pp. 57-82.

Fisher, Joe. *The Hidden Hardy*. Basingstoke: Macmillan, 1992.

Fowles, John. 'Hardy and the Hag'. In *Thomas Hardy After Fifty Years*. Ed. Lance St. John Butler. London: Macmillan, 1977.

Furbank, P. N. *Unholy Pleasure: or the Idea of Social Class*. Oxford: Oxford Univ. Press, 1985.

Garson, Marjorie. *Hardy's Fables of Integrity: Woman, Body, Text*. Oxford: Clarendon Press, 1991.

Gatrell, Simon. 'Wessex'. In: *The Cambridge Companion to Thomas Hardy*. Ed. Dale Kramer. Cambridge: Cambridge Univ. Press, 1999, pp.19-37.

Giddings, Robert and Erica Sheen, Eds. *The Classic Novel: From Page to Screen*. Manchester: Manchester Univ. Press, 2000.

Gilmartin, Sophie. *Ancestry and Narrative in Nineteenth-Century British Literature*. Cambridge: Cambridge Univ. Press, 1998.

Gilmour, Robin. *The Novel in the Victorian Age*. London: Edward Arnold, 1986.

Goetz, W. 'The Felicity and Infelicity of Marriage in *Jude the Obscure*.' *Nineteenth-Century Fiction* **38** (1983): 189-213.

Goode, John. *Thomas Hardy: the Offensive Truth*. Oxford: Blackwell, 1983.

Gubar, Susan. 'The Blank Page and the Issues of Female Creativity'. In: *The New Feminist Criticism*. Ed. Elaine Showalter. London: Virago, 1986.

Haraway, Donna. 'A Cyborg Manifesto' (1991); reprinted in *Contemporary Literary Criticism: Literary and Cultural Studies*. Ed. Robert Con Davis and Ronald Schleifer. Harlow: Longman, 1998, pp.696-727.

Harland, Richard. *Literary Theory from Plato to Barthes*. Basingstoke: Macmillan, 1999.

Ingham, Patricia. 'Provisional Narratives: Hardy's Final Trilogy'. Ed. Lance St. John Butler. *Alternative Hardy*. London: Macmillan, 1989.

Ingham, Patricia. 'The Evolution of *Jude the Obscure*': *Review of English Studies* 27 (1976): 27-37, 159-69.

Ingham, Patricia. *Thomas Hardy: A Feminist Reading*. Brighton: Harvester, 1989.

Jackson, Tony E. *The Subject of Modernism: Narrative Alterations in the Fiction of Eliot, Conrad, Woolf and Joyce*. Ann Arbor: University of Michigan Press, 1994.

Jenson, Margaret M. *The Open Book: Creative Misreading in the Work of Selected Modern Writers*. Basingstoke: Palgrave, 2002.

Korg, Jacob. 'Astronomical Imagery in Victorian Poetry'. In *Victorian Science and Victorian Values*. Ed. James Paradis and Thomas Postlwait. New Brunswick: Rutgers Univ. Press, 1985, pp.137-158.

Kucich, John. *The Power of Lies: Transgression in Victorian Fiction*. Ithaca, New York: Cornell Univ. Press, 1994.

Lawrence, D.H. 'Study of Thomas Hardy'. In *Phoenix: The Posthumous Papers of D.H. Lawrence*. Ed. E.D. MacDonald. New York: Viking, 1936.

Lerner, Laurence and Holmstrom, John. *Thomas Hardy and His Readers*. London: Bodley Head, 1968.

Longhurst, Derek. *Gender Genre and Narrative Pleasure*. London: Unwin Hyman, 1989.

Lucas, John. *The Literature of Change: Studies in the Nineteenth-Century Provincial Novel.* Brighton: The Harvester Press, 1980.

McFarlane, B. *Novel to Film: An Introduction to the Theory of Adaptation.* Oxford: Clarendon Press, 1996.

Mallett, Phillip, ed. *Thomas Hardy: Texts and Contexts.* Basingstoke: Macmillan, 2002.

Maynard, John. *Victorian Discourses on Sex and Religion.* Cambridge: Cambridge Univ. Press, 1993.

Miller, J. Hillis. *Thomas Hardy: Distance and Desire.* Cambridge, MA: Harvard Univ. Press, 1970.

Millgate, Michael. *Thomas Hardy: A Biography.* Oxford: Oxford Univ. Press, 1982.

Millgate, Michael. 'Unreal Estate: Reflections on Wessex and Yoknapatawpha'. In: *The Literature of Region and Nation.* Ed. R.P. Draper. London: Macmillan, 1988, pp.61-80.

Mitchell, Juliet. *The Stone and the Scorpion: The Female Subject of Desire in the Novels of Charlotte Bronte, George Eliot and Thomas Hardy.* London: Greenwood Press, 1994.

Moi, Toril. 'Feminist, Female, Feminine'. In *The Feminist Reader: Essays in Gender and the Politics of Literary Criticism.* Ed. Catherine Belsey and Jane Moore. London: Macmillan, 1997, pp.104-116.

Moore, Kevin Z. *The Descent of the Imagination: Postromantic Culture in the Later Novels of Thomas Hardy.* London: New York Univ. Press, 1990.

Morgan, Rosemarie. *Cancelled Words: Rediscovering Thomas Hardy.* London: Routledge, 1992.

Morgan, Rosemarie. 'Bodily Transactions: Toni Morrison and Thomas Hardy in Literary Discourse'. In: *Celebrating Thomas Hardy.* Ed. Charles P.C. Pettit. London: Macmillan, 1996, pp.136-158.

Morgan, William W. 'Gender and Silence in Thomas Hardy's Texts'. In *Gender and Discourse in Victorian Literature and Art.* Ed. Anthony H. Harrison and Beverly Taylor. Dekalb: Northern Illinois Univ. Press, 1992.

Moses, Michael Valdez. 'Hardy: The Archaeology of a Vanishing Life'. In: *The Novel and the Globalization of Culture.* New York: Oxford University Press, 1995.

Neale, Catherine. '*Desperate Remedies*: The Merits and Demerits of Popular Fiction'. *Critical Survey* **5**, no.2 (1993): 115-122.

Neill, Edward. 'Back to the Future: Hardy, Poetry, Theory, Aporia'. *Victorian Poetry* **36** (Spring, 1998): 295-305.

Neill, Edward. 'How They Brought the Bad News from Essex to Wessex: or, What We Talk about When We Talk about Hardy's Poetry'. *Victorian Literature and Culture* (1998): 489-505.

Neill, Edward. '"Oh, Keep the Dog far Hence": Hardy, Bersani and Biography'. *Oxford Literary Review,* **20** ([formally] 1998): 163-171.

Neill, Edward. 'Thomas Hardy'. In: *A Companion to Victorian Novel.* Ed. William Baker and Kenneth Womack. Westport, Conn.: Greenwood, 2002, pp.307-318.

O'Toole, Tess. *Genealogy and Fiction in Hardy.* Basingstoke: Macmillan, 1997.

Oppen, George. *Evolution and Poetic Belief: A Study in Some Victorian and Modern Writers.* Oxford: Basil Blackwell, 1956.

Page, Norman. 'Hardy and the English Language'. In: *Thomas Hardy: The Writer and His Background.* Ed. Norman Page. London: Bell and Hyman, 1980, pp.150-172.

Page, Norman. Ed. *The Oxford Reader's Companion to Hardy.* Oxford: Oxford University Press, 2001.

Paulin, Tom. *Thomas Hardy: The Poetry of Perception.* 2nd ed. London: Macmillan, 1986.

Pettit, Charles P. C. 'Merely a Good Hand at a Serial? From *A Pair of Blue Eyes* to *Far from the Madding Crowd*'. In: *The Achievement of Thomas Hardy.* Ed. Phillip Mallett Basingstoke: Macmillan, 2000, pp.1-21.

Pite, Ralph. *Hardy's Geography: Wessex and the Regional Novel*. Basingstoke: Palgrave, 2002.

Pykett, Lyn. 'Ruinous Bodies: Women and Sexuality in Hardy's Fiction'. In: *The Critical Survey* **5**, no.2 (1993): 157-166.

Pykett, Lyn. *The Sensation Novel: From 'The Woman in White' to 'The Moonstone'*. Plymouth: Northcote House, 1994.

Rivkin, Julie and Ryan, Michael. *Literary Theory: An Anthology*. Oxford: Blackwell, 1998.

Rooney, Ellen. 'Tess and the Subject of Sexual Violence: Reading, Rape, Seduction'. In *Tess of the D'Urbervilles: Case Studies in Contemporary Criticism*. Ed. John Paul Riquelme Basingstoke: Macmillan, 1998, pp.462-483.

Rutland, William R. *Thomas Hardy: A Study of His Writings and Their Background*. Oxford: Basil Blackwell, 1938.

Sacks, Peter. *The English Elegy: Studies in the Genre from Spenser to Yeats*. Baltimore: Johns Hopkins University Press, 1985.

Sarup, Madan. *An Introductory Guide to Postmodernism and Poststructuralism*. Brighton: Harvester Wheatsheaf, 1993.

Schiach, Morag. *Hélène Cixous: A Politics of Writing*. London: Routledge, 1991.

Sedgwick, Eve Kosovsky. *Between Men: English Literature and Male Homosexual Desire*. New York: Columbia University Press, 1985.

Seymour-Smith, Martin. *Hardy*. London: Bloomsbury, 1994.

Shires, Linda M. 'The Radical Aesthetic of *Tess of the d'Urbervilles*'. In: *The Cambridge Companion to Thomas Hardy*. Dale Kramer (ed.) Cambridge: Cambridge University Press, 1999. pp.145-163.

Stafford, Andy. *Roland Barthes: Phenomenon and Myth: An Intellectual Biography*. Edinburgh: Edinburgh University Press, 1998.

Sumner, Rosemary. *A Route to Modernism: Hardy, Lawrence, Woolf*. Basingstoke: Macmillan, 1999.

Thomas, Jane. *Thomas Hardy, Femininity and Dissent*. London: Macmillan, 1999.

Trotter, David. *The English Novel in History: 1895-1920*. London: Routledge, 1993.

Tuchman, Gaye (with Nina E. Fortin). *Edging Women Out: Victorian Novelists, Publishers and Social Change*. London: Routledge, 1989.

Turner, Paul. *The Life of Thomas Hardy*. Oxford: Basil Blackwell, 1998.

Underdown, David. *Fire from Heaven: Life in an English Town in the Seventeenth Century*. London: Harpercollins, 1992.

Wagner, Geoffrey. *The Novel and the Cinema*. Cranbury: Associated University Presses, 1975.

Webster, Roger. 'The Novels of Thomas Hardy: *Tess of the D'Urbervilles*'. In: *Literature in Context*. Ed. Rick Rylance and Judy Simons. Basingstoke: Palgrave, 2001, pp.135-153.

Wiener, Martin J. *English Culture and the Decline of the Industrial Spirit: 1850-1980*. Harmondsworth: Penguin, 1985.

Wood, Ellen Meiksins. *The Pristine Culture of Capitalism: A Historical Essay on Old Regimes and Modern States*. London: Verso, 1992.

Wright, Sarah Bird. *Thomas Hardy A to Z*. New York: Checkmark, 2002.

Wright, Terence R. *Hardy and the Erotic*. London: Macmillan, 1991.

Index